Joseph M. Fox

# The Brawl In **IBM** 1964

a memoir

Copyright Joseph M. Fox 1982
All rights reserved.

ISBN-10: 1456525514
ISBN-13: 9781456525514
Library of Congress Control Number: 2011907869
CreateSpace, North Charleston SC

# DEDICATION

To John J. Collins, Jr.

To Bob O. Evans,

To Henry J. White,

and

To the people of FAA who stayed competent throughout IBM chaos.

# TABLE OF CONTENTS

| | |
|---|---:|
| INTRODUCTION | 1 |
| | |
| BATTLE #1: IBM MARKETING vs. IBM DEVELOPMENT | 3 |
|    DEVELOPMENT DIVISION VP AGAIN SAYS 'NO BID - JULY 1963. | 6 |
|    DO NOT TELL THE FAA THEIR DESIGN WILL NOT WORK | 9 |
|    OUR NEW SALES V. P. | 14 |
| | |
| BATTLE 2 -THE 'ORANGE SODA' MEETING | 23 |
| | |
| SPINNING WHEELS | 33 |
|    A 28-YEAR-OLD PROPOSAL MANAGER? | 34 |
|    SALES V. P. MEETS WITH THE FAA | 40 |
|    IBM PRINTER FAILS IN ISLIP EN ROUTE CONTROL CENTER | 47 |
|    GROUP V. P. | 50 |
|    THE FAA VISITS IBM | 51 |
|    WITH THE FAA DIRECTOR OF RESEARCH | 54 |
| | |
| IBM PRESIDENT INTO THE FRAY | 61 |
| | |
| I MEET LEARSON- IBM's NEXT CHAIRMAN | 75 |
|    FIRST WEEKLY LEARSON REVIEW | 85 |
|    FAA BIDDERS CONFERENCE NOVEMBER 8 | 94 |
|    TO THE CHAIRMAN | 96 |
|    SECOND WEEKLY LEARSON REVIEW | 98 |
| | |
| CAN IBM STOP THE PROCUREMENT? | 105 |
|    IBM RESEARCH IS INTO THE ACT | 106 |
|    THIRD WEEKLY REVIEW | 112 |
|    IBM'S PROPOSAL 'CZAR' | 123 |
| | |
| DECEMBER - IN A FIREHOUSE ! | 127 |
|    CHAIRMAN: "WHY ARE WE SO FAR BEHIND?" | 129 |
|    AN AUDIT | 131 |

| | |
|---|---|
| NO TIME TO GET THE PROPOSAL PRINTED | 144 |
| CAN THE MODEL 50 KILL THE FAA VERSION? | 148 |
| FIREHOUSE REVIEW –NO MORE TIME | 149 |
| THE NEW YORK BOWERY 'PROPOSAL MACHINE' | 153 |
| | |
| CORPORATE FINANCE & LEGAL INTO THE FRAY | 157 |
|    COMPETITION | 163 |
|    IBM PRESIDENT MEETING | 163 |
|    WEDNESDAY, JANUARY 22. LAST DAY | 168 |
|    THE PRICE PROPOSAL HAS AN ERROR | 168 |
|    FEBRUARY 1964-WE WAIT | 171 |
|    TECHNICAL BRIEF OF THE PROPOSAL TO THE FAA | 172 |
| | |
| WITH THE IBM PRESIDENT | 183 |
|    CONGRESSIONAL PRESSURE | 199 |
| | |
| APRIL 7 IBM ANNOUNCES THE 360 | 217 |
|    FEDERAL DIVISION- AND CORPORATE - TAKE CONTROL | 218 |
|    NEGOTIATING WITH FAA – AND IBM | 222 |
| | |
| THIRD PARTY LIABILITY | 225 |
| | |
| IBM'S CORPORATE OPERATING BOARD -The "COB" | 233 |
|    THE IBM PRESIDENT'S REVIEW | 238 |
|    GET MORE INSURANCE | 249 |
|    IBM REORGANIZES | 249 |
| | |
| THIRD PARTY LIABILITY –IN OR OUT ? | 251 |
| | |
| MORE OBJECTIONS | 255 |
| | |
| IBM PRESIDENT FLIES TO WASHINGTON | 261 |
|    ONCE MORE TO IBM WESTCHESTER | 274 |
| | |
| THE POWERFULL FLY TO WASHINGTON YET AGAIN | 277 |
| | |
| ONE WEEK LEFT | 281 |

| | |
|---|---|
| POSTSCRIPT | 283 |
|    IBM REVENUES FROM FAA CIRCA 1976 –Estimates by author | 284 |
|    360 CLONES REPLACE THE 9020'S | 284 |
|    POWER IN A LARGE ORGANIZATION. | 288 |
|    FAA COMPETENCE | 289 |
|    THE UK GETS AN IBM 9020 FOR AIR TRAFFIC CONTROL | 289 |
|    I MEET TOM WATSON- CHAIRMAN OF IBM -1971 | 290 |
|    WE VISIT WITH THE FAA ADMINISTRATOR | 295 |
|    WATSON'S DEMEANOR | 296 |
|    WE BRIEF FRANK CARY IBM PRESIDENT | 298 |
|    OVERWORK ON THE FAA SOFTWARE? | 300 |

DECEMBER 16, 1960 – BROOKLYN, N.Y.

# INTRODUCTION

This is a MEMOIR, a true story. It is an account of IBM's effort to win the competition in 1963-4 for the computers to automate the En Route Air Traffic Control system of the United States. I was IBM's proposal manager.

Two mid-air collisions of commercial planes with passengers - in 4 years. Monday, July 30, 1956, -TWA and United take off within minutes of each other from Los Angeles – and collide over the Grand Canyon, and both fall into the canyon. All 128 people on the planes die. President Eisenhower sets up the FAA –the Federal Aviation Agency- and tells them to automate the en-route air traffic control system.

December 16th, 1960, Friday, a collision over New York City. A snowy morning. A TWA propeller plane is hit by a United jet. The TWA plane falls in Staten Island. The jet crashes in Brooklyn, a few blocks away from Prospect Park. All 128 aboard the planes die. And 6 more on the ground in Brooklyn. A 14-year-old boy is pulled –badly injured - from the United wreckage, in the Park Slope section of Brooklyn. He is the only survivor and is rushed to nearby Methodist Hospital - he talks with the nurses and doctors –but he dies the next day.

FAA is told to develop a new system to control en-route airspace, using "off the shelf" computers. The FAA role is to specify, procure and integrate the radars, the communications devices, the displays, the computers, the software - and the human controllers - into a working system. It performs admirably on this computer procurement. Any who doubt Government capabilities should read this tale.

# A Brawl in IBM - 1964

FAA asks for proposals from computer makers in September 1963. IBM is the dominant firm in computers. The chairman, Thomas J. Watson, Jr., is a pilot - and he wants IBM to supply the computers for the new system. But IBM is in the midst of finishing the development of one line of *compatible* computers that will replace its several lines of incompatible computers. This new 'family' of computers will be the IBM 360. It is a mammoth undertaking. Fortune Magazine in 1965 will feature the effort and label the story "IBM Bets the Company". The Washington IBM people are well aware of the chairman's interest. They have been working with the FAA research people and with the Air Traffic Controllers. And also with the IBM product development people.

# BATTLE #1: IBM MARKETING VS. IBM DEVELOPMENT

On a beautiful May morning, 1963, I leave home in suburban Maryland and drive down the elegant Connecticut Avenue in the District of Columbia, en route to the Mayflower Hotel, in Washington, D. C. I am very happy with the state of things. I am 7 years in IBM, 4 months as a manager, in IBM's Federal sales sector, and I am responsible for the IBM –FAA interaction.

I know what the FAA plans to buy. The FAA is telling all computer companies that it want a 'multiprocessor'. Multiple memories and multiple processors -CPUs, interconnected so that any processor can get to any memory unit. This is a new type of computer system. In the last 4 months I have briefed key corporate Vice Presidents in IBM. The VPs know that the chairman wants to win, and they tell me, "Joe, you will get whatever it takes. Everyone is on board."

I am heading to the annual sales "convention" for the IBM people working with the U. S. Federal Government. About 500 people will be there. A new VP whom I am yet to meet is in charge and will lead the meeting. I am 28 years old. Seven-years out of college and in IBM. A manager of several salesmen since January.

THE V. P. OF ENGINEERING.

As I enter the Mayflower Hotel on Connecticut Avenue, I spy the vice president of the Data Systems division, the individual in charge of developing the new line of computers, Bob O. Evans. I have never met Bob. I recognize him from photos. He is a big, heavy man – about 6 feet 3 inches.

Sam Kilner, my boss, had described Evans to me.

"His memory is phenomenal. He forgets nothing. He takes no notes, yet if you tell him a number on the first of the month, and try to change it 20 days later, he'll catch you.

'You said 47, not 57.'

And that is on any subject, not just the ones he's interested in. He can listen to a presentation, talk on the phone, dictate, - all at once. Then after appearing not to listen at all, he'll repeat the key points of the presentation, point out subtleties and contradictions, dictate action items, and dismiss the presenters or thank them, as the case may be.

If he doesn't like the presentation, he will at times call in his secretary and introduce the presenters to her. 'This is Mr. X and Mr. Y!'

They say hello to each other.

Then, he says to his secretary: 'Now that you know who they are, never let them in again!'

Kilner tells me that Evans has two kinds of subordinates. Those that do everything he says without question – and those who will fight him tooth and nail.

"And he uses the strengths of both."

*I will learn in the next several months that most of this is accurate.*

Evans is sitting in the lobby. I have never met him but I recognize him. I introduce myself. I begin to relate the needs for the upcoming FAA procurement. And point out that the FAA wants a multiprocessor. Several Compute elements interacting with many memories.

Evans stops me.

"I've heard about this. You say that our new line of computers will not sell."

"That's right."

"Well, the products are adequate for the job. You are paid to sell the standard product line. Sell it."

"Bob, the FAA wants a multiprocessor."

"It is your job, Joe, to sell the standard line. If you can't, you should get off the account and let someone who can sell take over. Multiprocessing will not work. IBM will not bid a multiprocessor."

"Bob, the RFP (Request for Proposal) will demand a multiprocessor."

"Then you have not done your job, Joe. Too bad. We lose."

I am floored. I play my trump card.

"But, Watson wants to win…"

Evans interrupts.

"That is your problem. Look. I am behind schedule. Nice meeting you. Good luck selling the standard line."

And Evans ups and leaves.

This is not good. Bob Evans is the most important technical person in IBM. What seemed under control 10 minutes ago is in jeopardy. He said, "IBM will not bid a multiprocessor."

I go to the meeting at the Mayflower Hotel. Ralph A. Pfeiffer Jr. is the new Vice President of Federal Marketing for the IBM Data Processing (DP) Division. He is hosting a gathering of the Washington sales force at the Mayflower.

I have not met him. He is now my boss's, boss's, boss. An organization change a month before brought him from IBM Westchester, New York, to Washington. It switched the sales group that I am in from the Federal Systems Division – called 'FSD' - and to the Data Processing Division, called 'DP'.

This is a crucial change. DP sells standard computers, priced and described in catalogues. FSD had been in charge of sales to the federal government for all IBM computers, announced or made to order. "Announced" is the key adjective. Responsibility for *standard* computer sales now has moved to DP, and Pfeiffer has taken over federal sales of standard computers- announced and priced. And all the sales people for FAA. And me.

The meeting is informative, but it is mostly to have Ralph introduced and the new organization defined. Hank White –my boss for the last 2 years - is in FSD. He was promoted to assistant to the president of the Federal Systems Division - a stepping-stone for people moving up the hierarchy. I filled his vacated position in January. And now we are in different divisions.

White had been in the sales job for only 18 months or so. Before that he had been in engineering management positions in the

A Brawl in IBM - 1964

Federal Division. He has been crucial to the effort with FAA. He organized the sales and technical team that I now manage. He left me a superb team. We are far overstaffed vis a vis the income from the FAA – they have but a few IBM computers installed.

The team has been assembled for the upcoming computer competition. We have two senior Federal Division technical people in the same office space in downtown Washington with our sales people. And White's division is paying for them. Sitting at the right hand of the division president, we had been in close contact with high-level IBM executives.

Kilner and I have been trying for 2 months to brief the new guy Pfeiffer on the FAA. We need him to continue to carry the FAA story in New York, where the corporate headquarters of IBM and many HQ's of its divisions are located. The RFP –Request For Proposal- from the FAA is scheduled to be out to industry this summer.

## DEVELOPMENT DIVISION VP AGAIN SAYS 'NO BID - JULY 1963.

Two months since I met Evans, but have still not gotten to Pfeiffer, but Bob Evans comes to Washington to visit with Sam Kilner and me. Kilner and I have yet to met and brief the new VP of sale, Pfeiffer. Sam Kilner invites Hank White to the meeting. I am delighted. White and I work well together. And Kilner I like and respect – he is stable, thoughtful and knows the IBM entities in New York.

After friendly opening hellos, Evans draws on the board a line of 5 different sized, compatible computers that he has in development. The line will be the IBM 360, but that name is in the future. Software developed for one model can run - unchanged - on all the others.

He shows two interconnected CPU's- a "duplexed" system. One computer can handle all the computing, and the second one is a spare- ready to switch to doing the air traffic control functions if the first computer fails.

"And we can hook up as many CPU's in a system as we want – to as many memories as we want." he says.

I am delighted. It can be a multiprocessor.

"BUT," he says, "we shouldn't sell it as a multiprocessor. That's like selling poisoned food! It would be irresponsible to bid it."

"*Oh.*"

He continues.

"The new line is best as a 'duplexed' system – one standby CPU to jump in if the first CPU fails. And the 'family' – the same instruction set across all the graduated sizes of the 360, small systems to very powerful big systems – the family takes care of any growth in the number of flights to be handled. As the air traffic increases and the to be mid-power model 50 (360 computer) can not handle it, we take out the model 50 and roll in the more powerful model 60, and the software will work - unchanged."

But I know that FAA does not want a duplex. A duplex will not win the immanent competition.

"Bob," I say, "with a multiprocessor, you just wheel in an additional CPU, connect it up, and off you go."

"Joe, do not sell multiprocessing. We can upgrade in eight hours, and the reliability is there. There are big problems with a multiprocessor."

"Bob, I know there are problems with the multiprocessor. I've written a 15-page paper on the problems and I have given a copy to FAA, and…"

"I don't believe you."

A short silence ensues.

*He is calling me a liar.*

*How do I respond to that?*

"You don't believe what?"

"I don't believe you wrote a 15-page paper on this."

I stare.

Evans says, "Get it for me."

I go to my office. I cannot find it!

I return.

"I'll have to mail it to you." I say lamely.

Evans smiles.

"I'll be looking for it."

Evans looks at the three of us.

## A Brawl in IBM - 1964

"Sell the standard line guys - or you'll be in deep trouble."

We then talk briefly about the upcoming visit to IBM Poughkeepsie –Evans's main location - by the key FAA people, - to hear about the new 360 line. The visit is to take place in mid-August. Evans agrees to be the host for the visit.

✯ ✯ ✯

After the meeting, White says, "Joe, you've got a job. You have to prove to Evans that a multiprocessor is better."

"Hank, I've tried, and . . ."

"Yeah, but you've been selling. Now prove it!"

"You know, Hank, you need an open mind to work with in order to prove something. I can't prove the sun comes up in the morning to someone who doesn't want to believe it."

"Evans isn't like that."

"Oh yeah?"

"Well, I want you to prove it."

I shrug, "OK."

I don't work for White anymore, but that doesn't stop White from being the boss.

And that is OK.

Kilner and White, DP and FSD, put into writing what they'd heard Evans say at the meeting –that the 360 line would be a multi-processor. The letters to Evans, dated July 23, said:

(1) A 360 with 2 processors would be announced.

(2) A 360 up to 10 processors could be designed specially.

White's letter also said they could win the business with what Evans described. But, neither one put in writing that Evans would not bid a multiprocessor. They punt.

✯ ✯ ✯

I decide to try to get Evans's own people to state that a multi-processor is the way to go. I arrange a meeting in Poughkeepsie, N.Y. – up along the Hudson River, two hours by car from LaGuardia

Airport. The labs of Evans's division –the Data Systems Division, called "DS" - are located there. If I can get the 360 engineers to study the issue and recommend a multiprocessor, perhaps I might sway Evans.

But I still need to get my own vice president, on board - the new guy, Pfeiffer. We must get him up to speed- the RFP is 60 days away!

We cannot get an appointment.

Kilner writes to Pfeiffer on July 25.

> The FAA RFP - Request for Proposal- will be out in September.
> FAA wants the first computer for a test system for its R&D Center, in mid 1964, and a computer system in one of its 22 Air Traffic Control centers by mid 1965.
> A multiprocessor is needed.
> There is great confusion about the 360 development status and abilites.
> Informally, it is a multiprocessor; in writing it is not.
> FAA soon will visit IBM Poughkeepsie to be briefed on the 360.
> This will be a $100,000,000 dollar computer order.
> The Chairman is personally interested.
> We should brief 0. M. Scott (Pfeiffer's boss's, boss's boss); Al Williams (President of IBM) and Tom Watson (Chairman) - A.S.A.P.

## DO NOT TELL THE FAA
## THEIR DESIGN WILL NOT WORK

Unable to see Pfeiffer, faced with an immanent procurement and with a flat "We won't bid a multiprocessor" from Evans, I decide to act on my own. It will take too long to get a letter approved by the new guy - whom I have not even met yet. I must get it to Evans before the FAA visit.

I send the letter to Evans and copy only White. It says that it is essential to tell the FAA people as much about the new 360 line as possible.

## A Brawl in IBM - 1964

And *"...we must not tell them that multiprocessing will not work or is not the way to go. FAA is committed to this approach. If we desire to express our concern, we can do so privately to one or two of the key people. ...*

*In conclusion, you must not, in your presentation, knock multiprocessing. To do so would do perhaps irreparable harm to our chances of winning the FAA business.*

That is a stake in the ground! Evans had better think twice about condemning multiprocessing in the briefing. It could -would -blow us out of the competition. And now it is "in writing." And the chairman wants to win. And I send Evans a copy of the 15-page paper showing multiprocessor problems. The one I had been unable to find during his July 15 visit.

Not copying Kilner and Pfeiffer on the letter is a deliberate decision. They would delay and water-down any memo, and review draft after draft - and time is running out.

✯ ✯ ✯

July 30, 1963 -I drive up to the IBM laboratories in Poughkeepsie N. Y., after taking the Eastern Airlines "Shuttle" from Washington National airport to LaGuardia in New York city. The Shuttle is an hours flight – every hour of the day - to and from La Guardia in New York and National Airport in Washington. One gets on the plane with no ticket - and buys the ticket on the plane – no reservation- just board and pay. If it would be over-sold, they usually run out a second airplane. It is convenient and easy. They use the 3 tailed 4 propeller airplane, the Constellation.

With me is Jack Collins who has taken the job I had until I was promoted 6 months ago. I am now the manager of the DP Washington-based sales group for FAA, the National Bureau of Standards, the U. S. Weather Bureau, and the weather division of NASA.

When we set out to get a senior salesman to replace me, the IBM personnel system had popped up the name John J. Collins, Jr. He joined us a month before. He had been one of IBM's outstanding salesmen in 1962, working in Elmira, in mid New York State.

"Who are these people we are meeting with, Joe?"

"The key man is Fred Brooks. He's the project manager for the 360. PHD. Reports to Evans Working for Brooks is Jack Keeley. He was *our* Federal Systems Division's manager on site with the FAA Research Center outside Atlantic City (N J) up till last year. We had 50 FSD engineers there, helping with the "test bed" that FAA was operating. We moved 40 families to the Atlantic City area and then we lost that contract – we moved them back to where they came from. I almost lost my job over that. I'll tell you more about that later.

"Keeley went back to FSD, in Kingston - near Poughkeepsie. Evans wrote to the FSD President, Don Spaulding, said 'the FAA procurement is going to pop, give me Keeley, I'll have him work directly for Brooks to assure that 360 meets FAA requirements."

"He's our man on the inside?"

"Right. Nice guy; smart; smooth. FAA loved him - but we have to watch him."

"Why?"

"He is new to DS. He doesn't know the politics, the players. It is tough to be bold in a new division. He'd been in the Federal Division for his whole career. But he's Evans' pick! So we'll use him as a messenger back to Evans - his own man saying 'we need multiprocessing.' He'll be at this meeting. Maybe we can get Evans's own people to endorse the FAA design."

"Will Evans be there?"

"No. He is out of town. But Fred Brooks will be here- he is the architect of the new line."

*Evans and Brooks in 1985 will receive from Ronald Reagan in the White House the National Medal for Technical Achievement for the work they are doing in this memoir period - creating the new line of IBM standard computers. That same occasion awarded Steve Jobs and Steve Wasniac receive the same medal for their <u>personal computer</u> work. And the Boeing team received it for the 747 airplane.*

## A Brawl in IBM - 1964

*But it is now 1963. 22 years before the medals – but for the work they are about.*

I fill Collins in on the 'test bed' at the FAA center outside of Atlantic City in New Jersey – an old U. S. Navy post. Dozens of old barracks refitted as offices, and several large lab buildings. The test bed has as its center an IBM 7090, the largest scientific computer the IBM makes. The test bed is to run simulated air traffic problems, to discover which functions help the controller and which functions do not - or are even distractions.

The Test Bed. Well before we put anything into controlling real airplanes, it is tested extensively. The major pieces of an air traffic en route system are simulated in the test bed. There are the radar systems. The controllers. The air routes- highways laid out in the sky and defined by radio direction signals. There are the pilots. There are the radio systems. And of course there is the software to drive the computers.

All systems must work together –or the overall system does not work.

The test bed consists of radars, displays, and computers to process all the info and route it to the controllers' displays.

So in the FAA site outside Atlantic City, in a very large room, one can watch the rudimentary predecessor of the future system in operation. With real FAA controllers. On loan from the FAA Operating Division. With the IBM 7090. With newer displays than the ones in the actual control rooms in 20 sites across the U. S.

How do we get the planes into the system? There can be scores of planes in the air daily – hundreds even. There are airplane *simulators* in the room. They show up on the controllers' displays the way they would were they actually coming in from the radars. "Pilots" sit at the controls of the 'plane' and do what the controllers tell them to do.

"AA921 – turn left onto route 17 and descend to 10,000 feet. Reduce your speed to 250."

Now in a real system it takes time to implement these directions. So the simulators send information to the 7090 computer at the times that a real plane would, with all the intervening locations, altitudes and speeds. The FAA has written the software to do all this.

The second by second results that are expected are printed in a document as thick as a phone book for New York City. Second by second – for all the units of the system. The controllers do their thing as they would in the actual center. The radars and the planes are simulated.

But – how do we get pilots to sit there and do this simulation over and over? And if the system 'goes down' – as it does very often – all the dozens of players in that room turn to reading and chatting. They do not leave – the system may come back up in a few minutes.

How does the FAA get the pilots into this test system? They hire *housewives* to be the pilots. They sit at the physical mockup of an airplane pilot's unit, and they turn the 'planes' left or right and push the throttles forward or back to fulfill the commands of the controllers. The computers in the mock-ups put out signals at the time that the plane would reach the altitude, the speed and the heading called for. And they send out all the intermediate altitudes etc. And the simulators fit the type of plane – jet or prop and model and make. And they then display on a screen what the controller would see.

The test bed works – and the developers of the new system learn what the controllers hate and what they like.

Back to our all day meeting in Poughkeepsie. The two FSD people that White and Federal Systems Division was funding on the effort make all the presentations to the DS product division engineers and software people. Problems and potential solutions are aired. The group seems to like the multiprocessor idea, and when Collins and I drive the two hours back to LaGuardia Airport, we judge the meeting had made progress. The DS people agreed to summarize the meeting and make a recommendation. Back to LaGuardia Airport and fly back to Washington on the 9:00 PM Shuttle. Home at 11 pm.

A Brawl in IBM - 1964

## OUR NEW SALES V. P.

July 31, 1963. I slouch in the chair in front of Kilner's desk. Sam Kilner, a boyish-looking 30-year old, is my boss. He's worked in DP Headquarters, in White Plains, N. Y., in Westchester, an hour north of Manhattan. I like Sam and particularly value his knowledge of the HQ communities of IBM.

"Damn, Sam! The damn RFP will be out before we get to see Pfeiffer."

"Patience, Joe. We'll see him."

Sam is always optimistic.

"It'd better be soon if he's to help us accelerate the delivery of the computer we need. Time is against us. Every day DS doesn't accelerate the effort is a day we lose, Sam."

I had told Kilner about the Poughkeepsie meeting. "They're not sparing the horses," I said. "They had a big group of great people there".

"That's good. Maybe Evans will mellow on multiprocessing if a few of his own people come to him and espouse it."

At noon, my phone rings. Kilner.

"We see Pfeiffer at 5. Ready?"

"Ready".

We go across to the IBM building on Connecticut Avenue, next to the Mayflower Hotel, between L Street and M streets at 4:45.

As we wait outside the office, I look at the changes that have been made. The new guy is making his presence felt. Walls are down; new carpeting, lights and furniture are everywhere.

*New executives always feel the impulse to make their presence known. New executives always seem to write a memo to all employees in their department or division or company. It is usually on some trivial matter. What it really said was, 'I am Here. In case you missed the bulletin board announcement.'*

At 6:00 we go in. We are introduced to Ralph Pfeiffer, a big 6 foot 2, a 220 pounder in fine clothes, IBM blue suit, and striped tie.

"Hello! Hello!" Pfeiffer booms, his eyes a-flicker with interest. We all shake hands.

"You've got 40 minutes," - pleasant but firm.

I start as dramatically as I can.

"Seven years ago two commercial airplanes TWA and United – full of people – collided over the Grand Canyon. 128 were killed. Three years ago, a TWA prop and United jet collided in midair over Staten Island. One fell on a government owned field in Staten Island. One fell in Brooklyn. All dead. 134 - and 6 more people on the ground.

Two mid-air collisions within 4 years. And jets are replacing the propeller planes, and their greater speed makes the situation worse. President Kennedy appointed a Presidential Commission to look at the system. The committee said 'Stop fooling around developing new computers and get on with developing a <u>system</u>!'"

"What's that mean?"

"The FAA had had a competition in 1958 for a computer to automate the system. IBM bid a version of our Air Force Air Defense computer. And lost. FAA bought a way-undersized computer. Ever since, FAA has been spending millions - speeding up the CPU, enlarging drums and things like that. They're all bogged down trying to get that undersized computer to go faster, do more. And the committee said: 'Stop'. You're wasting time. Get on with the system's task and buy off-the-shelf computers.'"

"Is that good for us?"

"Yes and no. Yes, because FAA has abandoned their futile attempt to grow the old machine. No, because it's not clear that we have a machine that is "off-the-shelf" that can do the job."

"What's off-the-shelf mean?"

"Right. Exactly. What does that mean? It seems to mean standard, priced, announced, stocked in quantity and you can walk in and buy one that is <u>on</u> the shelf for sale. It's taken 'off a shelf'".

I continue. "There are 22 centers around the US that house the controllers who tell the pilots what to do so as to facilitate traffic and avoid mid air collisions. Control Towers at airports have their own system to take care of the air space for take-offs and landings.

## A Brawl in IBM - 1964

They are the "Terminal Control" systems. They are not in this procurement. This is for the En Route Systems.

With 22 en route control centers in the country, and 6,000 to 10,000 controllers on duty at any time, and with 24/7 operation, the FAA will buy about 66 computers for this system. The system will display to controllers the position, identity, and the future path of the airplanes in the controlled space and part of the space over the oceans. It will alert the controller if it 'sees' a potential near miss or collision.

This will be 100 million-dollar procurement. Many computer companies are after this contract.

Watson wants to win. We are beautifully positioned – FAA respects us because we've done <u>everything</u> right for the last three years.

Pfeiffer shows no signs of hurry.

"How do you know Watson wants to win?"

"We had 50 IBM Federal System engineers at FAA's Atlantic City research facility. For 6 months. For ONLY 6 months. After we got there, FAA had to compete the effort. We lost it in January, due to ineptness on the FAA's technical people in writing the request for proposal. They really wanted us to win! That is not wishful thinking. Key FAA people *apologized* to me – they had lost control of the procurement - which was then run totally by the procurement staff and not the technical people. "We owe you one." I was told by a few of them.

"Within two days, Watson had a letter to the division asking why we lost. By the way, those 50 IBM engineers worked till midnight on their last day on the effort – to make sure they gave the new people as much information as possible. The FAA people were blown away by this impromptu show of support for the effort by the IBM engineers. All our people know that in the end it is lives we are dealing with. The people in the planes."

*(NOTE: 47 years later – 2010 –I was talking with a retired procurement official of the FAA and he asked me if I remembered that the IBM people had worked till midnight that last day. I assured him that I did remember. I take no credit for it – the engineers did it on their own initiative.)*

"Ralph, because of the high level interest, we've always over-manned this account. We have two superb technical people full time from FSD- and paid for by FSD - assigned to the effort. Ken Kowalke is an ex-Air Traffic Controller. We know what the controller sees and needs to do.

Charlie Oldani is a senior systems engineer. He 'sizes' the work the computer needs to do and then measures the ability of a model of a computer to see if it has the power to do the processing - before the radar sweep dumps in a whole new batch of data. He is superb.

We know what we need. We know what the RFP will ask for.

Ralph, there is a deep divide within the FAA - between the FAA Operations Division that has all the controllers, and the Research Division that has the mission to design the new system. We have both of these divisions very happy with IBM now. Jack Collins and I work with the Research Division, and John Finley and Earl Whitney work with the Operations Division.

Pfeiffer interrupts.

"How did the midair over Staten Island happen, Joe?"

"The official investigation blamed navigator error in the United plane. The plane had reported that one of the two DME systems (distance measuring equipment) was not working. They were not where they thought they were."

"But shouldn't the controller see that on his radar screen?"

"Theoretically, yes. But there were a lot of clouds, heavy snow - and the radar often doesn't see through the clouds. The report did not blame the controller. And there is a tendency to blame the dead. They can't fight the findings. But I don't know, really.

"Will the new system help?

"Absolutely! It will clear up the radar screen. It will put altitude and ID on each radar return. That's not there now. It will beep and flash to alert the controller if a collision is predicted. And it will eliminate the need for the printed flight strip"

I continue.

"IBM has a string of impressive accomplishments with FAA. We had built the 50-man force near Atlantic City that gained the respect of the whole FAA development team. We convinced them to get a

## A Brawl in IBM - 1964

7090 –IBM's largest scientific machine, to drive the test bed where procedures for the controllers were tested. We built and delivered- on time - a real time channel that FAA technical people said we could not do in a year. We did it in six months. Our engineers worked unasked till midnight on their last day, to make as sure as possible that the new company coming in could get to work quickly.

We are 'positioned' perfectly for this bid – except for the product to sell.

As luck would have it, the machine of the 360 line that fits the air traffic is the machine that is to be announced to the public last. It's the model 50. It has the least budget and fewest people and not enough detail."

Pfeiffer asks, "What about software?"

"Right. We need something, almost anything. We're so far ahead of the 360 that they've got nothing. We need a JOVIAL - or something like it. JOVIAL is the Air force language -of -choice for real time systems. It stands for Jules Own Version of the International Algebraic Language. And it is a very powerful compiler."

"And DS says...?"

"They've got nothing. We may have to contract it out of here."

"No way. That's not our strength."

"Now, the BIG problem, Ralph. – multiprocessing. The design the FAA has come up with is a multiprocessor. And, by the way, they have full time computer people from MITRE – MIT Research and Engineering. Full time on site with the FAA here in Washington. They are competent.

"Back to the computer specs so far. Some centers would have two central processing units, -CPUs - some will have three CPUs and some four. All the same machine make and model. All spare parts the same! All the same software- the application of tracking and displaying the lanes, locations. Simplified error finding and repair. AND any failures would be less disabling. This is the FAA design."

"The computers will predict the future locations of the planes AND predict when two planes would be close to colliding. They would display all this to the controller for him to take action."

Each center would have the traffic grow over the years - or shrink. They want a multiprocessor. All the same machine. Failures would be less disabling. Training would be easier."

I summarize - at 7:30 PM.

"So - in a month we will get an RFP (request for a proposal) for over $100,000,000 worth of computers. We know the requirements. IBM's reputation is outstanding with the FAA. BUT -the 360 is coming too late. We need to get delivery accelerated for the model 50.

{*There were to be 5 models of the 360 – named the Model 20, the Model 30, the 40 the 50 the 60 and the 70. The 20 was the least powerful and the 70 the most powerful.*}

Product. We know enough to pick the model 50 –and we need to get DS to design it as a multiprocessor, and support a bid.

"Competition. Burroughs Corporation has such a multiprocessor– called the D825. They have won a U.S. Air Force bid with it. They are the leaders in this competition.

"Ralph, you don't win one of these big ones because you're quick and lucky. You plot and plan and set everything up years in advance. And we've done this. When Hank White had my job, he had 5 full-time *senior* representatives on an account paying us almost nothing. We now have two senior FSD people doing FAA research for us - on FSD money.

"The product division has agreed that they can build the 360 as a multiprocessor –BUT - they won't. They say, 'bid two model 60's -a duplex'. And Bob Evans says flatly, emphatically, 'We will not bid a multiprocessor'. Will NOT."

Ralph slaps his forehead.

"This is incredible. How many people in headquarters know all this, Joe?"

"We've briefed almost everyone. On March 21, I went with Don Spaulding (President of FSD) and we briefed 0. M. Scott (Group V.P.). This year, I briefed Fred Brooks in DSD, the architect for the 360. We visited Brooks' assistant, Gene Amdahl. They told us that Federal Systems should modify the standard 360 line.

## A Brawl in IBM - 1964

We briefed a model 70 review group - the fastest of the new line. John Opel {IBM chairman in 1981.} was there. We said we'd lose the Air Traffic Control bid if we had no multiprocessor.

"OK." Pfeiffer gives directions.

"You've briefed Scotty once (the Group Vice President). Now we'll see him again in a few days –I'll set it up –I want this presentation and a letter from me summarizing where we are and what we want."

I drive home at 8:00 PM. Delighted.

The new guy is a doer! Going to see Scott next week! It had taken a long time to get to Pfeiffer, but the RFP release had kept slipping too. Pfeiffer had absorbed a great deal of information and asked good questions. And he was in motion – going to brief Scott, his boss's boss. Ralph was going to put his energy and reputation into this bid.

✣ ✣ ✣

On August 1, Thursday, Kilner and I work up a two-page letter to Scott from Pfeiffer, listing all the issues. Then we take the Shuttle to New York's La Guardia airport, get a car and drive to Westchester. We make flip charts till 1:00 AM. On Friday, we meet with Pfeiffer and "Scotty."

I give the presentation. There are no problems. We get Scott's support to disclose the 360 plan to FAA. We are to get IBM legal to approve such a disclosure of an unannounced computer.

We are to meet with Evans as soon as possible. I am delighted. As we are about to leave, Scotty looks at me.

"Joe, your job is to tell us what we need to win. Do not get seduced by the product division. You'll be working with them every day. They'll become your friends. They'll convince you that they can't deliver what you need. Stick to your version of what is needed! Do you understand?"

"Yes sir."

"Let us at this level decide if what they say they can do is all that they can do. You, Joe, do not know the reserves of IBM. And often the product division people do not, either. Don't compromise."

"I got it."
Scotty turns to Ralph.
"Let me know how the meeting goes."
I tell Collins of the meeting.
"He's right, Joe; you know that. You can't compromise! You must get everything! You never know which of 98 little items will tip the scale."
"I know, I know."

☆ ☆ ☆

In Washington on Monday, August 5, I stop by to see Carl Donnelly, the IBM Director of Air Force marketing, in the 1120 Connecticut Avenue building. Pfeiffer told me to get a run-down from Carl on big bids, as Donnelly had just submitted a bid for over 100 small computers for the Air Force.

Donnelly was in his late 40's, early 50's.

He turns somber as I come in, gets up and shuts his office door.

I am puzzled –this was no 'heavy' meeting.

"Ralph told me to tell you, Joe, what it's like on these big bids."

"Right," I smile, trying to change the mood.

Donnelly looks into space and shakes his head.

"It was awful, Joe, awful. The pressure is fantastic."

He pauses.

"You are caught in the middle. You know - or think you do- what you need to win, but they don't have it. They keep compromising, offering you this or that. And - you get to understand their problems. And you get to be their friend. They're nice people."

I listen, nodding.

"And if you blow the whistle on them by demanding what they can't give, you've severely hurt their careers."

Donnelly is somber.

"The pressure is awful. It got so bad, I cried."

I am not ready for this.

Donnelly is upset now –in fact, he seems on the verge of breaking down.

"I cried. And of course I was immediately embarrassed. It was awful, Joe. You have my sympathy."

He shakes my hand.

✾ ✾ ✾

The committee that had been assembled by DS to evaluate multiprocessing had worked intensively. Kowalke and Oldani -from FSD and assigned to FAA effort- participated and worked straight through the weekend.

The committee concluded:
(I) Multiprocessing was required.
(2) The model 50 could be modified to be a multiprocessor.
(3) The model 50 delivery could be accelerated to meet FAA requirements.

Evans' own people were saying that! We are delighted. Now to get them to brief Evans.

# BATTLE 2 - THE 'ORANGE SODA' MEETING

Tuesday, August 6, Pfeiffer, Kilner and I get on the Shuttle to New York, en route to meet Evans in his office Harrison, Westchester NY, an hour out of New York City. DS's labs were in Poughkeepsie, but the executive offices were in Harrison. Evans has offices in both.

On the 3-tailed Super Constellation propeller plane, I sit in a middle seat, between Kilner and Pfeiffer. I begin to brief Pfeiffer en route. It is only the second time I have met Pfeiffer. I tell him about the study results of the DS committee, that DS people had supported multiprocessing.

"An we've got to tell Evans that he must not attack multiprocessing when he speaks to the FAA visitors next week, Ralph."

"Why?"

"Bob is so strong and so forceful that he'll try to make multiprocessing look like the black plague, and..."

"If that happens, fine, Joe. FAA'll buy a duplexed computer."

"No they won't. I've used all of Evans' arguments on the FAA. They are not persuadable. Their mind is made up. The only thing that will come out of such a meeting is FAA convinced that we are not serious about multiprocessing."

"But Bob will tell them that we can build it their way."

"Telling them in one sentence that we can, and in 100 why it's stupid is inviting a loss on this program, Ralph."

"You don't think Evans can be impartial?"

"No. He hasn't been to date. And his people are petrified to admit they can make a multiprocessor work. Watch today. There'll be people in that room who completely agree with the us but they'll not say so because it might end their career."

"We'll see."

# A Brawl in IBM - 1964

Ten minutes later, I speak again. Ralph is reading his mail.
"Ralph, Evans gets pretty dominating at times."
"Fine." Ralph continues to read his mail.
I pursue it.
"I think he tries to win by sheer force of will. He..."
"Look, Joe, I'm no newcomer. If you don't have something of substance, let me work in peace."
I shut up.
I flip through the copies of the charts we are to use. After about 20 minutes, I write on a yellow pad some ideas about the software we need to bid – a compiler and support software.
I interrupt Ralph's reading.
"Ralph, here's a problem with the bid and an approach to fix it."
I show Ralph the brief words on the yellow pad, and begin to talk to them.
"We need a language for the programmers..."
"What's this mean?"
He points to the letters "SWR" near the top of the page.
"That means 'software'. We need..."
"Joe, I do not have time to guess at your abbreviations. If you want to show me something, spell out everything."
I say nothing for the remainder of the trip.

I had been in this manager's job about one month, in February of 1963, when my boss Kilner had come rushing into my office with a letter.
"Go see Charlie Benton (Pfeiffer's predecessor) on this. Today! I am going to New York; tell Charlie we want his support on this issue. Will he agree?"
I read the letter, understood it, and go across to 1111 Connecticut Avenue.
I can't see Benton, the secretary said. Too busy.
I hang around, pester, bother, and finally get in.
There are three other people in the office with Charlie Benton who seems a little annoyed. He knew me slightly.
"What is it, Joe?"

"We got this memo." I explain. Benton looks at the memo. Pauses.

"What is the date on this memo, Joe?"

"Uh, - I don't know." I wonder why the question.

"It's six months old!"

"Oh."

"You've got to get on the stick, Joe. You can't grab time on an urgent basis for something 6 months old!"

I am speechless. I am taking short steps backwards toward the door.

"Ah, ah..."

The other three people are watching, a little bemused, a little sympathetic.

"Thank you, Charlie."

I scoot out the door.

When Kilner got back, I told him about the incident.

"I should have seen the date, Sam."

"No, it's my fault, Joe."

"No, no. Mine."

Kilner talked to Benton later and related the conversation.

"Charlie, Joe is brand-new as a manager. You could be a little gentle with him."

"Hey. Let him learn what it's really like," said Benton. "If he's good he'll learn. He wasn't hurt."

✯ ✯ ✯

Pfeiffer, Kilner and I drive to Harrison to meet with Evans. A big building -two product division headquarters are here -DS, the Data System Division, and GP, the General Products Division. GP has the "small" computer mission and are not involved in the 360 nor the FAA effort. This division makes the most populous general purpose computer in the world at that time – the IBM 1401.

### A Brawl in IBM - 1964

*The "Border Fixation Law" was at work. Whoever first coined the word "divisions" to describe different groupings of endeavor in a corporation was predicting the warfare that occurs at the boundary. Both divisions assembled much of their talent at the dividing line, so as to fight the other one furiously. Each division believes that this area belongs to it to supply.*

Pfeiffer has two subjects to meet with Evans on this day - the FAA bid and another massive bid to the Air Force, called Autodin. Dave Fine –like me, three levels under Pfeiffer, - is there waiting. The secretary says that an FAA engineering group is already in Evans' office and so Pfeiffer, Kilner and I enter.

As soon as I enter the room, my spirits rise. There are the key people from the DS study team we briefed!

After hellos, I stand to give the briefing. My first chart is concerned with delivery.

> **OPTIMUM IBM BID**
> **BID MODEL 50**
> **INSTALL SEPTEMBER 1964**
> **ALSO PRICE AND DELIVERY FOR models 40 and 50 and 60 FOR MID 1965**
> **PROBLEMS**
> **No MODEL 50 IN 1964** –first Model 50 is scheduled delivery is a year later

"I can't promise any those dates," says Evans. "They are way out of line," .

"I understand." I say, and I turn to the next chart.

> **BEST ALTERNATIVE**
> 1. **BID MODEL 40 FOR SEPTEMBER '64**
> 2. **COMMIT MODEL 50 FOR MID '65**
>
> **360's STRENGTH**
> **IT WINS EITHER WAY!**
> **IT IS A MULTIPROCESSOR -CURRENT FAA FAVORITE**

## IT IS A FAMILY IN CASE MULTIPROCESSING DOESN'T FLY.

Now all hell breaks loose. Evans slams the desk.
"I will not bid a multiprocessor. It is irresponsible"
I remain calm.
"Bob, if we've got it, let's bid it."
"Look!" says Evans. "I'm trying to cooperate with you people and I get a letter from you (pointing at me) that tells me not to attack multiprocessing with the FAA when they visit next week."
"It doesn't say not attack..." I start to explain.
Kilner and Pfeiffer are exchanging glances.
I am caught. Not showing them the letter to Evans is a <u>big</u> mistake.
And it is now out and all over the floor.
Evans is loud.
"I'm going to get my shot at the FAA. I'm going to tell them they're NUTS!"
"And if you do, we'll lose," I say - quietly.
"No. You'll lose, Joe. You're crazy. It's you who wants a multiprocessor. You've got this thing all screwed up."
"Bob, the FAA is going to buy a multiprocessor. If you want to point out pitfalls, fine. If you hammer the idea to smithereens, you'll destroy our believability. We can't have our top technical leader be 99% against and 1% for!"
Evans glowers.
"Bob, your people agree that a multiprocessor is workable. We had a task force in Poughkeepsie the last few weeks and..."
Evans stands up, takes orange soda he'd been drinking filled with *crushed- ice.* –now drained of liquid - and *flings* the cup at the wall behind me. Ice pieces- not cubes - riddle the walls of room like BB's from a shotgun.
Pitter-patter, pitter-patter, pitter-patter on the walls.
Evans's people seem to shrink down into their seats.
No one speaks  - or moves.
Evans now punches the blackboard on the wall that separates his desk from the secretarial area. Chalk dust spews out.

# A Brawl in IBM - 1964

(Later, his secretary will tell me that the sudden crash right next to her head made her jump five inches. "I thought it was an earthquake." she told me.)

I break the following silence.

"Bob, you said in Washington two weeks ago you could build the 360 as a multiprocessor. Why are you fighting this approach if you can do it?"

"Because you're sucking us in," he points at me. "You damn well know that the FAA will get in trouble with their system and that IBM will bail them out. We will spend $5 million bailing them out and you know it."

"No, I do not know it. If FAA fails, then FAA fails. They are not some small company that will go under if we do not bail 'em out. We'd be stupid to bail them out. They spend $50 million a year on research and development - they are big boys."

Silence. No one says a word.

Then Pfeiffer speaks.

"I agree with Bob, Joe. If they get in trouble, then we will bail them out. Let's discuss the proposal effort that we want to get going. We will make the decision on whether or not we bid multi-processing later."

I stare.

*Does the new guy have no guts? Does he not understand that we <u>must make</u> the decision? There is no time to keep studying! The RFP is due out in 60 days! FAA is due to visit. We do not have time to "wait and see"? Didn't Scott – our <u>Group</u> V P- say 'don't compromise?*

Keeley, the DS FAA coordinator, later tells me that they – Evans's DS people - were going to speak up, but when they saw Pfeiffer "throw Fox to the wolves," they decided to be quiet. If the vice president of sales wasn't going to fight for the best configuration, then they weren't. They had briefed Evans on the task force results just before DP people came in.

They had supported multiprocessing!

At the end, he'd said, simply, "Thank you"!

And they'd ushered in Pfeiffer, Kilner and me.

Evans, impassive, says nothing to Pfeiffer's comment.
Kilner takes over the meeting.
He shows some charts that divide up the work on the proposal. DS would so this; DP will do this and that. Evans nods agreement to everything. I sit, sullen, trying to think of how to win this fight, or how to restart it! Pfeiffer suddenly switching has me at a complete stop.
I can think of nothing.
And I am furious with myself for not showing Pfeiffer the memo I'd written to Evans. They wrap the meeting up quickly.
Pfeiffer tells Evans he'll take a five-minute break before their second meeting, on the large Air Force bid, Autodin.

*Whence this idea of "Bail them out"? It is THE IBM 'SAVE'*
*There was an IBM legend –repeated over and over – " the midnight save in a blizzard to get the payroll done". It was a story told by the salesmen in every IBM office. When IBM salesmen got together for a drink after work, the old hands would relate their* SAVE *story.*

*It was how the salesman and the repair people fought their way over a mountain pass at midnight through a raging blizzard to fix a printer so that the customer could print the paychecks for the next morning.*

*The workers got paid. If not a blizzard, in other parts of the world it was a hurricane, or a flood. Newer salesmen pined for their chance to save a payroll.*

*This was the logic behind Evans's 'IBM will bail them out.' position.*

Kilner, Pfeiffer and I find a small, unoccupied office down the hall.
Pfeiffer is grim.
"You can't do that," he says to me, with a scowl.
"Do what?" I ask.
"Back a vice president into a corner in front of his people. Hell, you'll never get him to agree that way."
"Ralph, I told you he was going to scream at the fact that we are still convinced that we need a multiprocessor. Look! Time is running

out on this bid, and unless we start to move, it's going to be too late. Evans doesn't want to listen; he just wants us to sell the thing he is building. He..."

"It doesn't matter what he wants, Joe! You backed him into a position that he had only one choice ...to disagree with you."

Kilner jumps in.

"Ralph is right Joe, you can't win this fight head on; you have to finesse Evans."

"I've been trying to do that for months, and we are getting nowhere. Do you want to win this bid or not?"

This gets Pfeiffer even angrier.

"Stop trying to oversimplify the thing, Joe! Everyone wants to win."

A short silence finds the two of them glaring at me.

"You should have showed us the memo you wrote to Evans," Pfeiffer says evenly.

"I apologize for that. I was wrong not to show it to you."

Pfeiffer starts out the door.

"We'll review the whole thing next week. Stay away from the product division until the three of us meet again."

*"Stay away from the product division." ? ? ?*

*Whoops!*

*My job is in jeopardy!*

*Not that I will be fired, but I may find I am no longer the proposal manager for the FAA bid.*

*And I am angry. I knew there would be a battle. And I had warned the 'I'm no novice' new vice president. And he caved.*

*But ... I had not shown my letter.*

✫ ✫ ✫

Kilner and I have dinner that night. Over and over Kilner tries to convince me that we have moved forward.

My mind reels.

'Joe, Evans said he could make the new line a multiprocessor.'

'Sam, he has said –forcefully I might say? – that he is NOT going to allow a multiprocessor to be bid. And we can not propose one without his agreement.'

We go over and over these two points – over and over. Sam is happy with the meeting- I am morose.

# SPINNING WHEELS

The next day we –Kilner and I –go to see Scotty to update him on the Evans meeting. Sam and I are still debating the multiprocessing status as we wait in the outer office. "It was a good Evans' meeting. No it was a bad meeting".

Scott's assistant is on us instantly.

"You guys better agree on what you want to say. Or only one of you better go in there."

Silence.

I surrender and tell Kilner that I will be silent in the Scott meeting. Sam tells Scott we made progress.

We are about to leave when Scotty points a finger at us and looks very sober.

"One thing, one thing. I do not want you to be sympathetic with the product division people. They will try to tell you their problems; - the lack of time, the lack of components; lack of programmers; lack of this and lack of that.

Don't listen.

You are not paid to worry about their problems.

I want you to be tough! No compromises!

You are paid to tell the company what you need to win... and neither embellish nor compromise. Your job is to state what is needed to win."

He pauses for effect.

"Don't be sympathetic. Don't be lured into agreement. Understand?"

We nod.

Kilner goes to see the lawyers. I head for the Shuttle to go back to Washington.

A Brawl in IBM - 1964

I am worried about keeping my job as manager for FAA sales. Pfeiffer said "Stay away from the product division."

## A 28-YEAR-OLD PROPOSAL MANAGER?

How did I come to be in this position? At the ripe old age of 28?

I grew up in Crown Heights, Brooklyn, New York. I graduated from St. John's University in Jamaica, Queens, with a BS degree in mathematics, in June 1956. My parents came from Ireland.

I was a grocery clerk when in high school, in the A&P food store my father managed, a few blocks from where the United jet would fall after the mid air collision of December 1960. I played high school football for St. John's Prep in Brooklyn, with the final game in Ebbett's Field – home of the Dodgers. I was a file clerk in an insurance company in Manhattan after classes during college, a lifeguard in the summers at a surf club on the Atlantic in Queens, NY, and the head lifeguard in the summer of 1955. I never had to save anyone.

I was elected president of the Student Council of St. John's College in my senior year, and that got me into Who's' Who in U. S. Colleges. With a B. S. in math, and a brother–in law who knew some high-up IBM people, I got into IBM in June 1956 in New York City. I had no idea of what IBM did.

I was hired into the Jersey City IBM office as an "applied science representative", to assist IBM sales people with 'scientific' sales efforts. I was to commute from Brooklyn N. Y. to Jersey City N. J. Some friends opined, "They are telling you something, Joe".

I received a full year of great training by IBM – far more that the sales people or the systems support people. Then followed a 6-month stint in the U. S. Army, private-not even first class. I learned to type as an assistant company clerk in Fort Dix, N. J.

In January 1958 IBM moved me to Utica, N. Y. as a commercial sales representative in the Data Processing Division. I sold my first computer - to do payroll at the Revere Copper and Brass plant in Rome, N. Y. It was an IBM 650 computer, with a magnetic drum as the main memory. Core memories were not yet here. The software system was "SOAP" – the Symbolic Operating Assembly Program.

I was sent to class twice on the 7090 computer, then IBM's largest scientific computer. Not that I had failed the first time, but at that time there were no Operating Systems –no OSs - for computers. So one had to learn the intricate timing of the memories, of the processing time required execute each instruction, of the tape speeds and movements of the tapes and disks – stop and start delay times - and the timing of the input and output devices.

When I retook the class, it was 90% the OS, which made it much easier for the software developers – as long as the application was not 'real time'. The OS manages - and hides - the intricate timing of all the channels and memory, and much software work is avoided. The Operating Systems were not usable for real time systems. In a radar system the computation of one pass of the radar data must be completed before the next set of data overwrites the current ones – usually a few seconds. Loss of control of data could have catastrophic consequences. The developers must not permit confusion of the timing of the I/O and the computation in a system that has the potential of catastrophic consequences of failure. Air traffic control is a CCOF system.

In addition to the Revere Copper and Brass effort, I was working with the U. S. Air Force, at Griffiss Air Force Base, also in Rome, N. Y. The Air Force's Intelligence Laboratory was located on the base, and I worked on several large proposals, in 1958 and 1959. I was involved on the periphery of very large real-time systems, which had to be studied carefully to assure that the power of the computer could keep up with the flow of incoming data.

IBM asked me in January 1960 to relocate to San Francisco or to Washington, as a salesman. I picked Washington. It was the site for the headquarters of IBM's sales to the federal government. I wanted to be close to a division headquarters.

# A Brawl in IBM - 1964

In Washington I took a night class given by IBM Federal Systems Division –FSD - in government contracting. I learned what CPFF meant –Cost Plus Fixed Fee - and why it was the only vehicle fair to both the contractor and the government on large *development* efforts. I would see first hand that fixed Fee contracts on real time systems more than once put small software companies out of business. The course was invaluable for upcoming struggles.

My assignment in Washington was a 'special rep' to the U. S. Air Force. In effect, I was a lobbyist visiting the Air Force people in the Pentagon daily. I did not like the job and noticed that the FAA sales group had 5 senior salesmen – and the account had very little IBM gear installed or on order. After asking several people I was told that the chairman of IBM was a pilot – had flown for the U. S. Air force in WW2 – and he wanted to get IBM gear into the FAA air traffic control system. I asked Hank White, manager of the group in Washington with sales responsibility for the FAA and other civilian agencies to get me into his group, which had 5 senior salesmen on the FAA, as well as sales people on the U. S. Weather Bureau, and on the National Bureau of Standards. White was from Brooklyn and we meshed well. I became one of the 5 senior IBM reps on FAA.

Then, after 2 years, in January of 1963, White was promoted to be the Assistant to the FSD President. I was promoted to White's job. I moved into his office on the 7th floor of the 1120 Connecticut Avenue building.

Then, with the sales team in FSD and with White - an FAA zealot - at the FSD President's elbow, we had clout. But - then they moved the whole sales force for standard computers out of the Federal Division and into the Data Processing Division and Pfeiffer arrived. The political clout of the A.A. to the president of FSD –Hank White -was now greatly diminished, and the new V.P. of D.P. wanted to distance his group from the prior 'owners' –FSD.

One day Kilner called me into his office and introduced me to an applicant, and he said "Joe is an expert on real time systems".

I was surprised. I did not consider myself an expert on anything, but I did have some experience of "special bids". I'd managed the IBM bid of a special 'real time' channel that accepted information from the U.S. Weather Bureau's first weather satellite. I'd worked on BMEWS proposals, the Air Force's Ballistic Missile Early Warning System. On PRESS (Pacific Range Electronic Signature Study), a real time system for the U.S. Army range in the Kwajalein Islands. For the past 6 years I had been into all sorts of technical efforts on real time systems, requiring the most powerful computers available. Perhaps I did know a bit about real time systems.

There were eight levels of management between the Chairman and me. (See organization chart on page 302.) I was a lowest level manager, a 'first-line' manager. I did not manage managers, but salesmen and systems engineers.

✼ ✼ ✼

*Stay away from the product division, Pfeiffer had said.*
*Was I to stay in the FAA job?*
*Am I to be yanked? Demoted?*

Back in Washington, the day after the "Orange Soda Meeting", Dave Fine stops by my office. Dave was with Pfeiffer and Evans in the meeting after the FAA meeting. We got along well.

"Had a tough one, eh, Joe?" he says, - with some obvious relish.

"Yeah, you could say that. How did you know?"

"Ralph was still talking to Evans about your problem during my meeting."

"What did he say?"

"Ralph apologized."

"He WHAT?"

"Ralph apologized to Bob for your *belligerence*. You must have been beautiful. Ralph said, 'Fox is a little young...and tough to understand."

*My spirits sink. "-a little young..." –from the new VP.*

"But – Evans interrupted him. Said that he understood you perfectly. He just did not agree with you. Period. And that you were just doing your job and no apology was needed. He said he respected you."

*Evans just may have saved me.*

"What did Ralph say?" I asked.

"Nothing. I think he was so surprised by Evans respecting you that he just switched to my bid."

*I might keep this job, for a while, at least, - thanks to Evans!*

I tell Collins the whole story that weekend.

"Evans saved me, Jack. I was dying in the mud and Evans picked me up and washed me off."

Collins nodded.

"I admire Evans, Joe. He may kill us on this bid, but damn, he's fair."

✹ ✹ ✹

I had been setting up the meeting at which IBM would tell FAA about the new line. The date was set for August 14. I was anxious to get the R&D people from FAA to the meeting, and they were promising me they would attend.

The RFP was due out any day. The briefing *must* take place <u>before</u> the RFP was released. After release, FAA would be unable to go to go to any briefing by IBM or any of the other potential bidders. Procurement rules would prohibit it. Until after the proposals were in and reviewed.

On August 8, accentuating the positive, Pfeiffer writes to Evans - describing the upcoming meeting - stating how to handle the FAA visit. I am not copied- and I see the memo years later.

The memo states:

1. We'll tell FAA about 360 and the <u>family</u> concept –the small machines can execute the identical instructions as the large faster machines –and how FAA could take advantage of that.

2. That the 360 could be a multiprocessor.
3. That IBM sees that there are still unknowns in the use of multiprocessors. Recognizing these unknowns, it would be improper for the IBM Company in any way to commit a fully operating computing system or even to imply such a commitment.
4. 360 wins either way; it is a family – you can use one size at one site, a different size at another, and yet use the same software - or as a multiprocessor.

I judge it 'progress'.

At the last minute, FAA cancels the August 14 meeting. The 11th of September is set as the new date.

☆ ☆ ☆

The week after these events, I get a surprise boost – a vote of confidence from a very key player. From Evans.

I receive in the mail – from a friend in Poughkeepsie - a copy of a letter Evans has sent to his staff.

Subject: Multiprocessing August 14, 1963

Joe Fox and I have debated vigorously regarding multiprocessing. Anyone who has listened to the debates may conclude that Joe has not really examined the subject and this assumption would be tacitly unfair to him. He has assessed the merits and problems in multiprocessing as ... demonstrated by his paper. I have attached it for your personal review not only to clarify Joe's personal beliefs if there is any question as a result of our arguments, but also in hope that reviewing it might serve as a useful check on our present 360 plans or kindle new thought that might be valuable architecturally.

B. O. Evans

*Evans stating my paper might be a 'useful check' on the to be announced 360 plans and telling his staff to read it –*

## A Brawl in IBM - 1964

*WOW.*
Evans is helping me.
A fierce opponent – but he fights fair.
I get a copy of his letter to Pfeiffer - fast, - and a copy to Kilner.

✷ ✷ ✷

## SALES V. P. MEETS WITH THE FAA

Pfeiffer wants to meet with someone on the FAA's System Design Team – to hear with his own ears where things stand. We set up a lunch with Ken Gray, a design team member. Collins goes with Pfeiffer and me. We lunch with Ken, a key member of the FAA's technical team. My notes follow.

*Gray was definite. "If we find we can't program a multiprocessor – we think we can, by the way, Ralph –we'll partition the problem into pieces and use the machines as separate entities. The hardware may be able to be a multiprocessor, but we'll use it as though it weren't.*
*Ralph nodded understanding.*
*"FAA will buy a multiprocessor," said Gray – with finality.*

In the cab back to the office, I sit between Pfeiffer and Collins, relaxed. It had gone very well. Everything we have presented has been corroborated.

Suddenly, Collins leans forward and *snarls* at Pfeiffer. "Satisfied?"

Pfeiffer is startled, rises up a bit - then sinks back into the seat, and says, pleasantly, "Yes."

Later Pfeiffer and I are alone.
"Joe, is Jack always that intense?"
"Yes. That's what makes him so good."
"Is he good?"
"Outstanding. He came to understand multiprocessing in a month. It usually takes six. And the FAA people respect the hell out of him."

"How come Jack had a drink at lunch?"

*Oh-oh –trouble.*

IBM has an ironclad rule <u>against</u> drinking - and everyone takes it <u>very</u> seriously - one could get fired for breaking it.

"Well, Ralph, we never let a customer drink alone. You saw that Jack didn't order a drink till Gray had - and you and I had passed."

"You know the rule on drinking, Joe."

"Of course, but the customer had ordered one. The rule 'You don't let the customer drink alone.' takes precedence."

"Says who?"

I shrug.

"That's standard operating procedure here, Ralph."

Pfeiffer looks skeptical, but lets it drop.

It never comes up again.

✳ ✳ ✳

Pfeiffer summarizes the meeting in a letter to Evans.

This will summarize the major points resulting from my luncheon meeting with Mr. Kenneth Gray, FAA data processing consultant working on the FAA Systems Design Team, and our Joe Fox, FAA Program Manager.

Mr. Gray has been on the Systems Design Team since its inception and formerly spent several years at MITRE for FAA and the Canadian Government in data processing relating to the area of air traffic control.

By the fact of his previous experience and present position, Mr. Gray will exert a great influence on the RFP specifications and the ultimate selection of a computing system for air traffic control.

Mr. Gray made the following points and was quite clear in stating that he has had similar discussions with other interested computer manufacturers:

* FAA is adamant in having the program expedited because of the tremendous pressures being placed upon it by Congress, by the airlines, by the Airline Pilots Association, etc.

* The initial system will not be called upon to perform all functions, and FAA will not install a full system in the field initially.
* "Fail safely" and "fail softly" are critical items and must be provided in the system.
* He emphasized that the backup must be program switchable, (by software) not hardware switchable, into the system.
* He stated that initially they would not program in a multiprocessing mode; that they would start in a normal mode and progressively increase program sophistication.
* He stated that the number of ATC Centers probably would be reduced which would increase the minimum traffic load per Center to 300 track planes, with a maximum of 325.
* Mr. Gray is confident that he will be able to order and install a multiprocessing system. He stated competition would be very heavy for this bid.
* Mr. Gray felt that the bulk of the systems would be ordered in 1965.

As a result of the above points, which were made by Mr. Gray in our discussions, I believe we have the following alternatives:
1. Deliver model 50 in September 1964 and two model 50's with multiprocessing capability in Mid 1965 and one 50 per month thereafter, or
2. Deliver a model 60 in September 1964 and two 50's with multiprocessing capability in mid 1965 and one per month thereafter.

While the above represents our best thinking as the result of the meeting with Mr. Gray, it does not constitute the formal requirement, which can only be stated in the RFP. However, we do feel that Mr. Gray has accurately conveyed the essence of what will be contained in the RFP to be issued within 45 days.

Bob, I have a genuine appreciation for the challenge that these two alternatives represent, but I firmly believe that it *is* imperative that we make every endeavor to meet ... them. Would

you please give us your best estimate of the possibility of fulfilling FAA's requirements?
Signed by Pfeiffer

MITRE is a government think tank spun off from MIT. MIT is the Massachusetts Institute of Technology. <u>M</u>IT <u>R</u>esearch and <u>E</u>ngineering. Very capable.

There are two subtle points in the letter that I do not catch until the second or third reading. First is the point in the third paragraph that Mr. Gray had had similar conversations with other interested computer manufacturers. This will be a key point later in the effort.

The second is the first sentence in the third to last paragraph, which hedged the whole letter. It basically said, "BUT THE RFP IS NOT OUT YET."

Evans answers the Pfeiffer letter. Regarding marketing's insistence that a model 50 was the performance machine they needed, Evans writes:

"I hear but I am skeptical that enough is known of this problem at this time to confirm speed with finality. If this goes like many of its predecessors, the computing requirement will be explosive. Therefore, we in DS retain a 'tongue in cheek' on this point."

Evans does not comment on the multiprocessing requirement.

## THE FAA ADMINISTRATOR IS UNHAPPY WITH IBM

A new FAA En Route Center in Islip, Long Island, New York, is to be dedicated on Sunday, August 21. I do not want to go - I'd had enough overtime and travel, and I have three young sons and a wife at home. But Pfeiffer will go and meet the FAA Administrator.

I send Earl Whitney, a senior salesman, to go with Pfeiffer. Earl had been the key IBM person in getting an IBM 1401-1410 system installed at the center, controlling flight strips.

Problems arise. After all the speeches were over, Pfeiffer is introduced to Najeeb Halaby, the FAA Administrator.

## A Brawl in IBM - 1964

"I'm delighted to meet you," says Pfeiffer. "We've been working with your people and this is truly a great day."

"I'm surprised you showed up." says Halaby.

"I'm amazed at your company delivering such poor equipment. I've just been told that the equipment is not reducing the controllers' workload at all, and is indeed only being used 10% of the time."

Pfeiffer is dumbstruck.

"I've heard nothing about this. I will check into it."

Checking on the facts, it turns out that the center controller chief had not been informed of the installation schedule. Only part of the job had been scheduled to be ready at this point. And it is ready and working.

All is on schedule.

In large-scale computer installations, the functions should be automated in a gradual, piece-at-a-time fashion. All at once developments usually are very messy. But no one had told the center chief of the several step installation plan.

Executives do not like surprises. Even positive surprises in IBM were a flag that one did not have 'account control'.

We eventually get the true story to Halaby.

✼ ✼ ✼

On August 28, 1963, my family –with three sons under 6 years of age -moves from Fairfax Road in Bethesda to a new much bigger house in Rockville, Maryland, about 5 miles further out from downtown Washington. It is in a subdivision called *Old Farm*, off Montrose Road.

It is the same day Martin Luther King conducts the Civil Rights march on Washington - and delivers to huge throngs his "I have a dream." masterpiece.

✼ ✼ ✼

On August 30, Friday, I get a note in the mail from Pfeiffer.

TO: Mr. J. M. Fox, cc: Sam Kilner
SUBJECT: John Madden joins IBM as Manager of DSD Programming Technology.
In my discussions with Jerry Haddad, [vice president of DP] Jerry billed Madden as being one of the strongest proponents for multiprocessing that he has known. He feels that we might further our cause considerably by having a detailed discussion with him.

However, in thinking, about it, I am probably three months behind the great team of Kilner and Fox. Anyway, as you might have come to understand, "anything for FAA."

Ralph

*WOW. ...the great team of Kilner and Fox"*. And the letter is addressed to me. That is great news. I will keep my job.

But Evans is still not on board. He still has the future of IBM, the 360, in his hands.

Tuesday, October 2, 1963

I am on the Shuttle to New York. I muse over the events of September. I have avoided being removed from the FAA effort. The RFP is not out yet; that is good. It gives us more time. It always seems to be just about to appear, but it never does. It is now "any day".

Collins and I are up to Poughkeepsie to see the software people. At 5 PM we go over to the research lab where a major review – 100 people or so - of the 360 is underway. Scores of people stream out of the auditorium. We stop Carl Reynolds, the head of software for IBM and reporting to Evans.

"Carl, can we chat with you for a few minutes? We can find no one who knows a thing about programming a multiprocessor and we would like to get your ideas."

"Sure. Come on and eat with me; they're serving supper."

"Carl, let me warn you –Evans has told me to stay away from his people."

"Thanks for the warning. Let's eat."

We are seated for five minutes when Evans joins us. One can almost feel Evans' energy. He sits next to me, across from Reynolds.

# A Brawl in IBM - 1964

"I thought I told you to stay away from my people, Joe."

Reynolds jumps in. "I told him I'd talk to him- after he relayed your 'no talking' rule to me."

Evans accepts that.

Reynolds is his own man, and Evans is OK with that.

"We are not asking Carl for anything. We just need some guidance."

"Ha! You still think you are going to bid a multiprocessor system. You're nuts, - and irresponsible."

He continues to eat calmly while saying this.

"You are selling these guys in FAA a system that will kill them. They will never get it to work, but you'll be a hero because you sold it. Get off the multiprocessor kick."

"Bob, I can't. Without it we may as well not bid."

"You want to take a piece of garbage, put it on a paddle with a long handle, shove it into the FAA, and see if they eat it."

Evans was animated and went through the physical motion of pushing a long-handled paddle along he table. He has us all laughing, including Collins and me. But he is serious.

"If they get it to work, you're a hero. If they don't, well, -they asked for garbage –it is their problem".

He takes a bite of food.

"That is irresponsible, Joe. We will NOT sell poison! We don't work that way in IBM, Joe. We care about the customer."

He shakes his finger at me.

"You can't get away with what you are doing."

"Bob, if it won't work, let the U.S. Government find that out by trying. They say the Air Force made it work. MITRE is telling them it will work."

"It won't work!"

"FAA is going to find out, Bob –with IBM or without it."

"Without, Joe, without."

We stare at each other.

"You're maniacal about this, Joe. Crazy. You're not going to back off, are you?"

"I can't."

*Scott's said no compromise.*

"Well, you'll probably get IBM to bid –but it'll be over my dead body."

He pauses.

"And you'll probably do that, too."

I do not want to fight with Evans! Evans is DS! He is the 360. To fight him means fighting the whole damn division! His people either worship him or fear him. Either way, they do what he says.

Yet the only way to make peace is surrender– and that means losing the FAA order.

We finish our meals. Evans looks at me.

"Stay out of Poughkeepsie, Joe."

He turns to Reynolds. "Give him nothing."

And he leaves.

Reynolds looks at Jack and me.

"He doesn't like this bid, does he?"

We chuckle.

We discuss the ins and outs of multiprocessors and computers.

Reynolds is willing to try to help.

"You realize, Joe, that I can't do anything real for you without Bob's OK?"

"I know."

"Good luck."

## IBM PRINTER FAILS IN ISLIP EN ROUTE CONTROL CENTER

When I had been promoted in January of 1963, I took over the sales unit I had been part of for two years. Taking over peers is always a touchy situation. A former peer is now the boss. I am in management, and I try to handle my ex-peers with kid gloves. It is mostly OK.

But Earl Whitney is a senior sales representative who's been on the FAA account for years, and he is the oldest in the group by 5 to10 years. He had entered sales after a career in the maintenance of the machines. He is technically very competent. And he is also very difficult! He had no college degree and is out to show the world he doesn't need one! There are many like Whitney. They are very valuable, very competent. They are out to prove they are as good as or better than their peers with college degrees, and many often are.

Whitney is the key in this completely unexpected crisis. The 1401-1410 system installed in the new Islip, Long Island, En Route Control Center -where Pfeiffer had run into FAA Administrator Halaby –the computer system began to make infrequent errors –which could not be traced. Some flight strips were not being printed. That was a bit dangerous.

The flight strip in this system is a piece of paper on which is printed the information about one plane- giving its ID number, altitude, speed and heading, planned route, etc. It is a direct descendant of the strip that was in use back in the 1950s, where the controller <u>wrote</u> the information on it and moved it manually along the level flat surface of the radar display as the blip it belonged with moved.

The strips are about one inch high and 7 inches long, and they are placed in a plastic holder, and about 20 of them are visible at a glance by the controller as the sit now in an almost- horizontal rack. The controller can move an individual strip easily and does so to sequence the planes as they move through his space. A glance at the stack tells a lot about the planes arriving into the controller's space.

When a controller – one of twenty or so in the room -on one side of the Control room handed off a plane to another controller on the other side of the room, he would often place the strip and holder on the floor and send it slithering across the floor to the other side, where it was picked up and inserted into the new controllers stack.

Sometimes it was not intercepted by a distracted controller, and the strip would be found along the wall. This "sliding pass" of responsibility was frowned upon, but it still occurred, in the mid 1960s.

Rarely was a strip "lost". But while one was lost, an inattentive controller could be looking at his stack and perhaps not realize that there was a plane that was not represented.

FAA was not very concerned about the Islip missing strips. They reverted to a manual update system. But Pfeiffer was <u>very</u> concerned.

He was moving heaven and earth to get it fixed. A midair collision due to the computer system was possible –extremely unlikely, but possible.

Whitney and I are both sent to Islip for the duration –five days as it turned out, Thursday through Tuesday. Engineers from the plant are down to find the problem. The possibility that the strips are 'lost' from sliding was eliminated as the cause.

Whitney is in charge. This was his system, and he ignores me. But I couldn't leave - that would have Whitney talking directly to Pfeiffer. That would be trouble. Whitney thrived on giving management -all management- a bit of a run-around.

So I sit and wait - and call Pfeiffer once or twice per day, and Whitney runs the plant engineers sent to the site. The days drag by. I do nothing. I don't understand the details of the system that had been put together, and Whitney wasn't about to be helpful.

He jabs me every couple of hours with a "Why don't you go home?"

But I know the company would come unglued if something happened -a near miss –and Najeeb Halaby would call the chairman; – and I would be defenseless in trying to answer 'Why was a manager not on the scene?'

I sit and read newspapers, make phone calls, get coffee for the swarming IBM engineers. Day after day. Friday. Saturday. Sunday. Monday. They finally find and fix the problem.

✽ ✽ ✽

Evans on September 21 writes to Pfeiffer that he was "somewhat taken aback at the material in the letter. He writes that it is not clear that a duplex system won't sell.

He states that DS would not build an Operating System for a multiprocessor version of a 360 – and that DS had no plans to provide a JOVIAL compiler, and that a Model 50 delivery by January 1965 is impossible.

He ends the letter: "We can continue to lean on each other or we can jointly work to a plan around the material we can deliver."

# A Brawl in IBM - 1964

## GROUP V. P.

On the Shuttle to New York -yet again - are Pfeiffer, Kilner and I.

Rather than reply to Evans' answer to the Pre-RFP, we are going to escalate. We are en route to see Scott. He is a group V. P. and Pfeiffer's boss's boss's boss. See oganization chart on page 304.

The plane lands at LaGuardia.

*I left here two days ago. I must be crazy to be in this business. This project is destroying my life. I am forever traveling to Poughkeepsie or Westchester. Spending weekends at Islip. With 3 little boys at home."*

The format for all these meetings is unvarying. Enter; exchange greetings; put up the charts on the flip chart holder, usually built into the wall; Pfeiffer gives a summary of why we are there. Then I give the briefing –what's happened, what's new –and always finish with a chart labeled <u>ACTION.</u>

A list of things to be done and names of those to do them. I would often jump ahead of the listener's question, not allowing them to finish the thought.

"Do you think, Joe," Scott once asked, "DS can deliver..."

"No. No sir. Not unless...".

"...if the computer were built from today's components."

"Oh."

"No, I do not think so - they would have to redesign all the circuitry."

Later Pfeiffer counsels me.

"Joe, it's good to be quick and knowledgeable; it builds confidence in the listener. But you are too quick. Slow down! Pause for effect once in a while."

The magnitude of the bid is becoming clear – it is going to be very large, - and decisions must be made. I know that as a first line manager, I'll never be able to pull it all together.

I send a letter to Kilner.

'I cannot do this – we need a 'Czar' appointed. I am getting nowhere'.

We never discuss the letter.

## THE FAA VISITS IBM

The meeting in Poughkeepsie to brief the FAA is a complete success!

Kilner had been right; I wrong.

Evans gave a spectacular presentation to the FAA visitors on September 11.

I had until then seen only an adversarial Evans. In Poughkeepsie that day I sat and listened and admired. Evans' grasp of concepts, use of detail, - and his intensity- made for a mesmerizing presentation.

Evans had started with an overview of where IBM was in its product offerings. He drew a simple T on its side on the board and filled it in. On the top, the commercial line of computers, - the 1401, 1410 and the 7070 and the 7080 - and on the bottom, the scientific line - the 704 and the 709, and the 7090. The completed chart looked like this:

A Brawl in IBM - 1964

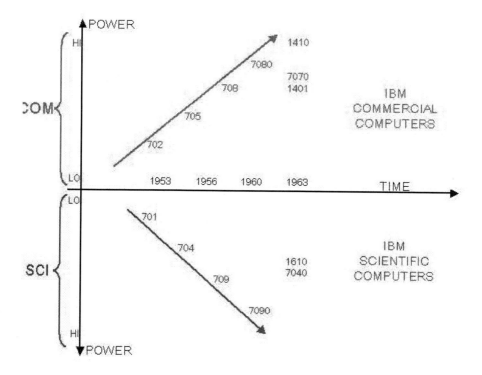

Evans Drawing of IBM Product Line

It represented the products IBM was delivering at that time. Each number was a computer, or rather, hundreds of computers.

"We can't continue to support this number of systems, of models. Each has different architecture, programs, operating system, support, and components. That means different training, different support, worldwide. It is too vast an endeavor.

He laid out detail after detail of where the different lines caused different parts, drawings, and organizations.

"We must consolidate these lines of machines. There is no way to continue to support such diversity."

He then summarized the new 360 line. A family of machines, each able to decode one set of instructions, the fastest one being 35 times faster than the slowest. A program to calculate payroll would be executed by any model of the 360- from the smallest- least powerful to the fastest.

It was a riveting, great presentation. Totally logical; totally convincing.

Evans knew every detail of the new line, and he could go on and on and keep the thing interesting.

*"IBM BETS ITS LIFE." FORTUNE Magazine in 1965 spread its story of the 360 effort over two issues. There had been fierce in-fighting in IBM over a one-line series of computers. The article quoted Evans, "There was blood all over the floor". But Evans had prevailed.*

All this dwarfed the FAA bid. The bid was a major diversion – at just the wrong time! It messed up optimizations. It threatened to undo hundreds of man-years of efforts!

I didn't deal with any of this. I thought of nothing but to win FAA.

Evans got to multiprocessing.

"We do not think you need multiprocessing, since you can grow with this line by buying the next bigger machine. All of the machines are compatible. And we think you will find it difficult to program a multiprocessor." He paused.

A Brawl in IBM - 1964

"But, if you determine that that is what you want, this new line will satisfy your needs. We can snap them together oh, up to 10 CPU's, if you need that many. So you have it either way with this new line."

I sighed with relief. We were over the hump –and Evans had committed himself. "We can snap together - up to ten of them."

Four FAA people had attended, key technical people and they had toured the labs and then Collins and I drove them to LaGuardia.

On the ride to the airport I know the visit was successful. FAA is jubilant -they would get a response for the multiprocessor not only from Burroughs, but also from IBM. There would be competition for the multiprocessor for the next air traffic control – en route – system.

*It is very important to have more than one bidder on a RFP. Often a federal agency would be required to re-issue a revised RFP if there were only one bid. And that could easily take a year or more.*

## WITH THE FAA DIRECTOR OF RESEARCH

Two days later I am to have lunch with Jim Mollenauer, the FAA deputy director of R&D. Mollenauer told me to meet him at the HQ of the Boy Scouts of America at noon. I look up the address in the phone book and arrive at noon - and I wait. After a half-hour – after thinking Mollenauer was just stuck in the meeting – I think again and duck into a store and look up in a phone book the address - again. Oooops. I am at the Boys Clubs of America.

*A 100 million-dollar procurement and I cannot even get to a lunch appointment.*

I grab a cab and go to the correct address on Connecticut Ave. It is 12 thirty. I stand outside and berate myself. Mollenauer is gone, I am sure. But after a minute or so, out he comes, apologizing for being late.

"No problem at all", I say, and we go into a nearby restaurant.

I ask what he had heard of the September 11th visit. He says that IBM really had impressed the people, had convinced them that the 360 was indeed "off the shelf", that the equipment was not a pipe dream, not a 'future,' but a real live honest-to-goodness contender in the procurement.

All good news.

"Joe, does IBM think multiprocessors are the way to go?"

I am on guard.

To be too open about the internal battle could let loose mischief.

"Jim, IBM is not of one mind. There are some who say that multiprocessors are very risky."

He thinks about this.

"Joe, let's set up a meeting for IBM to present the down sides of multiprocessors. Kind of balance the thing. All we have is the good side down here from the Systems Design Team and MITRE."

"Sure, Jim. You get the FAA and give me a date; I'll get IBM."

*Mollenauer never sets it up; I never pursue it. IBM can get itself on the wrong side of the Design Team too easily.*

Mollenauer says they expect competitive bids. He relates a high-level meeting with FAA where a major computer company had expressed optimism regarding the contract. When they described their equipment, FAA pointed out to them –politely- that they should read the RFP carefully, because their descriptions contained nothing of the multiprocessing features that FAA wanted. The company's people had reacted with some heat - and even indicated that FAA was a bit prejudiced on the subject.

What did I think? Is the agency being fair to all manufacturers?

I reply yes, that they are. It has been no secret that they want multiprocessing. That was a legitimate request; human life is involved. It was fair to rule out computers that did not have multiprocessing ability. And FAA had told everyone <u>clearly</u> what was wanted.

Mollenauer says that it looks like there may be but a two-company race for this procurement. A two-way race between Burroughs and IBM.

He mentions 5 or so companies. I express surprise that Control Data Corporation (-CDC-) is not in there. No, they seemed to have decided not to bid, and FAA did not believe that their systems were as modular as they had at first thought.

Mollenauer expects Burroughs to be ahead on price and delivery and he expects IBM to be ahead on technology and performance.

"And you're going to have to be quite a way ahead on those two to beat out Burroughs."

He asks what I think about the programming of the air traffic control functions – feeding the controller's displays, tracking and displaying all the information about the air planes - and the like.

Should IBM be hired to program the software for the system?

I say no, that a non-manufacturing company could better do the programming.

*Later the federal division lawyer Jack Ford tells me that that my answer was 'treasonous' to IBM. I reply there are times that you have to state your true opinion –or lose your credibility.*

A "PRE-RFP"

On September 26, Pfeiffer sends to almost every executive in IBM a "pre-RFP" that we have written. This was Pfeiffer's idea, and a good one. The Pre-RFP states we need the model 50 and multiprocessing. And lists the software we need.

Marketing is standing tall, sticking its neck out. It is willing to be counted! It is not waiting for the RFP. The document is 13 pages, packed with technical detail, justifying the model 50 as the machine needed. It contains details of the forthcoming RFP, with dates. It gives a business forecast and odds to win under several bid alternatives. It predicts what will be requested. It spells out every aspect of the bid.

Pfeiffer sends a letter to involved IBM executives.

Federal Regional Office Washington, D. C. September 26, 1963. By now you have had a chance to review the FAA "Pre-RFP" which I sent you. In anticipation of this RFP we have begun our proposal effort.

Mr. J. M. Fox of my organization is directing this activity and will have the responsibility for coordinating the total IBM effort. This will be a difficult proposal to prepare, but I feel that Mr. Fox, who because of his depth of knowledge of the customer and of the customer's problems, is the ideal man for this task.

He undoubtedly will be coming to you and many others in the company with extremely difficult questions to be resolved. In these instances Mr. Fox will be acting for me, and I am sure that you will give him as much assistance as possible.

✭ ✭ ✭

We take the Shuttle to New York to see Scott again. We had seen him on the 2nd of October.

Delivery of the 360 model 50 is now the bone of contention. The IBM plan at this moment is to announce the models of the 360 on a staggered basis. And the model 50 is scheduled to be announced last. Dead last. And it is <u>the</u> one the FSD analysts Kowalke and Oldani have determined is needed.

(The decision to announce them all at once is still months away.)

Nothing we said or demonstrated seemed to budge the 50 schedule. The RFP had been slipping for months. That helped our delivery problems. But "Wait for the RFP" is holding back the application of needed talent to many issues.

Scotty sends us over to see George Kennard, the president of DS and Evans's boss. We go through the charts for him. Kennard had been in the Washington area as a V. P. in FSD. I know him well – and like him.

Kennard states that there is nothing he could do. His resources are stretched to the breaking point.

Ralph Pfeiffer is very direct.

"George, we all have our problems. Will you or won't you get us a model 50 on time?"

"I don't know."

We go back to Scotty.

"We've got no commitment, Scotty. We've got a lot of sympathy, but no commitments."

Scotty calls Learson and asks him to get into the thing personally. "Things aren't moving, Vin."

From listening to Scotty talk on the phone, we could gather that Learson was being difficult. Scotty would start a sentence and get interrupted. He finally finished the call and turned to us.

"Vin promised to get into it. He's calling Kennard now."

We get up. Scotty holds us up.

"If this doesn't pop it, if we don't get a commitment, I'll go to Tom and Al," he says - again.

Tom is the IBM chairman; Al is Williams, IBM's president.

Neither had been into this struggle yet.

## WE VISIT FAA DEPUTY ADMINISTRATOR OF DEVELOPMENT

On Friday October 11, the team headed by Pfeiffer meets with Robert Shank, one under the FAA administrator. Dr. Fred Brooks gives the presentation. Brooks was about 35, bespectacled, round faced, short hair cut. Brooks is brilliant, one of the guiding minds behind the design of the 360.

Brooks had a gift that was the envy of every IBM salesman who ever heard him. He could explain very complicated things very easily. He would speak at the huge press conference describing the IBM 360 when it was announced.

Brooks does his usual crystal-clear presentation. The director of the Research and Development Division of FAA now asks, "Are you saying that FAA will be the first customer for this technology?"

Yes. We explain that there are other customers in the government who would probably order this technology before FAA did, but that it is likely that FAA would be one of the first deliveries of the series of machines.

The FAA people comment that this would be awfully risky and that they did not want FAA pioneering in computer development. The "Off the shelf dictum" is clear.

As the meeting is breaking, I follow one of the FAA men to the elevator – one of the key technical people. We are alone.

"Look – please, do not make the delivery a <u>mandatory</u> item. In your bid for the 50 people at Atlantic City, your people told me that the RFP was worded unfortunately, so that even though you wanted to keep IBM, your hands were tied. Be careful on this one. Please! State that you <u>desire</u> a nine-month delivery, not that it is required. Then, if you decide that you really require it, give it bigger weight in the evaluation."

The FAA man nods.

"Don't use the word 'require,'" I emphasize.

"I understand."

✯ ✯ ✯

I am sitting in my office on Monday morning, October 14, talking to my people when the phone rang. It is O. M. Scott.

"Hello, Scotty," I say, feeling awkward about calling a group vice president of the sixth largest company in the U.S. by his nickname.

"Joe," says Scott in his steady manner, "Ralph is in Europe, so I thought you were the next one to talk to. Have you seen Kennard's letter to Learson?"

"No."

"He wrote to Vin on the 9th. Ralph was copied. Take a look at it and call me."

"Yes sir."

I get a copy of the letter from Ralph's office. It's a lengthy letter, but two statements stand out.

One - DS doesn't see how to make the delivery; and two- DS is waiting to see the RFP before committing to accelerate the model 50.

I call Scotty back.

"I don't think it is a good answer, Scotty. He states that they will do the best they can. But no commitment; no progress. AND - they will <u>wait –wait-</u> for the RFP before deciding. I do not think things are moving, Scotty."

"OK, I'll be back to you."

# IBM PRESIDENT INTO THE FRAY

Tuesday, October 15, I am on the Shuttle, en route to Poughkeepsie. As I drive by Yorktown to get to Poughkeepsie, I decide to stop in and try to see Scott.

Pfeiffer was off in Europe, and I was "out of line" to see Scott without Kilner or Weiland, my bosses – between me and Pfeiffer. I did not even consider checking with the DP White Plains level people in the chain of command –Frank Cary and Warren Hume. They are not involved in this effort. I have never met either one.

But I am worried.

*'A lot of heat but not much work'* is a good summary of the IBM effort to date.

I stop to see Scott's assistant.

"Nothing's happening," I said.

"So?"

"I'd like to talk to Scotty."

He raises his eyebrows. Thinks for a moment.

"Think of an excuse."

"There's an article in this morning's New York Times about the Air Traffic Control System. Congress is blasting the FAA."

"And?"

"That'll cause more pressure."

"Enough of a reason," he smiles.

We go in to see Scotty.

I explain the pressure mounting on FAA. I am now completely relaxed at this level of management.

"What do you want me to do, Joe?"

"You said if DS and Learson didn't commit, you'd go to Tom or Al."

"Go out and write me a letter."

## A Brawl in IBM - 1964

His assistant and I spend an hour and produce the following draft:

To: Al Williams

We expect to receive the RFP for the FAA National Aerospace Utilization System next week. Our Federal Region people are in daily contact with FAA and have acquired an intimate knowledge of FAA requirements. These have been widely distributed within IBM and many groups have studied them. Every technical evaluation has clearly shown that the model 50 as a multiprocessor is the system we must bid. Delivery in January 1965 is the minimum we can accept if we are to be responsive.

Since July we have been urging DS to proceed on this basis. On August 12, I wrote Mr. Learson recommending that DS proceed just as though they were going to ship 50's. To date we have no firm commitment from the product division.

The situation has become grave. Three months have slipped by. Even though the RFP is expected momentarily, we cannot wait any longer. It is conceivable that the release date could slip again, even though Mr. Halaby (the FAA Administrator) is publicly committed to implementation.

Time is so critical that we feel IBM must proceed now on the assumption that 50s will be bid and delivered as required.

I recommend that the product division be directed to implement immediately a program to permit bidding and delivering two 50s with multiprocessor hardware in January 1965.

To the best of our ability to anticipate the RFP, this is the minimum requirement to be responsive.

Scott looks at the letter.

"The RFP has been coming 'next week' for months."

I wince.

"It is close now, Scotty. I'd like it to slip even more. Every slip helps our delivery problem."

Scott rereads the letter. There is a several minute silence.

He looks at me.

"Joe, are you ready to fight Evans in Watson's office?"

*Don't answer too quickly,' Pfeiffer told me.*

Finally, I say "Yes".
"Can you win?"
I pause - again.
"Will I get a fair hearing?"
"I promise you that."
"Then I can win."
"Then I'll sign the letter."
I am delighted.

I go on to Poughkeepsie.
I talk to Scott's assistant a few hours later. He is jubilant.
"It's a tough letter, Joe. He's changed it slightly, but he did it!"
"Thanks" I say.

*"And," I muse, "I did it without Pfeiffer."'*

I call Scott's assistant on the phone the next day.
"It worked, Joe, it worked! Williams' assistant told me that they felt the letter was so 'hot' they hand-carried it to Learson. And Learson read it - and didn't blow up.
'Scotty's right,' he said. 'I'll get into it.' "
I fly back to Washington the night of October 15 – on the Shuttle. I tell Collins of the Scott meeting, the letter, the Learson reaction.
"Progress, Jack. We're making progress."
Collins smiles.
"We're moving," he agrees.
I am on the 7 AM Shuttle, heading to New York. Friday, October 18.
There is a meeting in IBM Research. We had told Scott so many times that we could find no one in IBM who really knew multiprocessing that Scott had written to the head of Research. The answer had come back, giving three names. Keeley from DS will meet us at Yorktown and we'll talk to the 'scientists'.

## A Brawl in IBM - 1964

I loved to visit Yorktown. It was designed to be the home of IBM Corporate Research. But until the new HQ building at Armonk gets finished, corporate management resides here as well. It is very relaxed. People wore sneakers! Not the executives; the researchers.

I go over to the research part of the building and meet Jack Keeley. He is excited.

"Learson called me in yesterday and really pumped me."

"Did you tell him the facts?"

"Yes. Yes, and he called Evans on the phone while I was there and told him to do three things.

First, accelerate the model 50; second, make it a multiprocessor; and third, get a group together to provide support software." Support software was the JOVIAL compiler and other tools for developers of the final software that will feed the controllers in the centers.

I grin.

"We've won," I say, "we've won. Now we have a chance. Will the system have separate-stand-alone channels? Not integrated with the CPU circuits?"

Keeley says they will, that this had been decided just the previous day.

The rest of the day with Research does not add much knowledge. They were clearly very bright people –but they had not spent much time on multiprocessing. The Washington team did most of the presenting; Research listened.

They seemed supportive.

✭ ✭ ✭

On Saturday, October 19, Collins calls me at home.

"Joe, you've got to go up there to Poughkeepsie. We're being 'had', -gamed."

"What do you mean?"

"Nobody in the model 50 group is doing anything on multiprocessing. Zip. Zero. It's a blank."

"You're sure?"

"Sure."
"You and I'll go up Monday morning."
*Why are Learson's orders not being implemented?*

✭ ✭ ✭

Monday October 21, Collins and I are on the 7 AM Shuttle. I feel good –despite the fact that we'd had to rise at 5:30 AM to catch the 7 AM flight. We spend most of the day in Poughkeepsie with the two FSD people – Kowalke and Oldani -Washington FSD people -assigned to the effort.

Charlie Oldani is a senior the senior analyst who did the time calculations for the computer to process the 325 flights in 6 seconds, and Ken Kowalke - ex-Air Traffic Controller- was reviewing the whole approach to the processing and display.

We go over such questions as "Where do we put the fail-safe information so that when one memory unit fails another memory has the information?"

We do not know the answers yet. We are still thinking up the questions!

Gradually we are amassing data. The problem is the sheer scope of the information –and its preliminary nature. And the new line – the 360 – is still in flux.

The machine we needed, the model 50, was right in the middle of the line from a power –speed and capacity –and scheduled to be announced last! Therefore, it had the least definition at this point.

The 360 planned line was:

| MODEL: | Model 30 | Model 40 | Model 50 | Model 60 | Model 70 |
|---|---|---|---|---|---|
| POWER: | Least | 3 x's 30 | 3 x's 40 | 3 x's 50 | Most Power |

We learn in some cases more than the DS managers know. We are nomads, working out of no office, meeting each other for dinner and comparing notes. Occasionally we bump into each other in the huge buildings.

## A Brawl in IBM - 1964

There is no budget restriction to worry about.
I was never asked to justify any expense.
We just did it!

I am making plenty of mistakes. In mid-October, I announce an 'assistant proposal manager' - a man from DP headquarters staff in White Plains, N. Y., but this new number 2 lives in Poughkeepsie. Where the action is.

I figure I'd blunt any criticism that might come from DP headquarters by appointing one of their own, and I figure that anyone who lived in Poughkeepsie would be valuable because of proximity to the 360 development effort. And the man is also very good technically, and a hard worker.

Fierce reaction from my people surprises me. Kowalke and Collins individually told me I was crazy, that I was "ruining morale". When the taciturn Oldani came and said the same thing, I decide to undo the appointment.

I am embarrassed - and guilty, because it reflects unfairly on the person chosen. It was not the individual's fault; it was mine. I'd not prepared the way, not sold the idea, not set it up.

"I screwed up," I tell Kilner.

Very few people outside the project are aware of these events.

✼ ✼ ✼

Hank White and I talk at least once per week on the phone. He is the assistant to the President of Federal Systems, and my ex-boss. We communicate crisply. FSD has been freewheeling in its support of all Air Traffic Control needs. I had never been turned down for anything. Now, I need more people. So I call White.

"Hank, I need three more people for a couple of months."

I describe the type of talent needed.

"Fine," said White, "I'll get them for you, but let's do it the formal way this time. Go through channels."

"OK".

Then I pause.

"How do I do that?"

White laughs.

"You simply have Pfeiffer -DP-write a letter asking Spaulding -FSD- for the people."

"Oh. OK. Fine ."

*My first week working for Hank White in 1962 had been almost been my last.*

*I was to meet at the office with the briefing charts we had drawn up, then we would drive to FAA site in Atlantic City- a 4 hour drive- where we would meet with FSD management people from Kingston, N. Y. and review the issues with the customer.*

*We got to Atlantic City, and White asked me for the charts.*

*I had forgotten the charts.*

*His eyes widened.*

*Luckily, there was at that time commercial air service to Atlantic City from Washington and I was able to get the charts on a plane and to White in time for the meeting.*

*It was not an auspicious start to employment with a new boss.*

*Then we lost the 50-people contract late 1962. White was still the marketing manager and I was the marketing representative. Losing a contract of that size was significant, but worse, 40 of the 50 had just moved their households from Kingston, New York, to Atlantic City- only <u>6 months before</u>! Now they had to move back!*

*How had I screwed up so badly? The award went to the lowest bidder – much to the dismay not only of IBM, but also to the FAA technical management team. They told me they had "lost control of the contract." It was never supposed to go to the lowest bidder.*

*But the structure of the work effort determines the structure of the contract to be awarded. They had not been clear enough, they told me, in their description of the work effort.*

*The loss was expensive - awkward. I was embarrassed – I'd screwed up!*

✫ ✫ ✫

# A Brawl in IBM - 1964

On Tuesday, October 22, I go to see the DS manager of the engineering group of the Model 50, John Helt, in Poughkeepsie. I had met Helt once or twice, liked him well enough, and could communicate with him. Helt knows I am FAA.

"How do you feel about all this, John?"

"Great! We were to be the last machine in time, you know. Now we are the first or second. We've been accelerated. This is really great. I'm getting all the people I want. And things are going to move -I promise you that, Joe, things are going to move!"

I grin at him.

"Great! That's great. Do you think you will meet the 12-month delivery schedule?"

"Yes!–If we can get the components."

He is referring to the transistors and resistors mounted on a small ceramic chip that are to be the basic building blocks of the 360. The Components Division is to make these components, and some delays are being encountered. Called SLT, for Solid Logic Technology, the new chips are a breakthrough.

"Well, let's hope that Learson will get us them," I say. "John, what about taking the channels out of the main frame? Do you think that will be hard – hold you up?"

Helt looks puzzled.

"I'm not taking the channels out."

"Well, you can't take out only the memory," I say. "That isn't good enough. Keeley told me last week that DS is to take the channels out."

"Joe, I'm not taking the memory out, either," he says, still puzzled.

"John, Learson's letter says to make the 50 a multiprocessor in addition to accelerating it. Are you saying you are not going to do what he says?"

"Joe, I don't know anything about what Learson said or didn't say; all I know is that a letter I got from Paley –my boss's boss –is what I am doing. Accelerating the model 50."

He hands me the letter. Paley is Evans' right-hand man.

TO: John Helt
FROM: M. Paley
This is to authorize you to accelerate the model 50 as much as possible to meet the FAA delivery requirements. We are authorized to spend $2 million extra on this effort. Please give me a weekly report of your progress.

"John, he doesn't say what Learson said..."
"I don't <u>know</u> what <u>Learson</u> said, Joe," says Helt, getting testy.
"Well, I do," I say, now hard, "and I'm going to see that it gets done. I'm calling George Kennard right now," and I reach for Helt's phone. (Kennard is Evan's boss.)

*Collins was right!*

"Wait," Helt reaches for his phone. He doesn't want Kennard in the loop till he does some checking.
"Let's go see Pete Ford."
Ford was the man between Helt and Paley. Paley was Evans' right hand man.
"Maybe Pete has some other orders, Joe, but I'll tell you this –I am not going to ruin the model 50 by tearing it apart the way you want. We've spent years melding the parts together, designing to share circuits between memory, processor and channels to make it cost effective, to make it sell. I'm not going to take it apart. They'll have to get a new guy to run this thing if they want it taken apart."
His tone is low but firm.
"I don't care, John. That is between you and your management. I don't care. Let's go see Ford."
Ford is not in.
We see him after lunch. By then there are several people in the meeting, including Keeley. I wonder if I am going to get Keeley in trouble if I state the contents of the Learson letter. Should he have told me what it said?
Helt recounts the events of the morning; I sit quietly.
Ford looks at me.

"Why isn't what we are going good enough?"

"Pete, I've been through this a thousand times, and the damn thing has been settled by Learson's letter. We need a multiprocessor. Period. Either you agree to do it, or I call Kennard. It's that simple."

Helt speaks.

"I'm not the guy, if it is a multiprocessor. Then it isn't the model 50... and I am the 50 manager, not the FAA manager, Pete. I feel strongly about this and I'm not going to do it."

Ford looks at Helt.

"I understand." he swings around, "and Joe, I can't argue with you. I'm not up to speed. Let's get to Paley. He wrote the letter. Maybe he didn't understand Learson's direction -or maybe Evans didn't tell him."

A meeting is arranged with Paley for 5 PM.

"Where is it going to be," I ask.

"I don't know yet," answers Ford, "but we'd rather not have you attend, Joe. We have some internal "problems."

I like Ford's direct manner. The internal problems were real. Helt wasn't about to let them change the 50 without a fight.

"Okay. I'll see you first thing in the morning."

I meet with Pete Ford again the next morning.

"What happened with Paley?"

"Tell me what you want first," said Ford.

I opened up slow and easy, explaining the background of the bid. I follow the normal pattern. But I am expecting a showdown, a contest of wills with Ford, just like one yesterday with Helt.

But rather than start out with confrontation, I adopt the approach of starting low-key, relaxed, 'oh-by-the-way'. That had avoided some confrontations. Often the 'opponent' turned out to be willing to do what was asked. If I start belligerently, it often required saving-of-face. Then, -even if the 'opponent' were ready to concede- he might get his pride hooked and fight just for the image of it.

Ford listened quietly, answered quietly.

"We can't do it, Joe," said Ford, polite, - even apologetic. "We are not yet clear on just what is going to be done".

"Fine" I said, matter-of-factly, rising and reaching for his phone, "I'll tell Kennard and we'll see where it goes from there."

"Why can't you wait a few days, Joe?" asks Ford.

"Pete, you haven't been in on this thing for the last three months. The RFP is due any day. We may be too late now. Evans told me, in August, that the new line was a multiprocessor, now I'm told by Helt that you're doing exactly the opposite. I can't wait any more."

This very quietly, but with finality.

"Okay," says Ford -quietly. "You'll get a multiprocessor system. We'll start work on it right away. But John," motioning to Helt, "will not be the man who gets the software done. And Learson is not correct in thinking that we are responsible for programming. We aren't. You'll have to go directly to Reynolds for that."

"I understand, - and I can live with that."

Deep breath.

"Let me recap. You are going to accelerate the model 50 and make it a multiprocessor?

Right?"

Ford nods.

"Right."

"Channels separate, stand-alone boxes, with their own power supplies?"

I want a clear specification.

"Channels out, but it's going to ruin your delivery schedule," answers Ford.

"Without a multiprocessor, we should not even bid. I'll confirm this in writing, Pete."

I meet with Paley and Ford. They agree on everything that had been settled with Ford.

"But your delivery is going to be lousy, Joe," says Paley.

"Max, without a multiprocessor, we should not even bid."

The meeting over, I drive down to the building where a major review of the new 360 line was underway in the auditorium. I wait outside the conference, hoping to see Evans when he came out.

"Bob, do you have a minute?" I hail Evans as he comes out.

"Just one minute," says Evans.

# A Brawl in IBM - 1964

"Bob, I've been meeting with your guys and we are going down the right road, making the thing a multiprocessor, but the delivery now looks terrible. We can't win with that kind of delivery."

"Tough! I've got bigger things to cry about than that," and he swings away to leave.

I call after him.

"I'm not crying, Bob, I'm just telling you we are going to lose without a better delivery. Just don't say you were never told, Bob. You've been told we can't win FAA. "

"Tough. Life is tough, Joe."

I march off to the cafeteria, furious.

As I waited in line in the cafeteria, Evans comes along with two or three people and got in line behind him.

In a friendly tone, Evans asked "Is the RFP coming out, Joe?"

"Yes. November 7. And I need a software package, Bob. JOVIAL."

I don't tell him I've had the Learson memo read to me.

"No. Can't do," says Evans flatly.

"No?"

"No."

I let it go. I have to think about how to force the JOVIAL, or how contract it out.

"Are you all set on getting the proposal out? Can I help?" Evans asks -friendly.

*I am confused by the switch in attitude.*

"Yes, Bob. But I need a D S coordinator to help me with all the various departments in DS –your people, legal, pricing and so on. To help..."

"You've got Keeley to do that," snaps Evans, no longer solicitous.

"He can't do it. He..."

"Why not?"

"...has only been in your division for three to four months, and he just doesn't know the right people or channels. He does not know the Division's ropes. He can't do it, Bob."

"He's your man, Joe"

"He can't do it."

"Write me a letter."

Pause.

"Okay, I will."

✯ ✯ ✯

The RFP is due out any day.

"You just do not like Keeley." Collins had once accused me.

"No. No, I do like him. But he's too new to Poughkeepsie."

I had decided that if we were to lose this thing, the investigation to find the culprit and hang him would be the mother of all inquiries. I had decided to put everything into writing, for the upcoming audit.

I write Evans specifying in detail many of the changes that had to be made to the internal units of the Model 50. And of the inability of the product division to deliver a Jovial Compiler.

# I MEET LEARSON- IBM's NEXT CHAIRMAN

We are still in Poughkeepsie, on Friday October 25, working with the marketing people and the DS people. Everyone seems to be moving in the right direction now. Except on the software.
Collins is forceful.

"Go to Learson, Joe. You have to."

I leave Poughkeepsie about 2 PM and drive down to White Plains, headquarters of the DP division. I stop in to see one of the DP vice presidents, Jerry Haddad.

My status is now such that I am recognized and invited into the VP's office to chat. Haddad had been in the September Multiprocessing meeting in Poughkeepsie that preceded the Orange soda meeting. He had written Pfeiffer regarding multiprocessing.

"How are you doing on FAA, Joe?"

"Not so good, not so good. We just are not getting there. DS is stubborn and are not doing much to help get the thing done."

"What aren't they doing?"

I hesitate.

"Well," I say, looking at Haddad through tired eyes, "they will not get us the JOVIAL software."

"Why not?"

"Don't have the money or the people. And without it, we can't win."

Haddad picks up the phone.

"Please get me Mr. Learson."

"Vin? –Jerry. Look! DS will not give Fox what he needs to get the FAA business...No, I cannot explain the problem but Fox is here... OK, he'll be right over."

He swings around.

"Vin wants to see you over in Harrison. (Ten minutes away.) Get going."

"What shall I say?" I am awed.

I'd never met Learson.

"Just tell him the truth."

That seemed simple enough.

Just tell him the truth.

Learson's reputation was more awesome than Evans's. He was a contender to be chairman of IBM. (And would be the next chairman.) Tough, tough, tough! But fair fair fair.

I had been told that Learson was the one who got IBM into computers, He'd been in sales school with Tom Watson, Jr. when they were just out of college, and became friends. Young Tom fought his father, T. J. Watson, Sr., tooth and nail to get IBM into computers. In the late 1940's IBM had turned down Eckert and Mauchley of the University of Pennsylvania, and their machine - which became the Univac I of Sperry Rand.

Tom, Jr. was finally sent to Poughkeepsie to get the computers started, but he brought Learson with him. I was told it had been Learson's shrewd judgment of people that made IBM's comeback in computers so successful. He ran the place, I was told.

I drive to the IBM-Harrison building. I am glad Pfeiffer is in Europe –else I'd have had to call him and would in all likelihood I would have been told to postpone the Learson meeting.

I take the elevator to the third floor and go to Learson's office.

T. V. Learson, Vice President of Development and Manufacturing, is about 6 feet 4 inches tall. He is standing in his own office reception area, talking to a well-dressed man about 40 years old.

"Yes?" says Vin.

"I'm Joe Fox."

"Oh! I'm Vin Learson. This is John Hanstra."

Hanstra is the president of the other product division, General Systems, the one with the 1401 and not the 360.

What is the problem?" asks Learson.

"I can't get a commitment for the programming support we need to get the business. I need JOVIAL and…"

"Go down and see George Kennard. Tell him that you and he are to agree on a course of action to solve the thing or you guys come back and see me."

"OK. What I want…"

"Just go. Just tell Kennard what you want."

The meeting lasted about 30 seconds.

I go downstairs to see Kennard. His secretary does not want to let me in –Kennard is in a meeting –but when I explain to her that Learson has just sent me, I get in.

I relate to Kennard the conversation with Learson.

Kennard looks harried.

"I can't do it. We just do not have the people. These guys want us to do everything and give us nothing but budget cuts. I cannot do it."

Kennard is sincere and obviously harried. But I cannot compromise.

"Well, George, I…I…I've got to go back to Vin and tell him, you can't agree. I…"

Kennard picks up the phone and calls Carl Reynolds, head of programming, who was located in Poughkeepsie.

Reynolds says he'd see me…on Monday in Poughkeepsie… at 7 AM.

I groan. I've been out of Washington all week -and my in-laws were arriving from Ohio for a week with my family at this very moment. I am going to miss them this evening, - it is already 5 PM Friday, and I am still in Westchester, New York.

And now I have to be in Poughkeepsie at 7 AM on Monday morning.

"Can you make it at 7, Joe?"

"Not really."

Kennard talks to Reynolds again. Then to me: "Monday at 7, or Thursday?"

I surrender –"Monday at 7."

## A Brawl in IBM - 1964

Then I remember! I ask Kennard about a new coordinator for his division.

"George, I need a new FAA-DS coordinator."

I tell Kennard the reasons, and of Evans' reaction.

"I'll write Evan's a letter, but it is nasty to insist on a letter. I don't want to slam Keeley."

"I'll look into it." Kennard promises.

✫ ✫ ✫

I leave the in-laws and my long-suffering wife on Sunday at 9 PM. I get the 10 PM Shuttle -the last one for the day –and get to Poughkeepsie at 1 AM. I meet with Reynolds at 7 A M and we agree on the position that DS can <u>not</u> help us get a compiler.

One of the most confusing things about computers is that the computer is used as a tool to develop its own instructions. For years before a computer is put to work doing the job it is to do, it is used to do translation from an "easily-understood-by-humans" language to the murky, arcane language of the computer itself. The computer system in this mode is a tool to make tools. To make the computer perform the role of translator, two things are necessary. First, one must specify a language that is more akin to the human language than machine, and second, one must write the instructions to make the computer accept the "higher order language" and from it produce the more detailed machine language. This is done with software, a 'compiler', and a tool to build tools. A powerful translator.

The language and the compiler are two separate entities that will work together. The language is independent of the computer; the compiler is not. It is created specifically for a certain computer model and instruction set.

Fortunately, the FAA had stated a clear preference. If all things were equal, 'give us JOVIAL', they told. JOVIAL was defined by Jules

Schwartz of SDC for the Air Force's air defense system. JOVIAL stood for Jules Own Version of the International Algebraic Language. It was the U. S. Air Force's preferred language for real-time systems. The FAA had never used JOVIAL.

## A NEW DS COORDINATOR

At about 4 PM that same day, I go over to Evans' conference room to meet with Paley, Brooks, Helt and Ford. I don't understand why I have been invited to the meeting. It seems to be a meeting for Helt to complain that he does not want the job of managing this FAA system.

"I'm not the guy," he keeps saying. "I should keep the model 50 going."

"But this is the 50," said Brooks.

"No. Not when you tear out the memory and channels, it isn't!"

"That shouldn't be too hard," muses Brooks.

They go round and round, and I am pleased not to be in the middle of the fray for once.

I sit and watch. They talk about the ways of making the 50 a multiprocessor. It is clear that they are inventing as they talk.

"What if we do such and such?" "What if this comes out and this goes in?"

Paley turns to me.

"See, Joe. We have been working on a modular system."

"Yes, for at least three or four hours," I say, without emotion.

Suddenly, Evans comes in; he had not been expected.

He looks around the room, - says hello to everyone.

"What is going on?"

Paley answers, "Fox is criticizing our lack of multiprocessor effort."

Evans turns to me.

"Have you met our new FAA manager, Joe?"

"No, I didn't know you'd named one. That is great, Bob, it will help. Thank you!"

"Meet him, Joe. George Manson is his name. He's a good man – a tough man."

"Good," I said. "We need that. Thank you, Bob."

He walks over to where I am sitting and shakes his finger in my face.

"We're going to get you, Fox! HE'LL get you!"

His voice is intense. I just look at him.

The others watch.

"We're going to put your neck in a wringer and squeeeeeeeese," he says, making a wringing motion with his hands.

He steps back.

"We are going to get you, Fox," he repeats with conviction.

I just look at him, trying to stay expressionless.

Apparently, I am not as far along towards success as I have thought!

I look at Evans and say nothing.

"He says we have only worked on a multiprocessor machine for three hours, Bob," adds Paley, piling on.

I feel my eyes begin to fill with tears.

Maybe Evans sees that, for he suddenly changes.

"Look," he announces. "Let's leave him alone. He's only doing his job, and he isn't getting much help from us," and he walks out.

"Are we done?" I ask weakly to the group.

We are.

I leave.

I go back to LaGuardia and get the Shuttle to Washington. I take the next day off and take my in-laws on a White House tour. You could do that back then.

✯ ✯ ✯

A letter from Reynolds sums up the support software situation.

October 28, 1963
Memorandum for Mr. J. M. Fox
Subject: FAA Programming

This is to confirm the results of our one-day review of the programming requirements for the FAA bid by IBM. First, at the present time you do not plan to have IBM bid any multiprocessing programming. Secondly, FSD is planning to bid approximately 30 man-years of applications programming. This work will require a minimum assembly and utility capability with delivery of the machines. In addition, they will need a compiler whose data handling and bit manipulation capability is beyond FORTRAN IV and known present-day 360 FORTRAN plans.

This is what we needed. DS's support in software was nowhere near enough. Now I could go back to Learson with a 'no.'

I also received the memo naming the new DS coordinator:

October 28, 1963
MEMORANDUM TO: (DS Managers)
From Paley
SUBJECT: FAA Proposal -DS Systems Manager.

Mr. G. R. Manson has accepted-the assignment of DS Systems Manager for the FAA proposal, reporting directly to Dr. F. P. Brooks, Jr.

This responsibility includes all participation by the DS division toward the implementation of both the response and execution of an affirmative reply to the RFP, which is expected very shortly from FAA.

In executing his responsibilities, Mr. Manson will require the cooperation of the various systems managers involved in the direction of all supporting areas necessary for implementing the required configuration for this proposal. The specifics include recommended engineering solutions to the DP requirements in the complete detail needed for estimating, pricing and proposal preparation.

He will establish and coordinate the integration of this information to the proposal team.

He will, therefore, be the source also of all commitments to be made by the DS division and will be expected to reach the proper

# A Brawl in IBM - 1964

agreements with line organizations in those areas where work is to be done or supervised outside of Dr. Brooks' immediate shop.

The centralization of authority for FAA under Mr. Manson will assure the maximum best effort to be put forth by the DS division. Your cooperation in insuring the success of this effort is requested.

M. 0. Paley

Manson I discover is a veteran of the Stretch machine effort, which for years was IBM's most powerful computer. Outrageously expensive, only a few were sold. Deemed a failure for years, in the 1970s the Stretch was recognized as a technology and architectural beacon for the new line of computers, and its engineers and programmers were awarded IBM recognition.

✶ ✶ ✶

I tell Kilner THEY are going to "get" me.

"Joe, Evans has massive problems –HUGE! FAA is like a mosquito to him that flits in and buzzes and then goes away –seemingly –while he fights elephants."

"But we got Learson to call him."

"He talks to Learson five times a day. Learson is a giant to us but not to Evans. They are not going to get you."

Despite everything, October ends on an up note. The RFP isn't out - and that is good! Every day's delay helped us. We are slowly bludgeoning DS into action. There is movement. We'd reached the president of IBM.

October was a taste of what was to come: I had flown to and from New York twelve times in October.

✶ ✶ ✶

Now the RFP is expected momentarily. "Any minute!"

Normally, a proposal is entirely up to DP –the data Processing division - has sales responsibility for all computers. The product division is not involved. The products have been developed and announced. They are described in great detail in the "Sales Manual."

The sales team – salesman and technical support – knowing the customer need, using standard products, select a configuration, the size of the computer, its I/O and disks, - writes a proposal.

This FAA proposal is crazy. It breaks all the rules. There are no rules; it is all ad hoc. No one really knew how to run one of these.

On November 1 Friday Kilner and I meet Pfeiffer at 5 PM. Ralph had just come back from Europe.

"Welcome back. Good trip?"

"Very good, very good! The RFP is not out yet?"

"Not yet. Any day now, it'll be out."

"How do you know?"

"We check with three or four key people every day. We call the procurement people, technical people and the management people. We ask them simply 'anything new?' They tell us of bottlenecks or progress."

Pfeiffer wants a date.

"Joe, no one really knows when this RFP will be out?"

"No. FAA management is pushing like crazy to get this out. It just has to go through the appropriate checkpoints. They are feeling the press of Congress!"

"BUREAUCRACY!" declares Pfeiffer.

"But it works," I say. "Few things get left out."

"Don't they get tired of your calling?"

"No. We're their friends. We've worked side by side with them now for years."

Pause.

"Do they tell you things they wouldn't tell others, Joe?"

I get cautious. Danger here. Pause. Think.

"No. Not really. They're careful not to tell us sensitive information. They volunteer almost nothing. They'll answer questions - if they are not violating privacy and federal procurement laws. We've learned

# A Brawl in IBM - 1964

to ask the right questions. Any other company asking the same questions is given the same answers."

Pfeiffer seems satisfied.

I relate to Pfeiffer all the major events of the last two weeks of October.

I tell Pfeiffer about the Scott memo to Williams.

"Good work. Well done."

I tell him about the Learson meeting on software, about Learson's directions to Evans to make it a multiprocessor. About Manson. About the confusion in DS as to multiprocessing and who was working on it. I do not tell him about the "we are going to get you" threat.

IBM Reorganizes -October 31, 1963

There had been an announcement on all IBM bulletin boards on the 31 of October. A major reorganization had been announced. Learson, up till now Group Vice President in charge of all development, became Vice President of all Sales. He was now Pfeiffer's boss's boss's boss. Fox's boss six levels up. Scott became a division president in charge of the maintenance arm of IBM, and is not in the FAA effort any more. A new face to me, Dr. John Gibson, took Learson's old job, over-seeing the product divisions.

"What's it all mean?" I ask Pfeiffer.

"Well, Learson's in almost total control. He's so strong he'll run the product division through sheer personality for a while. He knows that place."

Pfeiffer smiles.

"Learson is our boss now. We brief him Monday, by the way. Eleven o'clock in Harrison. You," he points to me, "clean up your briefing charts this weekend with Jim Starnes (Ralph's assistant)."

"Ralph, the charts are fine. They..."

"I want them changed for Learson. My guy knows what I want. Call him at home and meet him this weekend."

I stare.

*Another weekend shot!*

"How do you think we are doing overall, Joe? Will we make it?" asked Pfeiffer.

"No. I do not see how."

I look from Ralph to Kilner.

"Ralph, we've got to get a bigger guy than me to do this job. Things are just not moving. We are not making any progress"

"No. You are doing fine. Just keep going... just keep going."

I leave Pfeiffer at 7:45 and go to my regular Friday night Contract Bridge lesson, two blocks away. It is the one social I have been able to attend regularly with my wife through the fall of 1963.

Sunday morning, I drive to 1111 Connecticut Avenue. I am not happy. It is a beautiful day. I am to spend several hours with Jim Starnes, Pfeiffer's assistant.

I hated to spend this beautiful Sunday in the office, yet again away from my wife and three sons, educating Starnes on the logic of the flow of the charts, and on the FAA situation.

These charts were not charts in the sense of diagrammatic charts. They were word phrases outlining a flow of logic. There was not a diagram in them.

After six hours, Starnes said my charts and logic were 'good', as they were.

"I know," I said.

"But we will have them professionally drawn, (meaning neatly, very neatly). Ralph will think the content has changed."

And that was exactly what Ralph thought when he saw them. Form was as important as content. To Ralph. Not to me.

## FIRST WEEKLY LEARSON REVIEW

I left Washington on Sunday, November 3, on the 10:00 p m Shuttle and went to the Tarrytown Hilton. The next day I met Kilner and Pfeiffer. They reviewed the charts.

"Much better, much better" said Pfeiffer. "How much time did you spend on 'em, Joe?"

"All day yesterday, Ralph. All day," I said.

They were 99 % the same charts they had started with.

At 2: 00 PM we were to meet with Learson and DS.

# A Brawl in IBM - 1964

The conference room at IBM-Harrison was on the third and top floor, and it was opulent. It looked like something right out of a movie set for Executive Suite. Lined with oak paneling, it was a huge room, the size of a small house. A table, at least 30 feet long dominated the center of the room. A multiple screen arrangement was at one end of the room and a projection booth was behind.

"Why are you whispering, Joe?"

"I didn't realize I was. It's this room. What a beauty!"

IBM had "picked up" the Harrison building after the Socony-Mobil merger had been turned down by the courts. It was a lush building. (I would see the conference room torn up a year or so later. I heard that IBM spent over a million dollars "de-plushing" the building!)

I am nervous. Even though I met Learson a few weeks ago, I am still a little awed by the upcoming meeting with him. Learson had a reputation for being a fierce man in a business meeting, and anyone was likely to get chewed-up.

Kilner and I lounged around the table, waiting. The DS people arrived —George Kennard, President; Max Paley, Bo Evans' right-hand man; and Pete Ford, the Manager of the engineers on the 360 machines. They too had a set of charts.

"Isn't Bob coming?" Kilner asked Kennard.

"No, he is out of town."

More small talk. But clearly they were going into the meeting as opponents. The conversation was stilted; never did they refer to the subject of the meeting.

Pfeiffer came in. Finally, Learson came in.

Learson sits at the head of the long table, and a quiet falls over the group. They all look expectantly at Vin.

They wait.

Vin looks around, then looks at Kennard.

"I guess you don't want this business, George. Your division has done nothing to get ready, to get ready for this bid since the summer."

He says this evenly, in a slightly joshing manner.

'Wow,' I think, 'this is going to be a blast and he is on our side'.

"That's not true," protests Kennard. "We have.

"No, no, I know you haven't," says Vin. "I've talked to Keeley. Nothing you say is going to change my mind. You haven't done anything."

"Vin, that isn't true! We have..."

"No, no. Nothing you say will convince me."

Kennard pauses.

"Well, okay," he says with a muster of resignation and indignation, "I thought we came here to see what we could do to get this business. If you won't believe anything I'm going to say, I won't say anything."

"Well, you have a point. I should be willing at least to listen to what you have to say."

He looks at Pfeiffer. "Let's see what you have."

Pfeiffer motions to me and I get up and put up the charts.

A few simple rules of conduct were to save me time and time again.

(1) Be polite at all times.
(2) Be stubborn on key issues.
(3) Be negative in a very positive, up-beat way. (This was not an easy trick.)
(4) Be extremely precise in all statements of fact, drawing a clear distinction between what was known and what was opinion.

This last IS the most important at these levels. To accidentally overstate or mislead by carelessness would bring justified outrage and cries of "you misled us." This was career death. The big guys would take disappointment; they would not tolerate misleading briefings and reports. Whether the misleading was deliberate or accidental was not pertinent.

I get through the first several charts without interruption. They showed those things that the RFP would demand "any day now." I describe the FAA problem and the need for three different sized systems for different sized en route centers.

I state flatly that the RFP will be out on Thursday, November 7.

When I get to the chart showing the various things that the system had to do -e.g., instructions for return to base directions for

# A Brawl in IBM - 1964

Air Defense aircraft, Learson interrupts. He points to a line, "What does that mean?"

I read the line. "Tabular and situation displays."

I had a good idea of what it meant, and I explain it. I was perhaps 90 percent correct. No one in the room knew any better, so the explanation went unchallenged. I was to realize later that Learson's interest in the answer was solely to judge by the answer whether or not I knew what I was talking about. If the determination was that I did not, I would have been in no more meetings with Learson.

But I pass the test and move on.

I flip to the next chart. It reads:

## NO ACTION BY DS ON MULTIPROCESSING TILL 10/28

Kennard is angry.

"That is a dig, an unnecessary dig," he glares at me. "I'm surprised that you would show such a chart. You want to make a fight of everything."

I answer calmly.

"It's not intended as a 'dig,' George. It is the truth. And it is shown because it is significant. Because it shows how far we have to go to win this bid, how late we are starting."

Paley and Ford both start talking before I finish.

"It is not true. There have been people working in this area for a hell of a long time."

"Who?" I ask, looking at them. "I've been in Poughkeepsie for the last few months and I can't find anyone who has been working on it! Maybe I'm a lousy looker, so you tell me! Who has been working on it?"

"Lot of guys," Paley asserts.

"Who?"

"Brooks", said Paley. "Brooks has been on it."

I speak evenly, without emotion or effect, flat as I can, relaxed.

"Fred Brooks started work on this October 28. His phone number in Poughkeepsie is 6464."

I point to the phone.

"Call him and check."

No one moves.

Ten or so seconds pass.

Learson asks, "Would anyone like to call Dr. Brooks?"

Silence.

No movement.

"I guess Mr. Fox has made his point. Let's continue."

I continue presenting, going thorough the desired delivery dates.

Learson tells the product division to report back to him on how they would accomplish the deliveries.

At one point Kennard says it will increase the budget 10 million dollars to make those deliveries.

"Different meeting!" Learson answers. "Bring that up in our budget meetings."

Paley holds up a sheaf of papers that look like memos. He looks to Learson. "Here are letters from Fox- as recent as October 19, changing the specs of what we're supposed to build. How are we supposed to know what to build if it keeps changing?"

Pfeiffer speaks with force.

"Of course it's changing. And it will continue to change till the bid goes in. What's new in that? Isn't that the way it always is?"

Learson looks at Paley.

"You haven't done the job to date. That is a fact. Now stop trying to hide that and let's continue."

I show the configuration that FAA wants. It consists of several memories, four CPU's and four channel units, all interconnected, all free-standing

Learson asks if any other company could deliver that.

"Yes!" I am happy to be asked.

"Burroughs has been building this kind of system for over three years."

"Hear that," Learson looks at Kennard. "They have had it for three years and you guys have been sitting on your fannies doing nothing."

He shakes his head.

I get to the need for a software package, and explain that a JOVIAL compiler with a COMPOOL facility is required.

Learson look at Kennard.

"Do you have any way to satisfy the need without writing JOVIAL?"

"I don't," answers Kennard. "We're studying whether or not it can be satisfied by a new Fortran language compiler."

"I met with Reynolds on that", I say, "and he says that it will not be known till March whether or not it will satisfy the requirement."

Kennard : "We want to study it some more. Maybe we can get an answer sooner than March. Maybe we can force a COMPOOL capability."

"When will you know?" ask Learson.

"I don't know when I'll know."

Learson tells Kennard, "By next Wednesday I want a plan to produce an answer for this requirement."

"I can't do it, Vin. That just isn't enough time, and these things can't just be decided by a statement."

"By Wednesday, George."

"I'd like to see you after this meeting, Vin."

"Fine, George, fine," - and Learson turns to Pfeiffer.

"Why haven't I heard of this JOVIAL before, then?"

I jump in. "Vin, the need for JOVIAL was clearly spelled out in the pre-RFP we sent you!"

Vin looks at me and smiles.

"I don't read my mail, young man."

"You're right, Vin", said Pfeiffer quickly. "We should have briefed you."

I shut up.

Learson looks at Kennard.

"George, I do not want this machine to be a part of the regular 360 line. I want it to be a special system, so we can price it any way we like."

"I don't know how to do that."

"Try!"

Paley then goes through a DS presentation. "Assuming that a contract is found in March 1964, we are going to try to determine what delivery we can get. Nine months –or January 1965 looks impossible, but let us look at it some more and get back to you."

He looks over at me.

"I hope you intend to bid the model 40 system for September 1964 delivery for program checkout! That should take some of the pressure off of us."

He waits for an answer.

"I don't know yet," I answer. "I want to see what the alternatives are."

Paley turns to the next chart. Two model 50s hooked together.

"This is..." he starts

"Have you seen this before?" Learson asks me.

"No. "

"DAMN IT."

Learson frowns at Paley and Kennard.

"Why haven't the DP people seen this system before? Why?"

"We just came up with it-over the weekend," says Paley.

"You came up with it five minutes ago," says Learson. "I do not want to have this happen again. I do not want to see a chart that Fox and Pfeiffer have not seen before."

He looks around the room.

"Gentlemen, we are going to win this business!"

Pause and silence.

"I want the feet-dragging to stop! From now on, we will have a meeting every Monday afternoon. Fox and Manson will get together every Friday afternoon. Then Ralph and George will get together every Monday morning. Then John Gibson and I will get together with you on Monday afternoon. That way I'll see just the disagreements –and I expect them to be few."

He smiles.

"We don't pay you guys the way we do and expect that you cannot resolve your differences. Next meeting, November 11. See you then."

He looks at Pfeiffer.

"Anything else?"

"No."

"Okay –let me spent some time with the DS people."

He and Ralph walk to the side of the room and have a private conversation.

The DS people stay in the room.

Kilner and I exit and grin at each other.

"Wow," I say with glee! "Yes."

Pfeiffer joins us.

"You stopped fighting the JOVIAL thing just in time, Joe. A little more and you may have been in deep water. But you did fine; you did fine."

We wait for the elevator.

"What is Vin doing with 'em in there? " I ask.

"Cheering them up. He's been hard on them and they have a tough enough job without the FAA bid. He's going to build them up a little. He's stomped them into the ground and now he wants to resurrect them."

As we leave, I had overhear Learson addressing Kennard.

"Is Manson up to this task? This is not an easy job!"

"He is."

"You're sure?"

"I had a long talk with him. He's ready."

I wonder what had been Manson's problem.

I tell Pfeiffer what I'd heard.

"What was wrong with Manson, Ralph?"

"His back. A very bad back."

The New DS FAA Manager

On Tuesday, November 5, I meet George Manson for the first time. I go over to his office at South Road Lab.

We are both very pleasant to each other.

"Hello, hello," smiles Manson. "We've got our hands full, don't we?"

"Sure do. Glad to have you on board."

"Well, it's a challenge, but we've had challenges before –and met them."

We chat about the proposal and get along well. No signs of animosity.

## THE RFP IS ISSUED- NOVEMBER 7

On November 7, the RFP comes out. Collins goes down and picks it up and gets several extra copies. The RFP is a set of documents, the main one being the work specification of 120 pages.

The RFP is a work of art. It is clear, structured, and easy to understand. FAA had written it with major help from MITRE, the government support group. Too many RFPs -government and commercial – are logical nightmares.

There are no surprises! Everything is as expected. And the delivery was stated as "nine months is desired!" "Desired", and not "required." This is crucial to us.

It is a historical moment of sorts, this RFP. If a contract is awarded, the effort would shape the Air Traffic Control System for the next thirty years. Occasionally in large procurements no acceptable bid is submitted, and the RFP might result in no contract. The procurement effort would start anew in the government agency. A loss of a year or more is not unusual in such a situation.

Airline passengers' lives and hundreds of millions of dollars are at stake. Done right, it will be a national resource. Done poorly, it can be more than an embarrassment; it can be a mortal danger.

A turn had been made. A new Airspace System is about to go forward.

※ ※ ※

The whole Washington team assembles in one room and we read the RFP together. After each section, we all comment on it. By the end of the day, we understand the RFP very well.

The proposal is to be submitted in two parts; the technical part due on January 6, 1964 and the price and terms and conditions part due on January 23rd. We groan – there go the Christmas holidays.

We dispatched one of our clerical staff to DS-Harrison via the Shuttle with five copies for the product division and we call Manson in Poughkeepsie and let him know it was on its way.

A Brawl in IBM - 1964

## FAA BIDDERS CONFERENCE NOVEMBER 8

On Friday, November 8, Collins goes to the 'bidder's conference that FAA conducts for possible bidders for the U.S. National Airspace System, NAS. There are 12 companies there:

| IBM | Philco | GE |
|---|---|---|
| Burroughs | RCA | Sperry Rand |
| Honeywell | ITT | Amerao |
| Control Data | General Precision | North American Aircraft |

Nothing new is learned at the bidder's conference. On an effort this complex, you'd better know almost all the answers <u>before</u> you walk into the conference. And you certainly do not want to ask questions –which might educate your competition.

We are surprised at the number of companies that attend.

## DS STONEWALLS.

On Friday, Collins approaches me.
"Did Manson tell you about Patrick?"
Bob Patrick is an outside consultant that I had hired to help in multiprocessing.
"No. What about Patrick?"
"Manson doesn't want him to see the RFP."
"Why not," I ask, bewildered.
"I don't know. He just doesn't want Patrick in on the thing."
"But Patrick is already consultant to DS. He already knows all about the new line..."
"I explained that to Manson. He doesn't care. He just doesn't want Patrick around."
Collins is sober.
"You're going to have trouble with Manson, Joe. He's a strong guy - and he's got his own ideas. You've gotten us from the frying pan to the fire in picking up Manson."
I call Manson.

"Do you know if you can make the thing a multiprocessor?" I ask.

"No, and I'm not going to investigate that until I study the RFP. Look Joe, we'll do what we can do, and I do not know when I'll know. You are wasting my time by calling me! I've got to go. Goodbye."

*Click.*

He hangs up on me!

I wonder how to work with this guy? Be nice; win him over?

No. No time!

The RFP is out! No time now to schmooze.

Be tough? This guy is not going to be scared into doing anything! It is going to be war!

I call Manson again and asked a question – "What do you think about section 4.2?"

"I told you to stop bothering me." Manson scolds me. "You're taking up my time on the telephone. I'll let you know what we can do AFTER I have determined it. You just sit back and relax, and we'll tell you what we can do in good time."

I ignore his comments.

"What do you think about the computer sizing?"

"We'll figure that out," says Manson.

"George, I have super guys from FSD who have poured over these problems for months. They can jump-start your people. I can have them in Poughkeepsie tomorrow."

"No. We will do it. Just stop calling me".

Click.

He's hung up on me again.

I don't know how to deal with this.

Who will gain the upper hand will depend a lot on circumstances, and on who plays the cards better.

It is DP versus DS. It is not even polite.

*"We're going to get you, Fox! We're going to put your..."*

The attacks only make our resolve greater. In addition to all other reasons to win, I'd also show these yahoos they couldn't intimidate us. I have two great fighters on my side -Collins and White.

I explain to Kilner that DS is just pure antagonism. I relate the phone calls, the hang-ups.

Sam does not believe me!

"Oh, come on. It can't be. It can't be like that."

I understand the disbelief. It is NOT the way IBM operates. Such ferocity was not found in DP.

## TO THE CHAIRMAN

Pfeiffer, knowing of Watson's interest, sends a letter to the IBM Chairman and the IBM President on November 11.

TO: Mr. T. J. Watson. Jr. - A. L. Williams

SUBJECT: Federal Aviation Agency

On November 7, the FAA released its Request for Proposal for computer support of the next generation Air Traffic Control System, with manufacturers, responses due by January 6, 1964.
We expect our prime competitors for this 150 million dollar business to be Burroughs, Control Data and General Electric, who are among the 12 companies expected to propose.

Success in winning this award will be dependent upon our response in five areas of evaluation:

1) System Capability
2) Delivery
3) Programming Systems Support
4) Technology
5) Price

We are currently behind our major competition in all but the technology area, as reflected by the following:

<u>System Capability:</u> FAA requires a system which provides modularity with 'fail-soft" capability.

In addition, the FAA must be satisfied that the equipment proposed is "off-the-shelf" by receiving with our proposal (I) program manuals, and (2) evidence of capability to meet the required schedule. In order to win this business must bid a system complex consisting of Model 50 type machines with multiprocessor hardware capabilities. To date the system which we will bid has not been determined, since the design for multiprocessor hardware has not yet been completed. DSD has promised us a system design by November 25.

Delivery. Based upon an estimated contract award of March, 1964, delivery will be required in March, 1965. DSD is uncertain that they can deliver Model 50 type machines with multiprocessor hardware on this schedule.

Programming Systems Support: We must provide suitable programming systems so that the FAA can begin programming by March, 1964, and debugging by September, 1964. This question cannot be fully resolved until we determine the system to be bid. DSD is aware of these requirements and is working toward an answer, but the schedule is extremely tight.

Technology: We feel IBM to have the advantage in this area, primarily due to our SLT circuit capability.

Price: This bid will be extremely price-sensitive. FAA will determine those manufacturers technically responsive to their requirements and then select the lowest bidder. We are certain that at least Burroughs will offer military-priced equipment, and expect the others to do so also. It is also certain that if we bid normal commercial prices we will be considerably higher than competition.

Knowing your particular interest in the Air Traffic Control problem and your desire to have IBM contribute to its solution, I felt that you should have the above information.

We are prepared to brief you in further detail.

   signed
   R. A. Pfeiffer, Jr.
   cc: Mr. T.V. Learson

This letter triggers an audit of the effort to date by the Chairman's office. The letter does not say IBM would lose – but it says we are behind in 4 of the 5 areas.

On Saturday, November 9th, the sales team reads the RFP all day.

A Brawl in IBM - 1964

## SECOND WEEKLY LEARSON REVIEW

Kilner and I catch the 10 PM Shuttle to New York on Sunday evening.

We are en route to the weekly meeting with Learson.

At 9 AM, we meet again in the spectacular conference room.

Evans is missing again. *Is he going to stay out of FAA?*

John Gibson has replaced Learson and is now Kennard's boss is there, and also Reynolds, DS head of Programming, and Manson.

John Opel, Gibson's Chief of Staff, is there. [Opel will succeed Cary as Chairman of IBM in 1981.]

Pfeiffer, Kilner and I are there.

Pfeiffer and Kennard have chatted before the meeting, fulfilling the edict that they meet before the big meeting. They have resolved nothing.

I put charts that sum up the RFP.

"It is exactly what we thought, to the last detail. We must bid the model 50."

Learson looks pensive.

"Have we investigated our present line, the 7000 series?"

The 7000 is the top of the current IBM equipment that the 360 is to replace.

All agree that that is not a sellable solution.

"Suppose you start from scratch with your requirement? Build a whole new system?"

"You'd be one year late," says Manson.

"And it wouldn't be 'off the shelf,'" I say.

The RFP states that the system had to be an 'off-the-shelf' system.

"What does that mean?" asked Learson.

"It means that the computer is not new; that it is not being built just for FAA, that it is not a developmental item", I explain. I relate that the Hough Committee, after the mid-air collision over New York, specifically faulted the FAA for developing computers instead of buying commercial machines.

"You think that the new line meets the 'off-the shelf' requirements?" Vin asks me.

"Yes, sir!" I say with conviction.

"I don't," says Learson.

"Ralph, you make sure that we don't keep going on this bid and find out six months from now that we never had a chance because we are not 'off-the-shelf.'"

"I'll get a definition".

"That's got to really hurt us," Vin says.

"Oh no! .., I react . "..we're in good shape actually, we..."

"Joe," Learson looks tolerant, "on a scale of one to 10, the other bidders will get 10 and we'll get zero."

"No, Vin. we've got a string of successful deliveries behind us. One after another. The large core memory for the 7090. The real time channels for the Test Bed . The 1401-1410 disk system at Islip. The technical leader for FAA on told me flatly we'd never make the delivery of the special bulk core memory. We made it - and he remembers it."

Learson is undented.

"Zero."

"Vin's right, Joe," says Pfeiffer.

I drop it. Late, but I drop it.

"Let's talk about the programming," says Learson. "George, you were to get something started by Wednesday. Where do you stand?"

"We are not going to write a new compiler. We are going to incorporate all of the needed functions in our new Fortran."

"That is one year too late, George," I say.

Kennard jumps on me.

"Where is the need for JOVIAL in the RFP, Joe? We can't find it in there."

"You're right," I admit. "There is no requirement for JOVIAL in there. BUT - it says that a COMPOOL facility is required. I wrote to Carl," I motion to Reynolds, "on October 19 and specified that we needed a COMPOOL facility"

(*I was telling them –I knew what was needed that far back.*)

"Then I met you and we set up a meeting with Carl for the next Monday in Poughkeepsie at 7 AM. (*I was telling them how hard I was working.*)

We had that meeting and several more and we all agreed that the only way to meet the COMPOOL requirement was with JOVIAL.

Reynolds speaks; "DS did not agree; Don Madden agreed".

*(Madden was a consultant, who worked for Reynolds.)*

"Oh, come on!" Pfeiffer is annoyed!

"What you are saying is that the President of the division and the head of programming set up a meeting between Fox and Madden to determine what was needed. And now that Madden agrees with Sales, you are throwing him to the wolves and saying 'he agreed' and you - the division - didn't.

Come on! He is your man; stick with his judgment!"

They don't answer.

Reynolds takes a different tack.

"Let's bid JOVIAL to FAA for a price."

"We are already in price trouble, Carl," I say.

Learson looked at Kennard.

"What are you going to do, George?" he demands. "It's your ball and this Fortran thing isn't going to work. What are you going to do?"

"I don't know," exhales Kennard.

I am amazed. Kennard had just about been told to write JOVIAL and he is still fighting.

*Why doesn't Learson just order him to do it?*

Learson slowly shakes his head.

"We debate and delay and debate −and the thing slips away from us. I can't get anything done around here."

Gibson leans over to Kennard and says softly, "George, we can decide later if it is a standard program or not. Take action to do it now."

Gibson is Kennard's boss.

Out of the blue, Manson changes the subject.

"We've analyzed the load of the traffic the RFP asks for and three CPU's will do the job."

He looks squarely at us −the 3 DP people, as though daring us to fight this assessment.

"So we'll build it that way −with only three CPUs."

And he quickly moves on, back to software.

I am startled! The audacity of what Manson is doing takes my breath away.

*"Meetingmanship" is at play. If Manson can "stampede" the meeting, get no opposition, and everyone acquiesces, then his "position" is tacitly accepted. Then it would be all uphill to turn the group around.*

*Speechwriters for politicians are very powerful, because if the politician gives the speech the way it's written, what he says puts a stake in the ground. It's his position.*

*People don't easily change their minds. There is an emotional investment in a decision. It is hard to reverse yourself. Possession is 9/10 of everything.*

*In How to <u>Win Friends and Influence People</u>, Dale Carnegie says that if you want to sell something, get the prospective buyer saying "yes" to a string of trivial items – then propose your item and ask for the order. The emotional grove of 'yes' is hard to overcome – the prospect is "conditioned" to say yes.*

I could not let the group accept the Manson position – even tacitly.

Three CPUs are not enough, I know.

I must attack the position – even if all I did was hold the question open. It might never be won - or even a subject of debate again, if it went unchallenged.

"Wait a minute," I say. "We need four CPU's."

Manson glares at me.

"Three will handle the load."

"Right, and we must add the fourth as a spare."

"Look at it, George," says Learson.

I am happy- the question has remained open.

Manson continues.

"Our main problem is hardware. I'm not sure that we can build a multiprocessor, and if we can, we sure as hell can't deliver on time. I think to talk about programming before we know what the system looks like is starting a big effort too soon."

"Not at all," I say. "We have to keep compatible with the new line or we won't be 'off-the-shelf.' If we stay compatible then we can start on JOVIAL now. Even if we change the system slightly, the work done in the next few months will be applicable."

"Look," Learson, a bit impatient, "solve the problem, George, to the satisfaction of the marketing people.

And solve it by next Monday. What's next?"

"Can we bid the model 40 with channels out," I ask, looking at Kennard. "No. Are you trying to ruin the whole new line? We cannot pull the 40 apart!"

I don't press. I am resigned to bid only the 50, but I wanted to try to get the model 40.

I didn't try too hard.

Opel comments that he agrees with Kennard, that to make the 40 a multiprocessor would be too big a job; since a multi-processor demanded that memory and channels be separate.

Learson asked why the 40 can't be bid instead of the 50.

Manson answers.

"It is too slow, Vin – and as you just heard - it's not a multiprocessor."

"Speed it up and tear the channels out?" asks Learson.

"We could double the speed," said Manson, but it will look just like a 50."

Opel says that any of the 360 machines could be sped up by a factor of 2, but no more. They'd been designed with this in mind.

Gibson asks, "Could we start a 'new' machine from scratch and meet the schedule?"

There is general agreement DS could not.

The meeting ended with Learson reminding Kennard to get an answer to the JOVIAL question.

The next meeting is set for November 18, the next Monday, in Poughkeepsie.

"George," Learson looking to Kennard," I want you to build this thing special. Different."

"I understand."

I didn't. After the meeting I ask Kilner what is going on with this.

Kilner explains that if the FAA machine were standard, it would have to be priced like all the other 360 machines. If it were 'different', it could follow its own pricing rules.

Make it standard, IBM could not win because of price. But, if we made it different, we might topple it of the 'off the shelf' status. A Catch 22?

After the meeting, we go to Learson's office in Harrison. Kilner and I wait outside while Pfeiffer meets with Learson. Learson is in the loop in all ways now –he'd been the boss of all the product people while they'd delayed –and now he is Pfeiffer's boss's boss.

Pfeiffer comes out of the office, cheerful.

He meets a staff assistant he knew, who asks him about the big Air Force bid. The one that

"We will win, " Pfeiffer is saying. " I have reasons to be confident."

I am surprised to hear Pfeiffer that positive. These big bids took funny twists. Crazy discounts. New machines. Politics. *"This state needs jobs..."*

Learson's secretary calls, "Phone, Mr. Pfeiffer," and Ralph takes it standing there at her desk.

"Hello –Pfeiffer."

He listens.

"WHAT?"

I can tell from the tone it was bad news –very bad!

"WHO?"

Listens.

"WHY?"

Listens.

"Who announced –the Air Force or Congress?"

*IBM had lost the Air Force 150 bases proposal!*

Kilner and I get out of there, leaving a note with the secretary that we are down the hall. We don't want to get caught up in this.

A half hour later, we get a call from the secretary.

"Mr. Pfeiffer is ready to leave."

"We'll be right there."

Pfeiffer is somber. We take the elevator down from the third floor.

I, restrained and sympathetic, offer: " I hope my career doesn't ride on winning the FAA order.'

RAP glares at me.

"Your career rides on your pleasing me. You do your job so I'm happy and you'll do fine."

I shut up.

We catch the Shuttle to Washington.

✯ ✯ ✯

Back to Washington on the 19th; back to New York on the Shuttle on the 20th. Wednesday.

Collins and I drive the two hours from LaGuardia to Poughkeepsie.

I visit several people, keeping my finger on things. Everyone is working furiously.

Manson is too busy to talk to me.

"Sorry, Joe. I'm busy. See you at the next meeting."

"We're supposed to see what we agree and disagree on, George."

"Tough."

# CAN IBM STOP THE PROCUREMENT?

In Poughkeepsie, I am wandering, killing time in a way, going from office to office to see what was going on. Much as I disliked dealing with Manson, I stop by his office.

Inside were Jack Keeley –the former FSDer on the FAA - and Jim Hewitt, the assistant to Kennard. I know Hewitt, a DP veteran who is smart and crisp. He has not been in any FAA efforts to my knowledge.

"Hello," I say. "What's up?"

They keep their backs to me, barely look at me.

"We're busy, Joe," said Hewitt, apologetic.

I stay in the doorway. I start to leave. Some sixth sense tells me to ask some questions.

"You're not on FAA, are you?"

Silence.

"Is it?"

"Yes, Joe," admits Hewitt. "But we'd like you not to bother us now. You'll learn of it in due time."

I am NOT about to leave now.

"Look." Belligerent yet calm, I attack.

"This bid is due in six weeks. I'm the proposal manager. If what you have doesn't get to me in time, I'll I have to report that to the INQUEST" (I stressed the word,) -"that at" (I pointedly look at my watch) "four PM on the 21st of November I asked Hewitt and Keeley to tell me what was afoot on the FAA bid and I later found out –too late to act on –and they refused to tell me anything."

I pause for effect.

"I AM the proposal manager."

A pause.

"Ok," says Hewitt. "We are preparing for a meeting with Watson tomorrow."

I am impressed.

*Nobody has met with Watson yet –but about what?*

"We're asking Watson to call Halaby (the FAA Administrator) and ask that the procurement be cancelled."

"Shit."

*These people must be crazy –Halaby would not –could not –stop the procurement.*

"On what basis can Tom ask Halaby to do that, Jim?"

"On the basis that the procurement is slanted, tainted, in favor of Burroughs. Only Burroughs can win."

"We can win, Jim."

"No we can't. We can't bid a multiprocessor."

*We were all the way back to start. Do not pass Go. Reset to zero. Start over.*
I look at them.

"DS is saying it can't bid a multiprocessor?"

"You got it."

"Shit."

"Now if you'll leave us alone, please –we've got work to do."

I go out to call Pfeiffer.

Pfeiffer is traveling. And cell phones are not in the world yet. It is 1963.

I call the assistant to Al Williams the President of IBM. C. B. 'Jack' Rodgers had been in Kilner's job in Washington before Sam, and I know him from those days.

Jack confirms that Watson would indeed be briefed tomorrow. Learson, Gibson and Kennard had met with Williams.

"Watson just might call Halaby, Joe."

"That's insane, Jack. You know that."

"I know and you know. Get someone to tell Tom Watson that. Get to Pfeiffer, or you could go off a cliff on this one."

Pfeiffer is still traveling- I leave messages for Ralph to call me.

*I'll get him in the morning. Ralph would know how to work this.*

# IBM RESEARCH IS INTO THE ACT

We had wrangled in one of the Learson meetings over the issue of which configuration was more reliable, the multiprocessor or a duplex. Learson had referred the question to Corporate Research.

That night, the 21st, I drove to New York, LaGuardia Airport, and picked up Hank White. We were testifying on the next day to the Research Division Audit Committee. White had some of his FSD people to present.

White listens as I tell him about the pitch that is to be made to Watson. He grows angrier as I go on.

"Those jerks in the product division. They waste six months arguing and now want Watson to bail 'em out. FAA won't listen to Watson. Even if they wanted to, they can't. The RFP is out. It's too late."

The next morning, we are in a small conference room in the Yorktown Research Center, meeting with a group of Research engineers and scientists, to present the reasons for having the channels and the memories in physical units separate from the main frame.

The meeting with Watson and the product division to prepare for the call to Halaby is scheduled for the afternoon.

I try to get Pfeiffer, and cannot. He is en route to Philadelphia.

I wait an hour and called again...still not there.

The meeting is going well with the research people. They agree with everything White, Oldani and Kowalke are saying.

How to get the message to Learson about the Watson meeting is driving me crazy. I leave the meeting and call Washington again. Pfeiffer is now due in the early afternoon.

"*Time to jump into the soup*," I decide, and I dial the Harrison facility.

"Mr. Learson," I tell the operator.

"Learson," is the one word identification I hear after the phone stops ringing.

"Vin, this is Joe Fox. DS is going to see Mr. Watson this afternoon to have him call the FAA Administrator to ask him to delay the procurement because it is biased in favor of Burroughs."

"I know that."

Cold. Not friendly at all.

*What is going on? Vin is our champion. Is he switching sides?*

## A Brawl in IBM - 1964

"Well, it's...it's not right, Vin. He can't delay the procurement. It is an official procurement."

"We'll see."

"And it is NOT wired for Burroughs." I am beginning to get angry.

"They've got the multiprocessor." says Learson.

"So do we!" I blurt. "At least FAA thinks so. Evans told the FAA we could make the 360 a multiprocessor – back in September. We can't now say it's unfair. It won't wash, Vin."

"Who told FAA we could do a multiprocessor?"

"Evans."

Silence.

"How do you know?"

"I heard him. I was there."

"You go down to Harrison right now and see Kennard and you tell him what you just told me."

"I'll call him right now."

"I said SEE HIM."

"Yes sir."

Click.

I am not about to drive to Harrison- about a half-hour - and find that Kennard wasn't there. I call, and interrupt a meeting Kennard is in by telling the secretary that Learson had told me to call.

I relate the conversation I had with Learson to Kennard.

"Joe, you must be mistaken. Bob couldn't have told the FAA that we could build the 360 as a multiprocessor."

"He did, George. I was there. He did."

"You must be mistaken."

"No. No, I'm not."

"Let me call Bob. How's everything else?"

"Well...bad. Manson is freezing me out. He won't answer my calls. Could you tell him to be more cooperative?"

"I'll tell him."

"Vin I said should come see you. I can be there in half an hour."

"No, no. I'm leaving for Poughkeepsie."

I go back to the Research meeting, wondering whether or not they'd get to Watson –whether or not Watson would make the phone call to the FAA Administrator.

*Damn them. They tell the FAA they can build it, and now three weeks <u>after</u> the RFP is out, three weeks, they want to stop everything. We deserve to lose the damn thing.*

I am depressed, and listen to the progress of the testimony to the Panel dispiritedly. Even Hank White can't cheer me up. I call Manson.

"Hello, George. How is everything?" I am trying to start off friendly.

"Look, Fox, what the hell are you telling Kennard –I 'won't answer the phone.' Bullshit! You get off that crap."

"Well, you haven't answered my last five calls and…"

"You don't say anything, Joe! All you do is blah-blah and waste my time with obvious stuff that I don't need you to tell me and …"

"Goodbye George."

And I hang up.

*We'll never get the damn proposal out. No way. These bastards have done nothing to get ready.*

The testimony to Research drags on. We all go to lunch.
Back again.
Deep discussion about reliability. I had heard all the arguments before. There was nothing new coming out of the Research team.
The phone rings in the crowded conference room.
"Call for you Jack," someone says to the chairman of the Research Panel, Jack Bertram.
"Hello."
Seven or eight side conversations start going on at once.
"WHAT? - WHAT? SHOT? WHEN?"
All conversations stop.
"The President?" …

All are watching Bertram.

"Is he dead?"

Silence.

Bertram faces the group.

"President Kennedy has been shot. In Dallas. He's being rushed to the hospital. No one knows how bad it is!"

The meeting recesses.

People drift off, listen to radios, call home.

After a half-hour, we reconvene the meeting. What else is there to do?

Soon the public address system at the Yorktown Lab is giving the brief announcement –"President Kennedy was shot and wounded by an unknown assailant in Dallas at 1:52 PM Eastern Standard Time. He has been rushed to Parkland Memorial Hospital and we will announce any further information we receive at once. "

The meeting resumed; we all are going through the motions, waiting for more word on the President.

I call Pfeiffer - and get him.

I relate the events of the morning and the conversations with Learson and Kennard.

Ralph listens, then tells me, "There will be no meeting with Watson today. They are all just sitting in his office watching the TV and waiting for news."

Watson knew Kennedy.

"Okay," I say, "I'll keep going on this thing and..."

"MY GOD," gasps Pfeiffer.

"What's the matter?" I ask, my heart in my throat.

"The President's dead," Pfeiffer says, emotionless, as though he were a radio announcer...or in a state of shock. "It just came over the radio."

I'll call you back," I say - and hang up.

I walk back into the conference room, and, trying not to be dramatic, make a simple announcement.

"The President is dead. It just came over the radio."

The room falls silent. A few hang their heads; others walked out, feeling the need to be alone.

I walk into an empty executive conference room to be alone. Sitting there in the large comfortable room, I felt very alone and overwhelmed. I cry softly for a short time.

They wrapped up the meeting and White and I drive to LaGuardia. I am getting mad now, mad at everything and everybody.

White and I get to the airport and it is jammed with people. We go into the bar and had a drink. It was about 5PM.

I notice a solitary man in the bar, watching everyone.

"There's an FBI man, Hank."

I point to the man. "I'll bet they are watching every airport in the country to see if it may be a bigger plot than just to kill Kennedy."

The trip home on the Shuttle is uneventful.

※ ※ ※

It rains in Washington, Saturday, hard. I go down to the Washington office just to see how eight out-of-town IBM people are faring. These people are from Boston, Brooklyn, Los Angeles, Cleveland, Atlanta, Jacksonville...and one from Dallas.

There are only about three of them in the office. The others are about their personal business and the three who are in the office are taking things calmly. I go home after about an hour.

On Sunday I, my wife and three boys go down to see the cortege take the casket to the Capitol. It is a beautiful, sad day. We get to Sixth and Pennsylvania in time to see the procession with the casket, drums and riderless horse. Although there is a crowd of over a million lining Pennsylvania Avenue, there is no laughter, no loud talking, nothing but somber faces and hushed whispers.

I have never seen a crowd like this; it is eerie. *'It suits the occasion'*. We hear on the radio that Lee Harvey Oswald has been shot!

※ ※ ※

The funeral is Monday, a national holiday.

## A Brawl in IBM - 1964

I go down to the IBM office at 1120 Connecticut Avenue. The funeral procession is to go down (or up) Connecticut Avenue on the way to the church. I am going half out of a sense of duty to the people from out of town, and half out of the desire to view the funeral.

After two hours, the closed office (it was a national holiday and I had to use a passkey to get in) began to fill up. The roofs and marquees of the shops along Connecticut Avenue filled with people. The roof of the marquee of the Mayflower Hotel across the street is filled with cooks and bellhops. They have a choice view.

I see a woman of about 45 years old actually climb a cat ladder –a plain iron vertical ladder bolted to the outside of a building –to a roof of a four-story building next door. She has on a fur stole and high heels, and she is not a young woman –but up she goes, hand over hand, until she gets to the roof and takes her position, watching with the others.

Someone has brought a portable TV to the office. As the Mass is televised, the band rolls its drums outside on Connecticut Avenue. The scene is electric –to see and hear the funeral services on the screen and to hear constantly the roll of the drums. With no interruption.

Once again I am struck with the solemnity of the group –now about 30 people in the small open office space –there is no talking but in whispers, and little of that.

The Mass must have lasted 45 minutes and during that time but one or two even move.

The Mass ends; the procession passes; the woman climbs down the cat ladder again –after first dropping her fur stole four stories down to the alley. As I watch I worry for her safety, but despite the high heels, she gets down without incident.

## THIRD LEARSON WEEKLY REVIEW

Now it was time to get back to the battle. The assassination and funeral had stopped all work –but the due date to submit the proposal has not changed!

We still must deal with the DS thrust that the procurement was 'fixed' for Burroughs, and we had to keep the chairman from calling Halaby, the FAA administrator. I talk to Pfeiffer. The weekly meeting with Learson is scheduled for Wednesday in Poughkeepsie, In Evans' conference room.

It should be a 'Shoot Out at the OK Corral'.

Kilner and I fly to New York on the Shuttle on Tuesday night.

We arrive at 8 AM at Evans' office on Wednesday, November 27, the day before Thanksgiving.

I go in and sit in the conference room next to Evans' office. I am alone, and I am very worried.

I cannot prove that Evans told the FAA that IBM's 360 was a multiprocessor. It is my word against Evans's.

Evans bustles into the room.

He and I are alone.

"One of us is going to die today, Fox."

*I feel very weary.*

"Fine. I'm ready to die."

"I mean it. One of us is going to die."

"And I mean it. I'm tired of all this."

I feel myself getting angry.

Paley and Kilner enter the room.

Evans' conversation with me is still semi-private. He lowers his voice, but not the intensity.

"You've been misrepresenting me."

"Not true, Bob."

"Oh yes, Joe! You've been misrepresenting me."

"NO. I've not. Name one instance."

"I'm not going to argue with you," said Evans, and he looks at his mail.

"YOU accused me, Bob. Give me an instance."

"Pfeiffer's letter of August 8th." ???

I have no idea of what is in that.

And I never get back to it –Learson walks in at that moment and the side conversation ends.

# A Brawl in IBM - 1964

The meeting begins –I switch my mind back to proving Evans told the FAA the 360 was a multiprocessor. I have no idea of how to do that. None.

Gibson, Brooks and Kennard enter. Behind them come Manson and Pfeiffer.

They all settle into chairs around the big conference table. I sit between Pfeiffer and Kilner. Next to Ralph is Learson. Kennard, Evans and Brooks are on the other side of the table. Paley is at the head and Manson at the foot of the table.

Learson opens.

"Okay! Let's get to the facts about what FAA was told and what it was not told."

He looks at me.

"You say that FAA was told that we could build a multiprocessor system in twelve months?"

"No. There was no mention of time. They were just told that we could build a multiprocessor system."

"That's not true," says Evans with quiet assurance.

I squirm.

*"Here it comes –the argument I cannot win –Evans is going to claim he did not say it. I can't win!"*

I groan inwardly, but said aloud, "I'm sorry, but you said...!"

"I said that..." starts Evans.

"Wait! Wait! " Learson takes charge. "Let's do it one at a time - and with less passion. You'll both get your chance."

Evans gets up and takes a piece of chalk, walks to the blackboard.

"I'll tell you exactly what I said," and he starts to do so.

"I began with the need for the new line..." and he goes on from there.

I wonder at his total recall. Everything he says is not only what he had said to the FAA, but it is in just the order he had said it, - and with the same inflection.

*Maybe I'm wrong, I think. A panicky moment.*

*"No, my people remember it as I do."*

Evans goes on.

"Then I got to the part about multiprocessors. I told them that we had never built one, but the problem was not a hardware problem but a software problem. I told that if necessary we could snap together up to ten CPU's and ..."

I gasp, clutch Pfeiffer's arm, and blurt, "He said it again. He said it again."

Several people speak at once...

But Learson has the floor.

"STOP! Stop right there," Learson commands.

Evans stands there, hand poised with chalk ready to go on, and looks at Learson, puzzled.

"What's the matter?"

"You just said it. You said you could build – no, would build –the new line so that it could be used as a multiprocessor."

"No! No I did not," says Evans, in obvious bewilderment at the point.

Kennard speaks.

"He didn't say that, Vin. He just said that maybe, if investigated..."

Learson cuts him off.

"George, I hear very well and he just said that the new line could be snapped together - 'up to ten CPU's.'".

I relax. It is over! Watson won't call Halaby.

"Vin," Kennard is not giving up yet, "he did not say that."

Learson, unemotional: "He did –and I heard it. Did you hear it, John?" he asks.

John Gibson, new vice president in charge of the engineering side of the house, Kennard's new boss.

Gibson, obviously not happy to be on the opposite side of the argument than his people, says

"Yes. Yes I did."

Vin quietly moves on.

"Let's continue. There is no question in my mind that FAA believes that we can answer the RFP. We cannot ask for a change in the spec or a later response date because of the bid being slanted away from us. What's next?"

"We need 4 CPUs in each system," says Kilner. "So far the design is for three. We need four. The memory speed is 2.5 microseconds, (one word from memory every 2 millionths of a second) and the cable lengths to the memory are so long that they slow the transfer enough that we lose a half a microsecond and therefore we need the fourth CPU in the system."

"The memory speed is 2 millionths of a second per word, not 2.5," puts in Manson.

"No, your guy told me it was 2!" I say.

"When?"

"Yesterday."

"Well, that is your problem, Joe. You go to the wrong people. You should ask me and you will get the right answer. Instead of going everywhere and getting bad information."

"No, George, it was your direction that I stop 'bothering' you on the phone. But the thing at question here is not where I got the information, but whether it is right or wrong. Now your guy told me yesterday", I emphasized the word, "that it was 2.5 microseconds."

Learson looked at Evans. "Is it 2 and a half or 2?"

Brooks answered, "Neither, it is 2.3"

Learson, slams the table, "No wonder he (pointing to me) does not know what the memory speed is –you don't."

He looks disgusted with the whole affair.

I persist.

"We must have the fourth CPU –for growth. Even if George's numbers are right, we must be able to grow with the system."

"Baloney." Manson says.

DS isn't going to buy that.

"It's in the RFP."

I am trying to stampede the decision, based on a high-level reason. "Besides, it's not hard to do four, once you've done three."

"You," Learson jumps on me, "don't' know that it is not hard."

Dead end.

"But I want you to look at it, George."

Success.

They adjourn the meeting so that Learson and Gibson could call Research and get the results of the review. They leave the conference room.

Kilner tells me to join him and meet with George Manson, in a side office.

"We've got to stop this warfare," Kilner tells me en route.

Amen to that I say.

"George," says Sam, "we've got to work more closely together. You and Joe have to work as a team."

"Why?" demands Manson.

Kilner is taken aback.

"Why not?"

"Because I've got a lot to do. I do not need Fox. I know what I've got to do and I'll do it."

"But not everything is clear. Joe should interpret things –what is important, what is trivial."

"I don't need an interpreter. I can read. I've got the RFP. I need time and Fox eats it up."

"But..." Kilner is almost speechless, "but... but you can't do it alone –you need us to help."

"No I don't."

We leave.

I am delighted. Manson has shown Kilner far better than I have just how entrenched the sides are!

Had Manson responded "Sure. Right. OK.", I would have been in bad shape. Kilner, who was not in Poughkeepsie very often, would have not appreciated my plight.

Kilner and I are alone for a moment.

"How many times must we win, Sam?"

"What do you mean?"

"We've won the multiprocessing fight at least nine times, but it always comes back. We won in July, in August. We won clearly in October when they agreed to put people on it. We won again today.

## A Brawl in IBM - 1964

But will we ever just win -period, no more, and get this damn division to start working with us instead of against us?"

"Just keep going, Joe."

"You heard that maniac, Manson, *'I'll make the decisions.' 'That's my job.'* He's crazy. I've got to steal around that bastard every day, every decision, to be sure he's not made some dumb-ass decision that'll loom up and kill us!"

"Easy, Joe, easy. Hang in there."

They all reconvened in the conference room.

Learson sat down, looked around the table. Announcement time!

"Research says a duplex system is as reliable as the multiprocessor and that it is too late to redesign the 50 and meet the delivery date."

*I cannot believe it.*

*'This reopens the whole damn mess!'*

Pfeiffer looks at me. His eyes said, *'How? and what now?'*

I shrug. For all my seething mind, I'd never imagined this!

Research had copped out! Their numbers, which Evans was writing on the Board, showed a tie! It was very complex. At least, I thought it was a tie.

But Research had then made a <u>management</u> judgment and said that the 360 model 50 was too far along in its product development cycle to redesign it in time for the FAA bid, or the delivery!

All the wasted months were being paid for. I think furiously –and come up with nothing. I say nothing.

Learson fishes out a dollar bill and gives it to Manson. He had lost a $1 bet that the multiprocessor would be more reliable.

Evans is driving panzer tanks through the opening.

"Just as I said. Just as I said. Let's present those findings to the FAA in the proposal. We'll prove it to them."

"What do you say, DP?" asked Learson Pfeiffer.

"I don't believe it," I say.

"Too bad," replies Learson. "It was a fair study."

Evans draws on the board two systems, one system with three CPU's with channels integrated into each CPU, and one system with them out.

"The separate channel system was 66,000 components; the integrated channel system has 42,000.

The 42,000 component, channels integrated, system is more reliable."

Then he draws a third system with just two CPU's with channels inside the CPU box, where one would do the whole job, and the second was a standby. A duplex.

"The duplex will be down eight minutes a year, and we should..."

"Can you show that?" I interrupt.

"Show what?"

"That it's eight minutes a year! Can you <u>prove</u> it?"

Evans ignores me. He continues on.

"This is the standard line. This is the way we should bid and..."

"Answer him," Learson tells Evans quietly.

Evans glares...but he answers.

"No. We can't prove it, but it's right."

Pause.

"Well, get us figures we 'can prove'," Learson ends that question.

Evans could have bluffed and said yes. But he didn't.

I am still in shock from the Research answer.

*Those dumb bastards!*

I don't know which way to argue.

Learson helps.

"Okay? We bid the duplex?"

Kennard does not hesitate.

"And bid the system with channels in the same box as the main frame. The R&D study is a toss up and the Research findings state that it is too tough a job to take the things out."

"Ralph?" Vin looks to Pfeiffer.

"Well, the key is the fact that the RFP <u>demands</u> that the channels be out. So all the study is fine but the FAA has made up their mind, and we will not be responsive if we bid any other way."

He hands the RFP to Learson, and points to the section that states the channels had to be out.

Vin looks at it silently for a long while.

## A Brawl in IBM - 1964

"Well," at last, "the RFP is clear. We've got to build it with the channel outside of the main frame. And as a multiprocessor."

Now the Product Division people are stunned. They try to argue, but Learson would not let them.

"That's it," he says.

And that was it!

Evans states that the costs of the FAA bid were 6.6 million dollars for the hardware, and $1.6 million for the JOVIAL.

Learson just nods.

"Okay. Let's summarize," and Learson does .

"We will make the 50 a multiprocessor. We will expedite delivery of a JOVIAL compiler. We will move up the delivery date of the model 50."

Several of the execs are making notes.

Suddenly, Manson speaks –politely.

"I think you are making a mistake."

*These guys never surrender!*

Learson raises his eyebrow and almost murmurs, "Why?"

No anger. No reproach. Just –'Why?'.

Manson launches into a well-reasoned argument on why not to accelerate the announcement of the 50. He doesn't bother with the multiprocessors. The heart of his argument is about the effect on the 360 line. He finishes.

Learson responds.

"Thank you, George. Those are good points, but on balance, my decision stands."

I am impressed. These big guys tolerate reasoned dissent –from any level. Manson was the lowest ranking manager in the room, - except for me.

The meeting ends. Pfeiffer goes off with Learson to Evans' office. He tells Kilner and me to wait.

I am spent.

But we've survived! Survived the Research report; avoided any call by the Chairman to the FAA administrator; clarified that indeed DS had 'told' FAA the 360 could be easily made a multiprocessor. And DS has been told "make the model 50 a multiprocessor".

*'It hasn't been a bad day's work.'*
But it is not over yet, this day.
The other meeting with Pfeiffer breaks up.
Pfeiffer and Kilner talk alone.
Pfeiffer comes over to me.
"Um, let's go into an office; I've got to talk to you."
He seems embarrassed and acts like someone with an unpleasant task to perform.
"Are you going to appoint a Czar," I ask.
It was clear to me that things could not continue this way. In fact, I cannot understand how they had let it go on like this for so long.
"Yes," says Ralph, surprised and relieved, "that was the thing we were talking to Research about. Research stated that there was a 'complete and irrevocable' breakdown in communications between Marketing and the Product Division and they recommend a Czar be appointed."
He pauses.
"What do you think, Joe? Don't take this as a lack of confidence in you. It's not. But we are not getting anywhere."
"No problem," I state. "I agree completely. It is needed, because I am at the point that I do not believe a thing DS says. As a result, I bring every decision into Learson to be reviewed. He doesn't have time to be bothered with every little thing. Who's it going to be?"
"Don't know yet. I'll call you. How's the proposal?"
"No good. No information, Ralph. We're going to have a hell of a time getting it out on time."
Now the day is almost over.
Kilner and I have a four-hour trip to get home - for tomorrow's Thanksgiving! A two-hour drive to LaGuardia airport, an hour flight on the Shuttle, an hour on the other end! We get home at 9 P M.
Collins and I fly back to LaGuardia on the Shuttle Friday morning, en route to Poughkeepsie. I get a call from Pfeiffer.
"We have a czar appointed."
I am delighted. I'd wanted a "supreme commander" full time since early October.
"Great."

# A Brawl in IBM - 1964

"Watts Humphrey."

"Oh."

I do not know Watts, but I know of him. He is in DPD headquarters in White Plains, a bright technical manager, a director, and one under a VP.

"He wants to meet with you Saturday in Washington, Joe. 10 AM; my office. I will not be there."

"OK."

I tell Collins about the new czar.

"Watts is from the technical group of DP headquarters. It really frosts me that they named a czar from DP."

"Why? "

"It's a reflection on me. I'm from DP. It's as though DP weren't doing its job –meaning me. I'm not doing my job."

"You're being too sensitive."

"No. They could have gotten a corporate guy – above both divisions. That'd have made more sense."

"Forget it."

Collins, as usual, is wise.

I fly back to Washington on the 6 o'clock Shuttle, headed for my 8 PM Friday night bridge lesson. And the meeting with Watts for tomorrow morning.

*At least they did not ask me to go back to New York.*

As we approached Washington, all I could see out the window was cloud. Down, down we settle. I could see nothing. Down, down, goes the Super Constellation.

Suddenly, the plane's engines rev up to full power. They are aborting the landing!

I am scared to death. The plane bucks and shakes as it tries to continue its downward course while the engines and control surfaces fought to take it back up.

Ten minutes seem like an hour, as the drowning hum of the four non-jet engines fill the passengers' ears. No one is talking. All are nervous, silent. We finally land.

I arrive at the bridge lesson at 17th and K street-at-8:30- a half-hour late, very tired, very hungry. No supper.

I never did learn to play bridge well.

## IBM'S PROPOSAL 'CZAR'

Saturday November 29, Collins and I drive into Washington D. C. from Montgomery County Maryland, about 10 miles.

"I don't like this at all," says Collins. "Why do we need a new man in the act at this time?"

"I don't like it either. But we have no choice. No choice. Let's just be sure that he does what we want him to do."

We meet Humphrey at the IBM 1111 Connecticut Avenue building. I know nothing about him but that he was technically competent. And the rumor in IBM is that his first interview for a job at IBM had been with Tom Watson, the chairman. I would later have confirmation of it.

We go through the whole story. It takes about three hours. I do not spare DSD, the Product Division.

"I just hope it is not too late to fix things"

"That's what I'm here for", Watts says quietly.

I like him, even though I resent that he is from DP. A Corporate czar would not have made me look ineffective.

"Well," I say, "you'll get the other side of the story from the Product Division."

"I have."

Watts is about to leave.

"Oh. I'll want to call on the FAA executives soon...to say I am on the project and make some first-hand impressions. Can you set that up?"

"No problem."

Watts leaves for the airport. I drive Collins home.

"What's he want to call on FAA for?"

"So he can tell the people in Armonk that it has to be 'this' way because HE heard it first-hand from the Agency. Just like Ralph did."

"Don't let him, Joe."

## A Brawl in IBM - 1964

"OK."

We had been embarrassed to have Ralph come down and repeat all the questions so that he could hear first-hand all we were telling him. To now bring in a new guy, at this late date, - ?

"They'll think you and are boobs, Joe."

Watts never did meet with the FAA. IBM took all his time.

He did a beautiful job of pulling together the technical and financial details.

At the highest levels.

He never got to the FAA. He never asked again. We never offered.

Watts Humphrey was a great czar. He buffered the corporate staff and the division staffs and let the proposal team do its job.

I had arranged to rent office space on M Street, next to the Bender Building, 1120 Connecticut Ave. - to house the effort to write the proposal. We had a full floor.

But - Collins tells me it will not work. "The knowledge is in Poughkeepsie, Joe - and it cannot be moved to Washington."

He is right.

So we move the effort to write the proposal to where the knowledge is – Poughkeepsie. 50 miles north of LaGuardia Airport.

✫ ✫ ✫

A month and six days left to create and print and deliver a1000 page proposal. In proposals of this magnitude, the team usually starts with masses of material prepared for other purposes. The team edits and adds to that material to come up with a proposal.

But there is no body of material! We are to be the first large proposal of the 360. We are going to have to <u>create</u> much of what normally is off-the-shelf.

The instruction set of the 360, for example, is described in dozens of documents in Poughkeepsie –but not one was at the level of abstraction needed for a proposal. We'd have to create one.

We work in Poughkeepsie, visiting offices of the key engineers.

NOVEMBER ENDS.

A month of assassination. A month of ferocious activity. A month of almost no progress! Of fierce antagonism. A new manager in the product division who is "going to get" me. A czar on board.

In November, I had flown to and from New York fourteen times! Thirty-four days to create and submit the proposal!

# DECEMBER - IN A FIREHOUSE !

December starts as November had ended. On Monday, December 2, Collins and I catch the 7 AM Shuttle to LaGuardia and drive to Poughkeepsie. We drive to a firehouse at Red Oaks Mill, about two miles from the IBM main plant and development labs. This will be our 'office' for December.

The <u>firehouse</u> has two rooms, separated by an 8 foot by 20-foot kitchen. One 'room' houses two fire trucks, shiny, red, vintage fire engines with hoses, pumps, and axes. The second room is a large, low ceiling 60-foot by 60-foot room designed for parties and meetings. On a slab of concrete. Cold.

There is no office furniture, no typewriter, no copiers, - just long picnic tables and chairs. There are 2 telephones in the kitchen, and a dozen or so tables set up in the big room. Most documents will be driven over to the labs on route 9 to be typed there.

In December, Poughkeepsie is gray. Little sun pokes through the clouds; the trees are bare. It is cold, snappy.

A proposal team routinely edits and adds to standard descriptive material to come up with a proposal. But there is no standard material! We are to be the first large proposal of the 360. We are going to have to <u>create</u> much of what normally is off-the-shelf.

The instruction set of the 360, for example, is described in dozens of documents in Poughkeepsie –but not one is at the level of abstraction needed for a proposal. We have to create one.

We work in Poughkeepsie, visiting offices of the key engineers, going back to the firehouse. I get a message to call Pfeiffer.

"Lo, Ralph."

"Hello, Joe. Do you have a new secretary?"

I am puzzled.

"No."

# A Brawl in IBM - 1964

"Well, my name has been misspelled on the last few memos you signed."

"Oh! I understand. We've established a little office here in the South Road Lab and I'm getting some secretarial support from the DS people here."

The explanation satisfies me, but not Pfeiffer.

"Well, teach her to spell my name."

Ralph Is not happy.

"OK."

Jack Ford, the lawyer from the Washington federal office, visits. He gets a call on one of the two phones. (Cell phones were decades in the future.) I hear him on the phone.

"What's the noise you are hearing, you ask ?" Ford says into the phone. "People. At least 50. And the noise is unbelievable. Can you hear it? It's like the ocean running over a pebbled beach. It is the people talking! Everyone is talking and they are all yelling –no one is calm. And the smoke is so bad from the cigarettes that I can barely see the other side of the room. I've never seen anything like it."

And it was cold! The room was so smoky that at least once an hour someone would turn on the exhaust fans and with a 'whoosh' - the smoke —and with it the heat —and working papers would fly toward the ceiling. People grab for them in surprise.

The firehouse had not been planned for constant occupancy; the concrete floor rested on the ground.

*How did the proposal effort for the air traffic control system of the nation end up in a firehouse?*

*It has remained a mystery to me all these years. My best guess is that the FSD technical Publications man assigned by White to help on the effort grabbed it as a last resort.*

At first annoyed, we come to realize that this intimate, tight space is ideal for resolving issues. The product division – DS – now brings top talent to the effort in the firehouse. Gene Amdahl, who would later form a computer company bearing his name and who had architected much of the line of 360 computers, is there at a table, coding the sample problems for the proposal. The code would be 'timed' to prove the computer could do the cited task in time to handle the constant flow of information from the radars and the controllers. There is no one who knows the instruction set better than Gene. The Washington team is encouraged.

Fred Brooks is here at times. He will write the classic book on software, *The Mythical Man Month*.

No issue remains in limbo, as the needed talent is but a few miles away in the main buildings of IBM on Route 9. Top people can be at the firehouse in 15 minutes.

## CHAIRMAN: "WHY ARE WE SO FAR BEHIND?"

The firehouse is jumping. Activity bubbles everywhere. Noise is a roar.

"Kilner on the phone, Joe"

I do not want to talk to Kilner. There is no help coming from there.

Kilner can not help now; no one in Washington could. Any call from there is trouble. More meetings. And I love Kilner.

"Lo, Sam."

"How is it going, Joe?"

"Bad, Sam. It's crazy here."

Silence. I am going to make Kilner carry the conversation.

"Uh. Well…Uh, look, we need you."

"Oh, no."

"Yeah. Pfeiffer has to meet with Watson next week –along with DS. It's the wrap-up of the investigation that has been going on."

"Yeah?"

"Joe, you've been meeting with Beitzel?"

Spike Beitzel was Watson's assistant and I had been asked to fill him in on the history of the effort to date.

"Yeah, that went fine –there should be no problems for us."

"Well, you know Ralph –and how ready and prepared he likes to be."

"Yeah?" I see it coming.

"Well, he met with Learson and Learson is mad. He says DS dropped IBM on its head."

"THEY DID, Sam! Of course they did."

"Well, Learson says –quote "DS disagreed; DS listened and agreed; they listened and agreed and did something else!"

"He's got it!"

"Yeah, but Ralph wants that spelled out in a briefing book by Monday."

"Oh no!"

"Can you come back tomorrow and we'll work Friday?"

"I can't leave here, Sam."

"Then we'll have to do it Saturday."

Pause...!

"Okay." (*SHIT! Another Saturday gone.*)

"Breakfast at 7 Saturday at the Mayflower Hotel with Ralph."

"Okay."

"Keep your spirits up, Joe."

"Yeah...goodbye."

Within an hour, I have another call.

"Pfeiffer wants you to call him, Joe."

Pfeiffer's secretary answers.

"Oh yes. He wants you, hold on."

"Joe, how is it going?"

"It's a shambles here. It's mad."

"Will you get the proposal out on time?"

"Oh- - yeah. We will –we must. I don't know how, but we will."

"Well, ask FAA for an extension, for a later proposal date."

"Are you CRAZY, Ralph," I blurt. "We ..."

"Joe," the voice is cold. A decision has been made. Somewhere. The Executive is talking.

"Joe - ask for an extension. Is that clear?"

"Yes sir."

"Let me know."

"Yessir."

Click.

An extension would slip the proposal delivery date, allowing more time to write the proposal. But, such a request is an admission of problems – no one wants to ask for an extension on such a big proposal.

I tell Collins – and he is upset.

"We can't, Joe, we can't."

"We have to."

"Joe, we'll look like utter idiots. We've been inside every move, every time. We - of all people - should be able to make the proposal date."

"Yeah, I know."

Collins paces.

"And it will hurt us bad, Joe. Bad. They <u>won't</u> give us an extension, and we'll look schloky. Dumb."

"Yeah, I know."

Collins looks at me.

"When?"

"Monday."

"I'll go with you. Rabb?"

Rabb was the technical procurement official for the FAA.

"Yeah."

We call Rabb and made a date for Monday, December 9.

## AN AUDIT

Saturday morning December 7, Kilner, Pfeiffer and I meet for breakfast at the Mayflower Hotel at 7 o'clock. Pfeiffer said that he had been with Learson the day before and that Learson could not understand how the product guys had been able for so long to do nothing on the requirement without DP knowing about it.

*I think: "Is this a joke? We knew! We brought it to Scotty and to Williams. Is Learson forgetting all the meetings he's been in with us? Of course we knew about it".*

But I say nothing; I just listen.

Learson has asked Pfeiffer to answer several questions.
1) Had DP made clear the need for taking the channels out of main CPU? He wants examples! Letters.
2) Had we considered the need for a czar earlier than the appointment of Humphrey?
3) Had the naming of the czar helped or hurt the satisfaction of what marketing said was needed? .
4) Why hadn't Pfeiffer answered Evans' letter that responded to the pre-RFP?
*Answer: We went to see him.*
5) Why did DP believe that during September and October DS was really working on the multiprocessor? *Because of the Learson letter telling them to work on it.*
6) What did DP think DS was doing; what do they now know they were doing?
7) Was DP misled? *Yes. "And we are not the FBI or CIA here, we believed them when they said they could hook 10 together".*
8) Pfeiffer tells us that Learson was angry over DS's lack of action.

I said, 'Amen!'.

Kilner and I spend a few hours answering the questions, filling in detail and collecting letters that had been sent. It is Saturday and I have not been at home much for a long time.

Kilner looks uncomfortable, wanting to discuss something else.

"Uh, Joe, the division is behind quota for the year."

I listen –*what the hell did that have to do with the FAA?*

"There is a letter stating that all sales personnel who have not made their 1963 quota will work every Saturday for a half day in the office – till they make their 1963 quota."

I had forgotten about quota for the last few months. Quota was the number of dollars of business that each salesman was assigned to achieve in the calendar year. All my people but the FAA people had made quota. And the FAA was buying nothing until the bid we were up to their necks in got awarded.

"So?"

"So your people must come in every Saturday."

"You're kidding!"

"I'm sorry, Joe –that's it."

"Sam, my people are on the edge of exhaustion. They are away from home every week –all week – and arrive back in town late Friday night –if then. This is crazy."

"Sorry."

"Sam, do you want us to stop the proposal effort and try to scramble for 1963 quota?"

We both know this was absurd. You can't sell computers in three weeks.

"No, no."

"What possible good is it going to do IBM to force these people in here on Saturday?"

Kilner doesn't answer.

I cave. I say I'll tell the people to be in there on Saturday.

The group Kilner manages encompasses the sales and technical support people who covered NASA, the FAA, the Weather Bureau, and the National Bureau of Standards, the Special Operations group covering the CIA, NSA, the National Security Agency, DIA, State and AID –agency for International Development.

At a joint meeting of all the managers reporting to Kilner, Sam announces the Saturday work.

I try to look inscrutable. I am disgusted.

Kilner is embarrassed, but he struggles through the announcement. Silence.

Then one of the senior salesmen on the NSA account stands up.

"Sam, on behalf of the salesmen, I want to state that we understand and pledge to do everything possible to support you."

Kilner is touched by the blatant 'yesmanship.'

A peer –my level -who manages the NASA sales team leans over to me, said, "I'm going to throw up," - and he stands up and leaves the meeting.

## A Brawl in IBM - 1964

To my everlasting disgrace, I come in on Saturday and have my people come in.

But we never came in for a second Saturday.

✫ ✫ ✫

At this moment, I have on my plate:
* an effort to <u>write</u> a myriad of facts about the 360, most of them in the developers' heads,
* a void in understanding multiprocessing
* a lack of any support software –no JOVIAL, nothing
* a delivery that was a full year late
* a request to delay the proposal; I was to sell the FAA on a delay
* the key VP who is going "to get me", and an official interface into DS who hangs up on me all the time
* a tired team in the middle of the woods in the winter in a cold firehouse
* an investigation of events by the chairman's office eating up time
* twenty days to get the proposal delivered to the FAA
* a family I'd barely seen in the last few months
* Christmas but days away
* a new czar to work with, -
* a price proposal I've not even thought about

This money we would get if we won this business was not that important to the <u>IBM.</u> Although it was $150,000,000, it would be spread over seven to ten years, and that was just not that much to IBM. It got lost in the hugeness of their 2-billion-per-year size –and growing fast!

But the chairman wants to win. I have powerful allies.
* The chairman wanted to win; his investigation was telling everyone that – loud and clear.

The rest of the company will begin to follow.
* Learson. He was a marvel in forcing facts and decisions.

* A new czar. I did not have to fight <u>every</u> issue anymore.
* The entire 360 model 50 engineering team is on the FAA job.
* Anyone I want from anywhere. I can get to help.
* Superb individuals from several divisions.
* A smooth functioning professional marketing team - Collins, Kowalke, Whitney, Oldani
* A tough mentor Hank White at the elbow of the president of the Federal Division.
* Unlimited budget –no one <u>ever</u> asked me to justify a thing.
* Outstanding support from Pfeiffer and Kilner. Gone the days when Pfeiffer would leave me in the lurch.
* Genius-level help from Brooks and Amdahl and others looking at the benchmarks!

"Benchmarks" –the processes to perform critical functions were coded on handwritten sheets- in the machine-level language of the 360 - and then assigned a time to process for each. The elapsed time it would take for all the processes was calculated and would be in the contract. On the basis of this, the company would guarantee the computer would do the job within the 6-second radar sweep. If it did not, the company would supply additional hardware, even a larger machine- at no coast to the U S Government. The guarantee would be a very unusual commitment.

✭ ✭ ✭

On Monday, December 9, Collins and I go to the FAA building at Independence and 8th to ask for an extension. We know exactly what to expect. We are comfortable with the FAA people after three years of effort.

On one occasion, a year earlier, an FSD IBM man from had complained to an FAA procurement man that the FAA was not doing such and such, and the FAA man responded:

"OK. I'll get Fox on it right away."

"Fox? He's our guy!"

# A Brawl in IBM - 1964

"Yes, but he'll fix things."

And I did fix that one.

Collins had found almost instant acceptance by the FAA people for his trait of straight talk and total honesty.

Salesmen who did nothing but sell lost credibility. We were not selling vacuum cleaners, but multimillion-dollar systems that were to keep airplanes from hitting each other. We never forgot the mid air collisions of the past few years.

Collins and I meet with Jay Rabb of FAA. Jay is a Southern gentleman, courteous, careful, and competent.

"Uh, Jay, what are the possibilities for an extension of the proposal due date?"

I try to be cool.

Rabb's eyes widen.

"No one has asked for an extension. Certainly you people don't need one. You knew everything that was in the RFP months ahead of time."

"Yeah, we did –but the new line is a bit hard to describe..."

We have to be careful here. If we make the new line look too new, we could tumble off the "off the shelf" status –if indeed we were there.

"Are you asking for an extension?" Rabb asks.

"No, no." A bit too quickly. "We are exploring possibilities. If we ask for an extension, we'll come in with a letter."

"I sure hope you don't do that," Rabb says quietly. We all know that if the contract is not signed before the end of the fiscal year – June 30, 1964 –FAA will lose its funding for that year. A major delay could ensue.

We leave.

Pfeiffer looks at me.

"Did you get an extension?"

"Ralph, they said if we ask, they'll say no."

"So you didn't ask?"

"I discussed it! You can't ask for an extension verbally, you must request in writing – and we are out of our minds to ask."

I pause.

"I met with the chairman of the Technical Evaluation Committee. He's got clout. He's going to say no if we ask."

Pfeiffer makes a face.

"And we should not ask, Ralph!"

Pfeiffer thinks.

"No one else asked?"

"No one."

"Sixty days is a very short time to prepare such a tough proposal." Ralph muses.

"Ralph, no one has asked. And that is why Gray told you all about the bid back in AUGUST --so that we wouldn't be delaying things now. Ralph, we'll blow ourselves off the 'off-the-shelf' status if we ask. No one else has asked. Rabb mentioned how we knew what was in the RFP when they visited Poughkeepsie on the September 11th. We can't ask. They'll say no if we do. No question."

"I'll get back to you," says Pfeiffer.

The extension is never discussed again. Pfeiffer handles it somehow.

On Monday afternoon, we get the Shuttle to New York and drive to the firehouse.

On Wednesday, the noise level in the firehouse is health threatening.

"Phone, Fox!" someone calls.

"Hello."

"Joe. Sam."

"Yeah, Sam?"

"I thought you'd like to know about the meeting with the chairman."

"Yeah, I would."

"We won."

"I figured we would. What happened?"

"I don't know for sure. Ralph called and said that DS got beat up bad."

I get no joy from this, nor does Kilner relate it with relish. I am too tired to be looking for revenge or punishment. I am happy that

# A Brawl in IBM - 1964

the 'record' at the chairman level would show DP to have done the right job! That was important.

"And," continued Sam, "he said 'DP got hit by an elbow or two as DS was taking a licking'."

"WHAT? What for? What's that mean?"

"I don't know. I can only quote Ralph."

"Damn."

"Yeah."

"Okay! Thanks for the call, Sam."

✶ ✶ ✶

In the second week in the firehouse, Whitney walks in. I am surprised. Although he reports to me, Whitney has not been 'on the team'. His customer, the operational part of FAA, had lost the fight within FAA to manage the procurement of the new system. They have a voice, but not the control. I had been ignoring the Islip system – and Whitney.

"Joe," says Whitney, "I'd like to help on the Input/Output section."

"You got it," I say without hesitation.

For Whitney to appear and take over the I/0 is a blessing.

✶ ✶ ✶

We work in the firehouse all week. I am there till Friday morning, when I go down to White Plains for the weekly meeting with Learson. Kilner is driving. Pfeiffer is in the passenger seat; I am alone in the rear seat.

Ralph asks Kilner, "How are the men reacting to the Saturday work?"

"Very well. They understand the necessity for it - and morale is good."

I wonder *"Who is Kilner talking about?"*

"Good."

Ralph is pleased; that is the answer he wanted.

I cannot let it go.

"My people think it is grossly unfair. They're working their butts off. They are away from home all week and it is unfair to take away their Saturdays."

Kilner's ears color a little. He doesn't like me - his subordinate - contradicting him.

Ralph swings around and looks at me, annoyed.

"They have got to understand that the company is in trouble. We need their help."

"The company has to understand, Ralph, that the people are in trouble. That taking away a man's weekend isn't the way to get him to put forth extra effort. My guys resent it. And they are right."

We drive the rest of the way in cool silence. My people work but one Saturday. I don't tell them to not show up, and no one asks where they were. And I work but one weekend.

But I should have refused to do even that. I had the clout to do that. I chickened out.

✲ ✲ ✲

The meeting with Learson shows the effect of the czar.

It is a calm, 'Here is where we are' meeting. Humphrey is getting commitments; I am impressed.

I rush to Washington - on the Shuttle - after the meeting. The bridge lesson.

At this stage that the proposal team is struggling to keep up personal lives. Weekends are recuperative periods, but the families were deprived of father/spouse not only during the week, but often on the weekend.

I make it to the bridge lesson only 20 minutes late. No supper. I tried to think of bridge, Goren. Point count. Finesse. *Finesse DS.*

I feel guilty being away from home so much. The burden of home is all on my wife. I try to be cheerful and peppy at home.

On Sunday, the 15$^{th}$, we are on the Shuttle to New York, and to Poughkeepsie.

# A Brawl in IBM - 1964

Monday the 16th.

The firehouse is hopping. There are dozens of meetings and several arguments going on. I move from one group to the next –sampling, listening, observing –noting who were the leaders, what the issues were. Who was smart, who retiring, who was aggressive, who was merely a hanger-on.

Occasionally I contribute, but not often. The details are usually too detailed and beyond my knowledge.

DS wants this –FSD/DP the other; field engineering something else, software people, a variation of one or the other. I listen and decide –there is no time to worry about whether or not I am right. Sometimes I confer with the people I judge to be the most competent. The observing pays off - and I go with their judgment. Usually I side with the team. Whitney has charge of the input/output design and he is good. All the effort at Islip on the 1401-1410 system is applicable. Whitney drives the non-standard, special engineering people to optimize the PAM's –the Peripheral Adapter Modules –that would match up with the seemingly innumerable, complex devices involved –radars, telemetry, telephone lines, displays, keyboards - scores of devices to be connected to, and not built by IBM, and to be hooked hook up in such a way that no one unit failure would cripple the system.

I had once mentioned to V. P. Scott that "since no one in IBM really understands multiprocessing, I'm going to hire a consultant." I expected him to help me find people in IBM who did know multi-processing. But he told me "Go ahead and hire a consultant."

After some searching we hired Robert Bob Patrick from the West Coast. It turned out he was consulting for DS as well, and he knew the 360 already.

Now, quietly in the offices back in the main building on route 9, Bob Patrick and Gene M. Amdahl are programming the benchmarks. I am delighted. Amdahl was one of the chief architects on the 360.

He spent a few days in the firehouse, poring over his code. Amdahl would form a computer company – Amdahl Computers- to rival IBM in the large computer arena years later. The desire on the part of Manson to keep Patrick off the effort had never come up again.

Inside the bay holding the two fire trucks, Collins and a member of the DS model 50 group have a short meeting.

Anyone entering would see two grown men sitting in the front seat of a fire truck in business suits. It is the only private place to sit.

They look like overgrown kids playing firemen.

I call a meeting of just the sales people, in the truck bay.

I have a 3-foot by 4 foot paper chart that summarizes where we are. We have a piece of scotch tape on each end of the piece of paper, and we tape the chart to the 6" hose of one of the fire trucks. I start to explain the chart to the group when a big man I don't know charges angrily into the truck bay.

"Get out, God damn it," he yells. "You cannot touch the fire trucks. That was the deal! Get those charts down -now!"

"But it's only two pieces of..." I stammer.

"Get them down and get out of this room. "

The man was barely rational. We all exit like guilty children. The man locks the truck bay. The bid is worth $150,000,000.

We can't use the truck bay anymore.

I never found out who the man was.

※ ※ ※

IBM had a rule- established because of painful mistakes - that every proposal of certain size had to be reviewed by an audit team. Called "Systems Assurance", the process was designed to catch over-commitments before they were made by over- zealous or sloppy salesmen –and it did catch many such errors. There were people assigned full time to carry out this assignment. Staffed by technically competent people, the systems assurance teams would arrive late in the proposal process and read the entire proposal, searching for errors, over-commitments, and vague statements.

# A Brawl in IBM - 1964

They arrive –two of them, unannounced – at the firehouse, on Thursday, December 19. Someone brought them to me.
"We're here to do the systems assurance."
I just look at them for a second. I wave my hand at the room.
"There it is."
They were puzzled.
"Where?"
"All over."
Silence.
"We cannot assure that. It's not together."
"Then don't assure it."
"You can't submit it, then."
"We'll see."
"You can't."
"We'll see."
They look at each other.
"Can we talk to the people who are the key designers?"
"Sure, but don't tie them up too long. We are behind schedule."
I introduced them to Kowalke and Oldani, who spend an hour with them.
In the early afternoon, they approach me again.
"We're leaving now."
"What do you think?"
"It's an incredible system. I've never seen anything like it. I'm not sure we are competent to pass judgment on it."
"You'll give me a systems assurance approval then?"
"We'll get back to you."
I never hear from them again.

✻ ✻ ✻

Reliability is the pot of gold at the end of the rainbow that FAA seeks. We chase it constantly, designing, redesigning, calculating.

Two things are driving us. The realization that there would be lives at stake, and since we all flew- the Shuttle- we understood the idea of safety.

The RFP demands that the bidder <u>guarantee</u> that the <u>system</u> would lose only one device at a time, and only once in 1,000 hours, and lose two of the same kind only once every 10,000 hours. If the equipment does not meet this goal, then the bidder must to deliver an extra unit free of charge to <u>every</u> FAA control center. We are talking about a lot of money.

Over and over this area we go. DS is stepping up to it with no reluctance. Carefully, but positively. This is a major departure from IBM's normal policy. IBM did not quote reliability, much less guarantee it!

The way one calculates the probability of successful operation is very complicated. The inherent reliability of every unit is calculated based on failure rates of every component that makes up that unit – transistors, resistors, connections, etc. Then the effect of redundancy is calculated. The probability that a backup unit would fail at the same time as the "live" unit it was backing up has to be calculated.

Now the theory of probability becomes key! And probability is a very counter-intuitive discipline. It is full of seemingly contradictory predictions.

For example, if you flip a coin 50 times and it comes up heads 50 times in a row, what is the probability it'll come heads the 51st time? Answer: 50%. The chances are equal; the prior flips have no effect on the 51st flip. Each flip is free of effect from the preceding.

The Request for Proposal asks that the winner guarantee a 1000-hour mean (average) time between failures (MTBF) for the unitized, non-redundant computer. That is one CPU, one memory, and one I/O control element. Then, for a fail-safe system - one with redundant CPU's and memories, etc. –they want a 10,000-hour MTBF. Just about thirteen months.

How long would it take to get a good statistical measure of a unit that was to fail but once every 15 months? Years of running and recording. Many years.

# A Brawl in IBM - 1964

The reliability guarantee and the method of proof measurement is a separate section of the proposal.

And if IBM agreed to meet this and didn't make it, extra redundant units were to be delivered free to <u>every</u> center and test site! This could be millions of dollars!

IBM has not manufactured the components yet to make the 360! And probability theory to measure the redundancy is murky, high level mathematics. The way to provide the redundant units varied across control centers. One center would need one out of two CPUs; another would need two out of three; others three out of four. And then memory needs varied. And then IOCEs differed.

And IBM is going to guarantee the reliability.

✧ ✧ ✧

## THE MULTIPROCESSOR GETS NAMED –THE "9020"

"Joe, we need a <u>name</u> for this computer."

I look at Collins, puzzled.

"A name! What do we call it?" Collins asks.

"Oh! I hadn't thought of that."

Up till now we simply called it the model 50. But it was now different from a standard 50. And we needed it to be different.

All non-standard boxes in IBM got a 9000 number assigned. I make a call; 3 days later the phone in the firehouse rang.

"Fox," someone shouts.

"Hello."

"Joe, your system is 'the 9020 <u>System</u>'. I've got about thirty other numbers for you, one for each box."

I like it.

## NO TIME TO GET THE PROPOSAL PRINTED

"There is not time to get this proposal to the customer by January 6."

John Jurkowski, on the effort for us from FSD Kingston, NY, is telling me he cannot get the proposal printed. He is responsible for getting the printed document out the door.

"We must."

"We can't."

"Find a way."

I have become the main operator of the table model 910 Xerox copier. I feed it for hours. I can take it apart and service it; I've become the copier expert.

"Why are you doing this, Joe?"

"Someone has to."

"Get someone. You've got better things to do."

"There are no secretaries here. I'll do it. It's therapeutic."

There were results one could see. Copies.

Whitney is in charge of the special Input/Output area; Kowalke had the software. Oldani had machine size and configuration, and Collins was coordinating everything. Maintenance schedules and spare parts are being written up; training; manufacturing; a general description of the 360 line. All this is underway, in competent hands. The group is working like a well-oiled machine.

But the proposal is to be about 1400 pages! It is spread all over the firehouse –and we must get it to the printer by Saturday! Fourteen hundred delivered pages, typed –in less than two weeks.

## DECEMBER 15, SUNDAY

We get the Shuttle to New York late Sunday night and drive to Poughkeepsie. Collins and I open the firehouse the next morning at 7 AM. There are usually five to ten people waiting for us. We close –lock –the firehouse at 1 AM. We have a 20-minute drive to and from the motel.

"What should I do with this?" "Is this okay?" "Can we put this section in front of this?" "Who is doing maintenance on this?" "Does it make sense to say this when they put this here?"

We are both exhausted.

# A Brawl in IBM - 1964

Our priority is simple; get out a proposal. Unless it gets in <u>on time</u>, the game is over.

This last week in the firehouse is crazy.

We eat one meal per day –a huge supper.

Collins has a cold, and a bad stomach by Thursday. I am holding up well.

There are only a few days left!

Jurkowski keeps pestering me.

"Joe, I need to start papers into the print shop in IBM Kingston <u>tomorrow</u> –or we don't make it"

"Nothing is ready, John. "

"We have to start paper into the printer, Joe. We must print up 1400 pages!"

"John, I don't know what to do."

Jurkowski wanders off.

The technical group is told, "This is it – write down what you got –now. "

We read.

And read.

The format laid out in the RFP now saves us! It specifies every section in detail. All we have to do was assemble it all. The request for proposal – written by the FAA and MITRE team - is a fine piece of work.

✫ ✫ ✫

The signs of Christmas are everywhere. Christmas songs; Christmas trees.

It is all a blur. Constant talking; constant writing, constant decisions.

"What do you think it'll look like, Joe," asks Collins.

"The proposal?"

"Yeah."

"You know, I don't know. It should be okay."

"I don't know either," says Collins. "We don't even have a prior proposal to look at with the 360.

Well, we'll know soon."

After getting nothing from me, Jurkowski fixes the problem!

"Joe, I've a fast-turnaround, commercial printing firm that will do the job if we get them paper by Saturday!"

"Great work, John," I beam, relieved and grateful.

"It is in the Wall Street section of Manhattan. Can you get the rough draft there by Saturday?"

"Rough? Yes."

The firehouse has enabled us to see - to actually see - all the elements of the system come into being. In one corner the engineers are designing; in another the programmers are doing the same; and over there the maintenance people; and there the reliability team. The applications people take the results of all and mill them into a sensible approach to what the request for proposal asked for!

When I thought of it later, I realized that since no one had worked on making the thing a multiprocessor till October 24, the effort to conceive, design, and write it all down - and type a 1400-page proposal in less than two months could not have been done without the firehouse!

How many phone calls, meetings, memoranda, and briefings had been avoided because when a programmer wanted to know how the channels worked under A and B conditions, he leaned back in his chair and asked the designer at the table behind him! The collection of talent in the firehouse was unique! Some of the best engineers and programmers in the company –indeed in the world -had been cooped up in that firehouse for a month.

It has to be good! It has to be, damn it. So many people have sacrificed so much for so long that it has to be good!

✵ ✵ ✵

Jack O'Connell of DS has awarded a contract to CUC - the Computer Usage Company - for the JOVIAL compiler. He has brought in his section of the proposal on time and excellently done.

A Brawl in IBM - 1964

And there had been a fire! Well, a false alarm. The phone had rung and some of the engineers had left their tables and jumped onto the trucks! And roared out. The rest of the people just watched.

One night, as the engineers and marketing people had stood around the 4 foot x 6 foot green blackboard mounted on a wooden tripod, -the whole thing vibrating violently at the slightest impact of the chalk –as they stood around this center of knowledge, and as the marketing people watched fascinated, two groups of engineers slugged it out verbally as to whether the system drawn thereon would work.

A stranger next to me is observing the discussion and watching the board. He stood there for ten minutes or so and watched the argument ebb and flow.

Finally he turned to me and asked: "Where do I register to vote?"

I plead ignorance and watch him leave the firehouse!

I look at 35 or so other people still in the firehouse and wonder how many other complete strangers are in the room. Anyone could be in here!

I ignore security. One more function is not what I need. Besides, who would even be able to find the firehouse –who would believe that IBM's efforts were in a firehouse?

## CAN THE MODEL 50 KILL THE FAA VERSION?

In September and October Collins had conducted a campaign of "living in Poughkeepsie." He'd go from office to office in the engineering building. After a month or so he was a familiar face.

Now, two engineers stop Collins in the hall of the 702 building, where he was getting some documents. They take him into an empty office and close the door.

"Jack, you've been straight with us –and we want to warn you –Helt and others are going to Learson this afternoon to prove to him that the FAA bid will destroy the model 50. That they've got to stop the FAA bid."

"Won't work," says Collins.

"Jack, be warned –they've got a good pitch. And, Jack, please don't tell anyone we tipped you off."

Collins fills me in. We are in the firehouse.

"DS is going to Learson today to show that if they bid and win the FAA job, delivery of the model 50 is so bad they'll have to drop it from the planned announcement. The manager of the model 50 – Helt -is happy as a pig in mud."

"Why?"

"He wants the 50, not FAA –and, Joe, I am told he can prove it."

"They'll get shot down."

"My sources say the 50 manager is really confident. He's ecstatic that the FAA bid has moved people and money onto the 50; now he can close down FAA and build his machine."

"They'll lose."

That night about 7 PM, with the firehouse at one-half density of people, mostly the DP people from out of town, the manager of the model 50 group enters.

"Joe, he's a smiling Christmas tree – and all dressed up for a party - while we bust our butts here."

Collins was not happy.

Then someone called for the model 50 manager.

"Phone, John."

He takes the phone.

He turns and glowers at the people in the firehouse.

"You sons-of-bitches," he mutters and leaves.

The FAA effort is like a whirlpool swallowing the model 50, swallowing the chip production for the first year of the 360. Helping the FAA effort is seen in some quarters as treachery. You were a traitor if you helped the proposal. The sales team was occasionally told, "I'll help you if - and only if –you don't tell anyone I'm helping you!"

## FIREHOUSE REVIEW –NO MORE TIME

On Friday, December 20, at 4 PM, the last day in the firehouse, with Christmas just four days away, legal, contracts and financial people are in the firehouse. They are to review the proposal -and approve it for submittal. Humphrey is coming.

A corner of the firehouse is set aside for the meeting. We gather around a collapsible table and immediately bog down in trivia. Legal declares that the proposal must not state that IBM has 1.2 million square feet of manufacturing space.

"Why not?" I demand. "It's pertinent."

"It's selling our bigness," says the lawyer.

We squabble. Humphrey says leave it in.

We tell the group what is in the proposal. They could read only scraps of sections, - the pages are all loose.

Collins and I are to stay over and work here on Saturday. We'd be a day late to the N Y City printer.

The group looks at several minor items. DP and DS clash on almost every item. Five o'clock. Five thirty.

I am happy that everyone wants to go home to Christmas parties. They agree to things more readily in their haste to go home. But the wrong people want to go home!

Humphrey stands up suddenly, in the middle of a discussion. "I'm really enjoying this," he says, "but I've got to go."

We are taken aback. This is the *final* sign off of the proposal.

I am aghast! This means another, later, meeting. It cannot be.

If only Humphrey would outlast this team, we could finish this review. Humphrey explains why he had to leave.

"We are having a party tonight."

The group rushes to disperse. Most of the sign-off team have a two-hour drive back to the Harrison area and home. It is the Friday before Christmas.

Within minutes, at 6 PM, only a few DS people are still there. The DP team has no place to go. We will try to pull the myriad of pieces of paper into a meaningful sequence and get the whole thing to the printer as soon as possible.

Collins and I gripe to each other.

"Damn idiots –worthless waste of precious time."

There are a few people still in the firehouse. A stranger approaches me. Strangers are commonplace in the firehouse.

"You seem to have a low opinion of Data Systems," says the stranger, meaning the product division.

I should have ignored the comment. But I didn't.

"You bet I do. Look at these quarters. Who is here to finish this critical proposal? Damn few DS people."

I stare defiantly at the man, ready to fight.

"Well, I think you're right," offers the stranger. "DS is not doing its job. I don't know how you guys stand it".

Suddenly, I start to cry.

The stranger is startled. I am sobbing.

I back away. Collins comes over; I wave him off. I am in the entryway of the firehouse, sobbing.

A dozen or so people are still there –they are embarrassed.

I get out of there. I go out the door, move about 20 feet into the parking lot, and sob.

I do not know why I am crying. But I cannot stop.

John Cousins and Pat McGuire, two FSD veterans from the efforts in Atlantic City, come out of the firehouse, heading home. Embarrassed by my crying, they approach, stop.

"Joe..." says Cousins.

"No, no! Leave me alone."

Not knowing what to do, they leave.

I finally stop crying.

'Damn,' I think, 'how do I go back in there? How do I become the leader again?'

I walk in. Everyone looks at me, ten or so professionals, mostly from DP.

"Let's go one pass through everything we have, starting with the introduction."

I sense relaxation. Things are okay.

Collins walks with me to the table.

"You okay?" he whispers.

"Yeah! "

That is the last of that.

It is never mentioned again.

Why had something suddenly overtaken me. I had gotten sympathy from a stranger –I never did find out who he was –and this had triggered an emotional flow I could not control. Fatigue, stress and animosity ...who knows?

*"Avoid sympathy; it softens, and speak of your troubles only when they are over." Anonymous.*

✡ ✡ ✡

We are in the middle of Poughkeepsie, in the middle of the winter, in a firehouse.

It is the Saturday before Christmas –next Wednesday. And there are hundreds of pieces of paper scattered on a dozen tables.

The morning can only be described as black.

We are keenly aware that it is the Saturday before Christmas - and I had not yet bought one present. Collins and I go to breakfast, and Collins gets sick.

The long days and nights have gotten to him. He leaves and goes back to Washington.

I go to the firehouse. It looks as it must have looked on so many Saturday mornings after a big party!

Chairs and tables are in disarray; ashtrays are overflowing and paper is everywhere –on tables, on chairs, and on the floor.

I had no idea of who would be working on this Saturday and who wouldn't.

I am in trouble.

Whole sections of the proposal are scattered over a table –an engineering section. I look at it. There are no page numbers! It is 200 or so pages long - and interspersed with the typewritten pages are hand-written yellow sheets. I try reading a section and discover that I cannot make sense out of it. It is too technical!

I teeter on the brink of panic, and then frustration, and finally self-pity. But, Oldani is there.

Russ Roblen, a key DS engineer stops by. Seeing the morass, he spends three hours straightening out sections of the proposal. I will never forget Russ Roblen. We would never have finished without him.

We gather up the pieces of the proposal that we will deliver to the printer in lower Manhattan. But not today! We'll be lucky to finish by Sunday night.

It isn't the best approach. That would be to call Kennard –or even Evans or Manson –or Watts - and point out that we had been abandoned to do all the work. Demand DS people to get in there and help! They had a few thousand people in the Poughkeepsie area!

But I am past fighting.

It is a gray December day, cold and quiet -and dismal.

✱ ✱ ✱

We get the Shuttle and I got home at 8 PM Saturday. Jurkowsky takes the proposal to the printer in lower Manhattan.

## THE NEW YORK BOWERY 'PROPOSAL MACHINE'

On Monday morning December 23, 1963, we are on the Shuttle. Upon landing, we take a cab to lower Manhattan. To the Wall Street area, to an old loft building.

We go to the Allan Wayne Printing Company in the financial district of New York City. They specialize in the service needed – speed with quality.

They occupy two whole floors of an old, smallish building. They hire only male typists. They had 20 or so electric IBM typewriters on one floor, in a huge room that takes up the entire city block. And there is a dormitory on the next floor up. The way they get their incredible productivity, and the reason for males only, is the dormitory!

The typists work day in and day out for a week or more, sleeping and living in the dormitory. Typing continues through the night,

# A Brawl in IBM - 1964

often through the entire night. After a week or so of intense work, a typist –paid by the hour – would collect his paycheck and take off for a week or so.

The IBM proposal coordinator, John Jurkowski, has done his job superbly. I knew nothing about the switch to the Wayne Company except that he told me to go there. I had no idea there were outfits like this.

The Allan Wayne people save us. They ask the IBM team to use the conference room and the lounge, but stay out of the office and the dormitory. No problem.

We sit all day in the conference room and read every page as it comes off the typewriters, and reread it again in context. The typists are much more than typists - they catch grammar and punctuation errors, and even errors in logic. Time after time, they come to us.

"Don't you mean this?" And they would suggest a change. Yes was a common answer.

The week at the printer is a picnic compared to the firehouse. It is downhill. If it weren't for the fact that we are away from family during the holidays, it would have been a lark. The proposal takes shape, two three-ring binder notebooks –easier to make last-minute changes –split into a technical and a management section.

We take the shuttle home on Tuesday evening, Christmas Eve.

Christmas at home.

Then we take the shuttle back on December 26, Thursday. Collins, Kowalke and I arrive in lower Manhattan at 10 AM.

For the next seven out of eight days, we live in the lounge and the conference room of he printer. We work New Year's Eve till 6 PM and then got the shuttle home to Washington, and then the shuttle back again to New York on Thursday January 2.

We work Saturday, the 4$^{th}$ all day in New York, till 6 PM. Keeley is there; Roblen is there.

The proposal <u>will be submitted on time</u> - and it is for a multiprocessor –and a good one! No matter what happened now, we'd been able to design a new kind of system. The squiggly lines on the rickety blackboard in the firehouse are now straight and sure.

The 9020 is a lovely piece of work!

We spend Thursday and Friday in New York at the printers. One of us will have to stay through Saturday morning, January 4. At 6 P M Kilner – who has been a big help in NYC this last week - and I have flipped a coin to see would stay. I lose and do not leave New York until the 3 p. m. Saturday shuttle.

Sunday is a day of rest. At home.

On Monday, January 6, 1964 we deliver the technical proposal to the FAA on time - in three large cardboard boxes, carrying them into the FAA building like groceries.

The proposal had been driven to Washington over the weekend.

✯ ✯ ✯

In the first week of January, I get a letter from the DP Division president, Frank Cary, congratulating me on getting the proposal in. I have never met him, and he has not been involved. He is Pfeiffer's boss. He will become IBM Chairman of the Board in the 1970s, succeeding Learson. I figure that Pfeiffer had written the letter and had Cary sign it. And I appreciate it!

# CORPORATE FINANCE & LEGAL INTO THE FRAY

Now a new world, a total change of location, and of players and issues.

The price and terms and conditions section of the proposal is due on January 23.

The proposal submitted on the 6th of January took care of the technical issues - for the moment. Now it was price and terms that are to be hammered out and proposed.

And this would be via the lawyers and finance people in Westchester, N. Y. With Group staff.

What is Group staff?

The business of coordinating all the marketing and development is too large to fit in one division so several divisions reported into 'Group Staff', and issues that could not be decided in a division were brought to Group staff.

The Washington team now consists of Pfeiffer, Kilner and me. The technical people drop off the effort and go back to their 'normal' jobs. DS engineering also enjoys a respite.

I caught up with what Pfeiffer and Humphrey had been doing. Pfeiffer had written to the IBM Chairman and President again on January 2, 1964.

January 2, 1964 TO: Mr. T. J. Watson, Jr. Mr. A. L. Williams
SUBJECT: Federal Aviation Agency

This has reference to my letter of November 12th and your request to keep you apprised of our proposal efforts in response to the FAA's Request for Proposal.

As requested by the FAA, the technical section of our proposal will be submitted on January 6, 1964, with the pricing and delivery section to be submitted by January 23rd.

A Brawl in IBM - 1964

As you know, our success in winning this award will be dependent upon our response in five major areas. Following is our present status in each of these areas.

Systems Capability
We expect to be competitive in this area.

Delivery
The RFP requests delivery of a large or medium size system and possibly, in addition, a small size system in twelve months. We will quote delivery of a medium and a small size system in fifteen months. (This is an improvement over the eighteen-month delivery we discussed at our last meeting with you.) We will quote an eighteen-month delivery on the large system. Our liability to meet the requested twelve-month delivery for all size systems is a disadvantage, perhaps a major one.

Programming Systems Support
Our support in this area will be impressive. However, our delivery of the JOVIAL system and its documentation will be late. This will not be a major disadvantage.

Technology
Our SLT technology will give us a competitive advantage.
At this time we do not have a price, however, we expect to receive one momentarily.

Summary
In view of our proposed responses in the areas of systems capability, technology and programming support, and since we are not responsive to the delivery requested, we feel that pricing has become the over-riding issue.
As soon as we have completed the proposal in all its detail, we shall advise your office.

*signed*

R. A. Pfeiffer, Jr.
cc: Learson, Gibson, Hume, Cary, Humphrey

And Humphrey has been working on the price with the president of IBM. He documents a meeting with the president of IBM, Al Williams.

January 3, 1964

The following are the conclusions of a meeting with Mr. A. L. Williams on Friday, January 3.
1. Only one system would be proposed to FAA.
2. The total program costs would be reviewed to see if they could be reduced.
3. All pertinent costs would be incorporated and a flat price would be determined based on the total program quantities, incorporating a suitable level of profit.
4. In determining total FAA program costs, developmental costs of more general value should be excluded.
5. It is recognized that there are many potential technical benefits from this project. These should be quantified whenever possible.

The fifth item was in there because we hope to write off some costs against research and not charge the FAA. This would lower the price!

While Humphrey works the price issue, I am in Westchester working the terms and conditions on Wednesday, January 8. The vast majority of people in IBM do not understand how government procurement works. DP sold <u>standard</u> equipment, carried on a government approved schedule or list, and the order simply cited the schedule and price. On the GSA standard contract. (GSA was the General Services Administration.)

The legal and contracting staffs of DS and Group Staff do not want any special clauses. Period.

"Let the FAA buy as the government buys our standard line. *Use the GSA contract*"

## A Brawl in IBM - 1964

I patiently explain a dozen times that this procurement is a *negotiated*, custom procurement and all the standard stuff just doesn't apply.

I fight silly little battles.

I want to put the size of IBM into the proposal. No. That is selling bigness.

IBM is the dominant entity of the computer business. It had signed in 1956 a "consent decree" to end a United States anti-trust suit. One result was that the lawyers in IBM have a great deal of clout. When they said something couldn't be done, it wasn't done. Selling bigness is not done.

One of Watts's people had been working on the terms and conditions section of the proposal all during the time that we had been in the firehouse.

Watts's man is more interested in having people like him than in getting what is needed. I meet with him briefly on the subject of getting time to test on the early 360s in the IBM lab before delivery of the system to the FAA.

He tells me "I think I can get about 4 hours per month in the lab. I'm calling the man in charge of that right now. Pete Ford. You know Pete?"

I say I did –and that 10 hours per month would be much better.

I listen to one-half of the phone conversation. It is clear that he is not going to push Ford for anything more than four hours per month, which is pretty small.

"Can we get four hours of time per month, Pete?" he asks into the phone.

"Ask him for 10 hours," I say. Watts's man ignores me. I repeat myself.

He shakes his head. He makes a wry face, indicating that things are going well and I will screw them up if I interfere. I sit quietly for the remaining several minutes of the phone call. Just before Watts's man hangs up, I say, airily, "Let me say hello to Pete."

I take the phone.

"Hello Pete."

"Hi Joe."

"Pete, can we get 10 hours a month?"

Watts's man jumps up and glares at me.

"No, no," he says.

"Sure, Joe," says Ford. "No problem."

We hang up.

"You've got to at least ask," I say. "Sometimes they'll say yes! We got 10 hours."

The decisions are being made, at high levels, and Humphrey keeps me informed.

The 9020 is to be a special machine, derived from the 360, but separate from it. All units that are not to be in the 360 price manual can be priced without the full burden of costs that the 360 units will carry.

All IBM units got assigned some costs of IBM marketing, software, management, advertising and so on. But the 9020 will not be charged with these costs.

And it will not be sold to anyone but FAA.

"*FAA only, FAA this once only,*" I am told. Williams has so said.

"Why FAA this <u>once</u> only?" I ask.

The lawyers explain that there is a Renegotiations Board, a government unit in Washington that reviews corporate profits of large corporations each year. (*This board no longer exists.*) Williams doesn't want to lose money on the first 9020's under one contract, and years later <u>seem</u> to be making unconscionable profits on the last 9020's. Put into one contract, all the costs will be fairly applied to all 9020s.

"Sounds good to me," I say.

And there is to be no marketing support of FAA except for a small project office to be set up in FSD. No DP salesmen are to call, or give schools. All service will be charged. All this seemed agreeable.

There are some things that everyone agrees IBM should not give on, like the clause that gave FAA the rights to any patents, or data that resulted from the contract.

FAA asked for a 5% royalty on all sales of this equipment. Once again, we hew to the "off-the-shelf" definition, that this was IBM's standard line and therefore no royalty.

"The company," reports Watts, "will agree to the following:

## A Brawl in IBM - 1964

  Reports Clause
  FAA in Residence Clause
  Documentation Clause
  Acceptance Test Clause
  Systems Integration Clause"

These are major changes to IBM's way of doing business. Humphrey is doing a great job.

Then Watts lists what IBM would not agree to:

  Price Information Clause
  Separate Maintenance Pricing
  10% Payment Withholding Clause [until the computer passed the tests)
  Design Drawings Clause [IBM will not give the drawings)

All these are still not settled, but Watts feel that we would get an answer soon.

On Thursday, we work till about 8 PM.

On Friday, I work with the lawyers and financial people till noon, then Shuttle back to Washington.

They set a meeting for Monday, the 13th in Yorktown, with the president of IBM. Many questions remain. How many systems to price the non-recurring costs over? This now becomes the key question. Two other issues among the two dozen terms and conditions seemed to be troublesome.

First, the government was asking for cost analysis. But IBM certainly does not want to show its entire commercial cost structure to anyone outside IBM. It shows such numbers to precious few inside.

All the units of the multiprocessor are to be fixed price. Including the special Input Output unit the PAM. It interfaces to the outside world.

FAA procurement wants to buy the PAM Peripheral Adapter Module fixed price; other bidders have objected.

So FAA reluctantly agreed that the PAM would be CPFF –cost plus fixed fee.

But now IBM would not bid that piece CPFF.

"What do we do, Joe?" the DS and Group Staff people asked. I shrug.

"We're caught. We can't show them the cost backup for the modules anyway –bid it Fixed Price."

We will stumble on this later.

Now the overall price is to be set. What price was needed to win?

## COMPETITION

On Monday, December 30, a group assembles at 1111 Connecticut to assess the price competition to be expected. Watts is there, and people from pricing in DS. I am in lower Manhattan. People from all over the U.S. are there –from Cambridge, Massachusetts; from Los Angeles. IBM employees who had been in competition with the Burroughs multiprocessor are there.

Sales of the Burroughs multiprocessor –the D825 - are scrutinized. The Air Force's Backup Interception Control –BUIC – bought 38 systems. This is public information.

They estimate that Burroughs' "list" price for the D825 for FAA is 6.5 million, but Burroughs could discount 2.2 million, based on the Air Force prices. This is anything but an exact science. It is a process of gathering pieces of information here and there. It is the only way to do it, but not very precise. It is looking at public information and drawing conclusions.

Important? Look at the national scope of the attendees. Anyone with knowledge was asked to help. The result –the group expect Burroughs to bid the FAA system in the 70-75 million dollar range.

## IBM PRESIDENT MEETING

On Sunday, January 12, I leave for White Plains on the 10 p.m. Eastern Airlines Shuttle. Jack Ford, Washington legal, and I are going up to the Westchester area. I hope I can get into the Williams meeting. I had never met him.

## A Brawl in IBM - 1964

We land LaGuardia in the middle of a big snowstorm, sleep at a motel near the airport and drive up to the Yorktown facility early the next morning. IBM executives had moved into' Yorktown IBM Research while the IBM HQ building at Armonk was being finished. We arrive at Yorktown at 9 o'clock for the 9 o'clock meeting.

We are the only ones here! Everyone who lives in the New York area is snowed in. Stuck in their driveways. Pfeiffer, due to meet us at 9, arrives at 11.

The meeting with the president of the corporation is cancelled. Ford, Pfeiffer, Humphrey and I work trying to figure out what to do on the pricing schedule. The bid is due January 23 –ten days.

We meet all day in several different locations within the headquarters complexes. We rush down to New York City, to 590 Madison Avenue (IBM's 57th Street location) to meet with the president of the corporation. I am not allowed in the meeting. I am told that Humphrey proposes that the IBM swallow $20 million of the cost. IBM would sell the systems below cost in order to gain the knowledge and experience that will go with building and delivering such a system. Williams wants to think about why and how to justify such a decision.

There is a meeting with the president of IBM in Yorktown. I sit outside and wait. I read magazines and fret. I am not used to this role – sitting outside waiting.

The building has no coffee machines, but a coffee cart makes the rounds of the building once per morning and afternoon.

I wait for about one hour, and the coffee cart comes around. A secretary goes in and out of Williams' office, ferrying in coffee.

The door opens and Learson and Gibson come out to get their coffee themselves. Learson stretches, as if he has just gotten out of a car in which he had been riding for along time. He looks at me.

"What are you doing here, Joe?"

"Waiting for the meeting results, Vin."

"Well, come in, man! Come in."

I could have kissed him, but say, simply " Great." and I go into the president's office.

Learson introduces me to Al Williams, president of IBM, as the "salesman on the account."

That is close enough.

Mr. Williams is a heavyset, quiet-speaking man. Soon after I get into the meeting, two people, Humphrey and a financial man, get into a side discussion while Mr. Williams is talking. Williams raises his hand and says, "I'll wait." There is no hint of sarcasm. His manner evidences that he believes he should wait until these other two people reach an end of their interaction. The other two are abashed - and immediately apologize for having gone off into a side conversation. The effect is dramatic. Williams had, in effect, reprimanded the two.

It was the first time I had ever seen anyone so completely in command of a situation, take such effective corrective action, and yet be such a gentleman.

The meeting settles several minor issues.

For the remainder of the week we wrestle with getting the documents ready to be typed and inserted into the growing proposal.

✯ ✯ ✯

Monday January 20th

I leave my Rockville, Maryland, home at 6 AM, get the 7 o'clock Shuttle and arrive at Harrison, New York, at 9:15. I spend the day with headquarters personnel –lawyers, businessmen, financial staff, strategists. We work until 11 PM.

<u>Tuesday. The 21st – two days to submission.</u> All day at Harrison. We work until 2 in the morning with the secretary and chief legal officer of the corporation, Hank Trimble. We plow through clause after clause, word by word. The staff people are out to protect IBM; Humphrey is out to win the contract. We clash on every clause. Humphrey and I lose almost every fight.

At the very last minute, George Newmann, counsel for the Data Systems Division, puts in a clause labeled "Third Party Liability".

# A Brawl in IBM - 1964

I ask what third party means. Newmann explains. Should two airplanes crash, survivors might first sue the airline, secondly the government, and then any manufacturer whose equipment could be considered to have contributed to the crash.

Hence, the *third* party. Perhaps a maker of an altimeter. Or the maker of a computer.

I step out and call the Federal Region lawyer, Jack Ford. I need help.

"What does the clause say", Joe?

"It's not a clause, Jack. It is merely the name of a clause. It says 'Third Party Liability-' period – three words. It says, in effect, 'Before we sign a contract, we expect to agree on a clause on Third Party Liability Indemnification.' "

"Joe, there are more and more lawsuits where an injured party sues not the manufacturer but a component supplier. For example, the brakes on a Buick fail and the injured person sues not only Buick Division of GM, but the company who made the brakes. Buick-GM is the second party; their brake supplier –who had no dealings with the injured party –is dragged in as the third party."

"What's that got to do with us –here."

"Well, the number of these suits is rising. Newmann wants FAA to indemnify us. If someone is killed, and the survivors come after us, we will be protected. The FAA will pay any judgment against us."

"What if it's our fault?"

"Then we are still liable. A maker is always liable if found negligent. But people could come after us even if the computer had nothing to do with the accident. It will be very hard to prove we're not involved. It costs money to defend yourself. And the suers often go after the "Deep Pockets" in the mix. After the affluent parties"

"Jack, we don't have this clause for our 1401-1410 at Islip."

"I know, Joe. Don't worry about this clause. Newmann is a great lawyer- and he is reasonable."

✡ ✡ ✡

The 9020 –our system of multiple Central processing units – CPUs- is a curious mixture of standard and special equipment. The tape drives, printers, large core memories, channels and other units are standard machines. These machines would be in IBM's standard government contract 'schedule.' With standard prices and terms. The special units would not be on any list. They could not be rented.

But the standard units were not announced yet. Not in the sales listings that all IBM sales people get. So their prices are higher than they probably will be when the 360 is announced. On the special units, the price is to be lower than commercial.

Late on Wednesday night, the 21st, Pfeiffer calls me and tells me that we have a price.

"105.6 million."

"Oh."

Bad news.

"Yeah. It's the best we could get."

We are both subdued.

That price won't win. Williams does not accept the $20,000,000 "learning benefit" that Humphrey had proposed.

We believe it to be 30-40 million above Burroughs. Too much.

"Well, we'll just keep plugging, Ralph."

"Yeah. Good, Joe. Good."

We configure the computing equipment into three different sized systems:

The A system would handle 325 flights at a time in their sector.

The B system -200 flights per hour.

The C system –100 flights per hour.

Oldani does the sizing.

The A system is to cost $4.4 million –9 of them are bid.

The B system for $2.7 million –16 of them.

The C system for $1.9 million -12 of them.

Extra systems are in there for training and development –37 in all.

A total of 105.6 million!

A Brawl in IBM - 1964

## WEDNESDAY, JANUARY 22. LAST DAY

The proposal is due tomorrow! Ford, Humphrey and I work until 2 AM.

Last items are finally signed off.

An IBM aircraft is standing by to take Humphrey and me -with the proposal - to Washington.

But should the weather be bad, and the plane late, IBM will miss the date –and be out of the competition.

Game over.

Just in case, a copy of the letter is faxed to Washington. The letter contains the overall price, which will be hand- carried to FAA headquarters. The supporting backup to the overall price may then be delivered and accepted later.

It is a furious effort. IBM-Harrison is in a panic.

What has been left out? Do we have enough copies? Is it correctly typed? Are the pages in order.

There are about 20 addenda and supplements to go into the letter.

This is not a normal function for the division and group staffs.

The executives give Humphrey complete responsibility. What he says goes, and no one is bothering to check anything.

At 11 AM, Thursday the 26th, we rush to the airport in White Plains New York.

The IBM corporate plane awaits us.

*After being in the stark firehouse ('Get that chart off that truck. Get out of this room.'), we are important after all. I had never even seen an IBM plane.*

Kilner and Collins are waiting at the airport with a car to drive us over to the FAA. The financial proposal is delivered on time.

## THE PRICE PROPOSAL HAS AN ERROR

The effort normally now passes from the bidders to the FAA. It is now in their hands. Marketing should relax. Procurement rules prohibit sales interaction while the government evaluates the bids.

But- hold it. Not quite! It is not to be!

A 'mistake' in the IBM bid is to keep us in the proposal mode.

IBM's bid offers 96,000 words of 2 microsecond memory (one word every 2 one millionths of a second) at a price far cheaper than buying one 96,000 word memory that was 10 microseconds. The slower memories are priced as standard IBM products, - and the faster memories are not.

It makes no sense for anyone to buy the slower, more expensive 98,000 word units.

Three faster memories are cheaper and 5 times faster.

No one has foreseen this!

The Washington team takes one look at the prices, and immediately begins to change the proposal.

"Joe, how did you let this happen?" asks Collins.

"I don't know, Jack. It was wild. We did not get the prices till late. We just missed it."

I go to Pfeiffer.

"Ralph, we've got to get it changed."

Pfeiffer is not happy at all. He doesn't want to go back to New York and open up the fighting all over again.

But - it will cut the IBM price by some 10 million dollars! Ten million!

We could go from 105 million to 95 million. It just might get us close enough.

"How did this happen, Joe? Why didn't you see it coming?" Ralph asks.

"Ralph, I wasn't in all the meetings. We didn't see the prices. We were on the outside."

Pfeiffer reluctantly agrees to get the price changed.

I call DS and Watts, and make appointments to go back to Westchester the next week.

It continues.

✯ ✯ ✯

## A Brawl in IBM - 1964

On January 29, I brief Pfeiffer on the FAA. We have no real information, but I show the best estimates of the bid.

| | |
|---|---|
| IBM | $94,000,000 |
| Burroughs | $59,000,000 |
| CDC | $117,000,000 |
| GE | $93,000,000 |
| Others ? | |

We believe GE has not bid real multiprocessors.

"Ralph, all bidders are on tap for a detailed technical presentation to FAA. We'll get one week's notice."

"Are you ready?"

"Yeah. We're practicing now. And we'll go into high gear when we get the notice."

And now I get to a ticklish issue.

"Ralph, we must get the FSD professional negotiators into the action –if we pass the first dropout cut."

"No. No FSD. You do it."

"I can't."

Pfeiffer smiles.

"You can do anything, Joe".

"No. No, I can't. I can't land this fish, assuming we have it hooked. Ralph, all the IBM people who understand government competitive contracts are in Federal Systems. Not in Group Staff. Not in DP.

"Do we have a chance, Joe? At 94 million – if we get the memory thing straightened out?"

"No – it is still too high. Burrough's price we think is 59 million for the Air Force ...but... if they are over-confident, - if a discount is added back, we see them maybe at 70 million...? - and with 9% profit, they are at 84 million.

"And...?" asked Ralph.

"That's close enough, if it's right."

"That's still 12 million dollars difference!"

"But it's less than 15% difference. A government procurement can be awarded at 15% higher - for more quality. It's not the dollar value, but the percentage."

Pfeiffer is interested.

"You think we have a chance? Really? "

"Well, it's slim –but yeah."

I write to Group Finance.

MEMORANDUM January 30
TO: Mr. John Schwamb, Manager Pricing, Group Staff
SUBJECT: FAA/NAS Proposal

We intend to tell FAA by February 5 that they should disregard LCM and use 32K main memory for the A System. We must submit a new price for the A System based on this configuration. Would you generate a price for us by February 3?

FAA is moving very quickly on this procurement and we must get this in by the 5th.

In late January, Humphrey is promoted out of his DP Headquarters post to Group Staff. He sends letters to Pfeiffer, Kennard, and Gibson. He sums up his recommendations on:

1. Systems Design
2. Peripheral Adapter Module (PAM) .
3. Implementation Schedule
4. Manpower Plan

## FEBRUARY 1964-WE WAIT

January ends as a month of accomplishment. The technical proposal was submitted on January 6$^{th}$ and on January 23$^{rd}$ the price and terms and conditions proposal was submitted. But it also ended on a negative note –the price was so high that we believe we are out of the competition. And it didn't end crisply –the prices for memories came out in a bit of a bizarre fashion, and the proposal did not quite make sense as it now stood. There is unfinished business to be done.

February finds us trying to change the bid, to get the big memory out of the proposal. It should have been simple, but nothing on this effort was to be simple. We tell Group Finance that we want to change the large proposed memory.

But now Group Staff Finance comes out of their corner swinging. Bill Quinn tells me, on the phone, "Not only can't you write such a letter, Joe, but if you raise the issue we are going to recommend that the whole bid be withdrawn!"

Silence.

"Are you crazy?" I ask. "On what basis?"

"Too risky. What if there is a crash? And there's no profit in it!"

"But we put it in only a month ago." I am almost shouting, "You signed off."

"I made a mistake. If I get another shot at it, I'll do my damnedest to withdraw it."

Pause.

"Bill, it's idiocy to leave it the way it is. We look like jerks. How do I explain this to FAA?"

"Sorry, Joe, that's your problem."

It should not have been difficult to resubmit the proposal with the prices corrected - but it was proving to be very difficult. The urgency had gone out of the FAA bid in IBM Westchester County, the headquarters for most of divisions and of course for the corporate headquarters.

After the big push to get the whole thing submitted, the human thing is to want to let it rest.

Trying to get people to even talk to us is a problem.

## TECHNICAL BRIEF OF THE PROPOSAL TO THE FAA

More pressing than fixing the LCM mistake –the FAA wants a presentation on the proposal.

I am delighted that neither Manson nor Humphrey comes down to the meeting. It is mine to run.

The team meets for the whole day the day before, practicing. We are in the 1120 Connecticut Avenue conference room.

A myriad of technical details must be presented and discussed. I would select one of the IBM attendees to answer each question.

The team works like a well-oiled machine.

It is the marketing team –Collins, Kowalke, Oldani Whitney –plus essential new comers –Claude Davis from the DS model 50 engineering group –and Don Burnstine from the Field Engineering Division. And Jack Keeley, who had managed the IBM effort outside of Atlantic City N J for years, who has a deep in knowledge of the FAA. And Jack O'Connell from Poughkeepsie, who would handle any questions regarding the support software.

Davis is brilliant, articulate, warm and relaxed. He handles questions in a friendly down-home way, with a slow southern drawl. I have no hesitation to turn a question over to him to answer. He has fine judgment –he knows what not to say, what to avoid lest it open an abyss.

Burnstine is a six foot two inch, bow-tied Brooklyn-ite who shouldn't have been at these meetings –his division wasn't needed here. But Burnstine has contributed far beyond his division role. He was a key contributor during the firehouse days and now he is still contributing design ideas. I am delighted.

I am being given a free hand. No one is second-guessing me. All the hours in the firehouse are paying great dividends.

Reliability, multiprocessing, programming, support, speed, loading, software, failure modes.

All day we practice, imagining questions, selecting the person to answer, that person answers, we critique.

"What do you say if they ask you what happens if a memory goes down?" asks Jack Collins.

"I don't know," answers Burnstine. "We haven't figured out yet how we are going to isolate the equipment."

Why isolate? Because a 'sick' unit might send out erroneous signals that would infect well units.

Burnstine and Davis, along with Kowalke, Collins and Oldani, work out details of how they would build a fail-soft system. At approximately 1 AM the group finishes.

In those few hours, Davis and Burnstine have done more of the high level design the FAA system. In all the weeks and months spent in the firehouse, we had only put down on paper a high level description of what a system should do. It was this evening when, looking down the barrel of a gun, we arrive at the details by which we could implement those concepts that we had described in the proposal. The team was working beautifully together; the 9020 is a fine system – or will be, if ever built.

We arrive in three cabs at the new FAA building at 800 Independence Avenue. After decades in the old Navy temporary buildings built along Constitution Avenue near 17th Street, FAA had moved into a new building. They all seemed to like the new building, but I thought that the charm of the old temporaries was a loss.

At the last minute, Pfeiffer says that Carl Weiland, Kilner's boss, will go along to the briefing. Carl was totally unprepared for this, as he'd been in no meetings, none. I never knew why he was told to attend. Maybe they were nervous about letting a 29-year old head a $100,000,000 presentation. But I like Weiland, and I expect no trouble.

The meeting goes almost according to according to our practicing.

Jay Rabb, silver-haired, dignified and courtly, lays out the ground rules in his southern drawl.

"This is a technical briefing. The people you are briefing have not seen the business section of your proposal. Please do not divulge any information from it to us."

The FAA group staff is a mixture of the R&D Division, the I&M Division –Installation and Maintenance – and MITRE, the government support think-house. NAFEC was the name for the FAA R&D entity outside Atlantic City, New Jersey –National Aviation Facilities Experimental Center.

We write summaries. The meeting was very informal and a genial atmosphere pervaded. The meeting lasted from 9:30 AM until 9:00 PM, with four coffee breaks and one lunch break. No price or policy matters except RFI - radio frequency interference- were discussed. On a technical basis, all the IBM attendees believe that we impressed them greatly with our understanding of multiprocessing, Isolation and Reconfiguration, Lock-out Instruction, Reconfiguration, Instruction Reliability, the 7090 Simulator, the Executive Routine.

FAA (J. Seitz) made the point that the loss of 32K of memory at a time –for one failure - is a sizable loss, and asked why we had not bid 16K memories. Our answer –price, an excessive number of cables, drivers, etc.

The discussion turned to why we had not taken the LCM out of the A-325 flight configuration when we had taken it was out of the B-200 system. [The only one of the 3 configurations that had an LCS was the A, for technical reasons.] We pointed out that we were in the process of writing to FAA to change the A system configuration. They understood what we were attempting to do.

Mr. Dunn asked if we could possibly deliver an "8 units of 32K memory A system in 15 months. I said we would investigate and expressed hope that we could.

Radio Frequency Interference - RFI:

Radio Frequency Interference is the term given to the effect of radar emissions (for example) on the computer. Would bombarding the computer with radar waves cause errors - knock some electrons loose?

FAA asked if IBM would take responsibility for meeting the requested RFI specification without a test.

Our proposal referenced the fact that our 1401/1410 at Islip, and the 7090 at NAFEC, were encountering no problems and that the 9020 was to be equal in this regard.

We had given FAA a figure of what the 360 would withstand. In the meeting, the FAA asked if that was IBM's figure.

"Yes," I say.

"Then your machine will not operate in a room with fluorescent lights."

"OH."

Burnstine calls Poughkeepsie at the break and tells me what had happened. No one ever had asked that question before, so the engineers stated a figure they thought reasonable. But then every

# A Brawl in IBM - 1964

successive level of management had cut the radiation number the machine would withstand in half - until they had come up with this absurd number in the proposal.

I go back into the meeting and told FAA IBM would guarantee the machine would work in any RFI environment.

At the next break, Weiland grabs me.

"Joe, you don't have the authority to guarantee that RFI stuff."

"I know."

"Are you crazy?"

"Look, Carl. If the machine doesn't meet the spec, we'll coat the covers on the machine with some material. Lead paint. Or we'll screen the wall the radar is hitting with lead panels. The machine has to be in a benign, air conditioned room – people will be in there. It's not going to be a problem."

Weiland just looks at me.

It is a ticklish moment.

Weiland could order me to go in and hedge. It would make us – and especially me - look bad.

"I can get IBM to accept the risk, Carl."

Weiland smiles. "Okay,- you better be right."

I smile.

It never becomes a problem.

## FAIL SOFT UNITS:

On three separate occasions during the meeting, the fact that we had bid three elements in several areas where only one element was required was discussed. FAA indicated (privately) that some other bidders had not followed the RFP, and that either these companies would be evaluated with additional elements or IBM (and others) would be evaluated without the third element. Our technical proposal on page two outlined this problem.

We offered to submit updated reliability and price figures, taking the third I/O Control Element out of the Band A systems (25 IOCE's), the third Compute Element - CEs - out of the B system (16 CE's), and the third LCM (large core memory) out of the A system (9 LCMs).

FAA stated that they did not desire this information at this time and would notify us when and if they desired it. I stated that we would naturally be most disturbed if FAA contracted with another company for a system which did not meet the requested third element for "fail soft", without IBM having an opportunity to re-quote. All members of the FAA Board agreed that they should not do this and recognized our position.

I do not believe this will slip by to our detriment, and I will make sure it does not. I believe FAA will smooth the inconsistencies for the technical evaluation, and for the first pass at price evaluation. If two companies are close at that point, they will request further information.

SOFTWARE:

A great deal of time was spent on how FAA would start programming without the JOVIAL Compiler for the 9020 being fully specified, and without a physical 9020, and with only a simulator-assembler. Ken Gray made the point that we offered nothing with which FAA could debug a multiprocessor. We conceded this, and stressed the debugging of straight line operational or executive routines.

Mr. Gray was not fully satisfied; MITRE personnel and others did not seem too concerned.

PROGRAMMING ASSISTANCE:

FAA asked: "Would IBM be interested in assisting FAA programmers even if not selected as the hardware manufacturer?"
Yes.
*This would, of course, be FSD, not the DP division.* And a separate contract.

DELIVERY

The discussion got to our delivery dates. I state our delivery.
15 months for the first system,
17 months for the second,

and 21 months for an A system with LCM.

FAA personnel are shocked.

There is a 30-second silence.

Mr. Kingsley leaned over and said to Mr. Gray, "That's bad, isn't it".

Mr. Gray says to Mr. Kingsley, "I want to reopen the status of the 9020."

After a diversion on some other question and a coffee break, Ken Gray asked "This model you spoke of -is it a 'lab curiosity' or a production model"?

We had earlier, in response to a question, stated the status of the 9020- a flow model of the Compute Element in being; memory about to go into test. We had gotten by the question.

We stated the facts regarding the model.

Mr. Gray desired to know the facts regarding the I/O Control Element, the memory, the LCM. The state of design, design drawings, circuit tests, models, units in being etc. are discussed.

I prefaced the answers by a short discussion of why we were at 15 months. In the context of their prior 360 briefing, where the new line was discussed as the A, B, C, D, & E. machines, I stated that due to priorities long established, the model 40 and model 60 machines were scheduled to be built in quantity <u>before</u> the model 50- which was the basis of the 9020 system.

I pointed out that the 9020 would not be identical to the model 50 machine; that 29 B machines (model 40's) would be in existence by January I, 1965, and that this fact was in writing to FAA in the January 23 letter -prices and delivery.

I went into detail on the component shortage for the 360 and the 9020, and that the 9020 probably would not be accelerated unless we won this competition.

We emphasized that they were getting a thoroughly tested machine delivered, and that IBM was willing to contract for- no, we would <u>guarantee</u> - the Mean Down Time and Mean Up Time and mean Time to Repair figures requested. (We would have to deliver units free of charge to supplement the installed systems in all centers if we did not meet the reliability requested.)

Mr. Gray stated that he felt better about the status of the 9020.

However, the entire IBM team judged that we did not regain all of the ground we lost with our late delivery.

Mr. Gray stated that, prior to any contract, FAA would have to visit Poughkeepsie and thoroughly review our status.

In short, were we "off the shelf"?

Don Burnstine wrote a summary and covered the delivery discussion:

> Sometime later the question of delivery schedule came up. Up to this point in time, the meeting had been going extremely well. The relationship between the customer and us was excellent with a total atmosphere of cooperation.
>
> We had a very, very good feeling that we were making many points technically -that they felt we had a thorough grasp of the problem, etc.
>
> At the point in time where Fox mentioned that our delivery was 15 months, there was a silence so thick you could cut it with a knife. They were absolutely shocked.
>
> Not so much because we hadn't warned them that we were not off the shelf, but that we were so late. We had the feeling up to that time they were totally on our side and really felt that we had something going for us.
>
> After the discussion of the 15 month schedule as opposed to 12 months which they requested, and actually our 15 months is even worse than their 12, by more than 3 months, because our 15 month schedule only says that we will have it physically sitting on the floor at their site, rather than installed and tested, which is what they asked for.
>
> I feel that if anything will lose the contract, it is going to be that fact that we are late.

*(So, as we had said all along, delivery might kill us! During the fall of 1963, the 9020 was competing for the people, for the top talent of the company. Now it was competing for the scarce circuits.*

*The late delivery resulted from the new solid-state technology status. Before the 360, transistors were marshaled onto "cards" –small rigid carriers about the size of a playing card (the ace of spades) and interconnected on the cards by wires and with resistors, etc. With the 360, there was now a "chicklet component" mounted on the card. The transistors were inside the "chicklet". The density of work per square inch was greatly increased. But these "chicklet" components were new – and IBM was falling behind the production goals set for them.)*

My memo:
SUMMARY AND CONCLUSIONS:
(1) We impressed FAA with our knowledge of multiprocessing. Gray commented privately that we had come along way in a short time.
(2) FAA and MITRE personnel like our system.
(3) Our reliability discussion satisfied them.
(4) Before any award, we would have to expose FAA, in Poughkeepsie, to our status regarding the 9020.
(5) March 1 is the date that the technical team will report, and prices will be considered then.
(6) Their shock at our delivery indicates that competition is earlier, and that they are placing great importance on delivery.
(7) We must submit very soon our revised A configuration and prices.
(8) The DS personnel did an excellent job in working with the customer, and in presenting the hardware requirements of multi- processing.
(9) Decision will be based primarily on delivery and price, despite some aside comments to the contrary by Mr. Gray, regarding the fact that low bidder would not be automatically "in", and management would not be so price conscious.
(10) Any delivery improvement and options -e.g., one 9020 with a single Compute Element in 12 months -should be explored, and if possible, forwarded to FAA in writing.
(11) We almost came off the "off the shelf" status, and are precariously perched thereon.

✯ ✯ ✯

We felt that we had done very well, indeed. We had smashed into the rocks of delivery, but we had been ready for that. We knew that that remained as one of the items that had to be cleared up.

Now it was time to clean up the garbled bid –to straighten out the memory mistake. I felt a new urgency, as the FAA people had mentioned to me that IF we were going to change, the sooner the better.

The FAA people had spotted the inconsistency.

It stuck out like an alp.

✢ ✢ ✢

I begin to go to New York with Pfeiffer.

Everyone involved in this matter keeps repeating that FAA "had requested that IBM change its configuration".

If I said it once, I said it a hundred times –"FAA has NOT REQUESTED that we change our configuration. OUR comment about changing has elicited their statement that IF IBM is going to do so, do it quickly.

IF is the very crucial word they used. The rules of procurement PROHIBIT them asking us to change our proposal, because they would have to offer all competitors of the same option."

Pfeiffer is on the phone with Learson, and he tells Learson that FAA had requested that IBM take this action.

When he hangs up, I point out to him- once again -that FAA had NOT requested that we change the proposal.

Pfeiffer explodes.

"Goddamn it, Joe, I understand nuances. I'm capable of understanding nuances, and will you stop saying that!"

"Goddamn it, Ralph, I know you can understand nuances, but half the time you don't take the time to listen to what I'm trying to tell you –and what you're saying to Learson is NOT correct - and it ... is ... IMPORTANT."

Pfeiffer smiles. "OK."

# A Brawl in IBM - 1964

*Nuances are one of the secrets to survival. The executives don't get anywhere near as upset at mistakes as they do at what they feel is "gamesmanship", or sharp practices. The worst thing you can do is get something agreed to on the basis of incomplete or, even worse, misleading information. Then your veracity and integrity are in question. Were IBM to be told only after a resubmitted bid that that FAA had NOT REQUESTED this change, I would have been shot for 'misleading' the headquarters.*

I correct Pfeiffer for this reason. Two months down the road, the vice presidents would remember the reason for the change in the bid. They had minds like steel traps. It had to be very clear up front.

We can't get agreement to adjust the proposal! No one seems to be willing to make a decision. Finally, Humphrey sets up a meeting with the president of IBM, Al Williams. Watts is still active and essential to this effort.

# WITH THE IBM PRESIDENT

The meeting is set for 1 PM Monday February 17. Pfeiffer and I fly up on the Shuttle from Washington on Monday and meet with Humphrey an hour early to make sure that we would have everything in intelligible form.

Humphrey is worried. The system prices had been arrived at by spreading the development cost over 47 systems. Ten systems were to come from buyers other than the FAA. The lawyer from Product Group – George Newmann - had insisted to Humphrey and me on Thursday, February 6th, that he had heard distinctly Mr. Williams instructing Mr. Kennard and Mr. Humphrey that the system would be priced "for FAA only", and that no other systems would be sold. If this were true, the highest number of systems that the cost could be spread across in order to arrive at a unit price is 37.

I thought the lawyer was right. Humphrey does not know how to break this news to Williams. He has no recollection of being instructed to spread the cost only across 37. It is clear that if we go to 37 systems, we would have to formally notify FAA that we were RAISING the price. That would end it all, I believe.

The meeting starts.

Watts explains the background, the status of the negotiation, the problem with the memories and the twist in pricing that had occurred.

Humphrey comments that Mr. Williams is aware that the system was priced on a quantity of 47.

"No," said Williams, "it's 37."

"No, sir," says Humphrey, "it is based on 47."

Williams is very calm.

"I distinctly remember giving instructions to have this system priced for FAA only."

# A Brawl in IBM - 1964

He turns to Jack C. B. Rogers, his assistant. "Make a note that we should look into the reasons why my directive was not followed out in pricing this system accordingly."

Looking back at the group he states that, obviously, we would have to raise the prices of the system that had been bid less than a month before. I look to Pfeiffer for help. Pfeiffer looks concerned –but says nothing.

Bill Quinn from Group Finance speaks.

"We should withdraw the bid"!

Williams is surprised.

They discuss whether or not IBM could legally withdraw the earlier bid, which was stated to be valid for 90 days. It is decided that the words would have to be carefully stated by the lawyers to assure that the new proposal <u>which we would submit with higher prices</u> would clearly supersede the old proposal.

There is a question as to whether or not the FAA must accept the new proposal and the new prices in light of the fact that the old proposal stated that the bid was valid for 90 days.

I have on my inscrutable face; inside I am in tumult.

*These people are crazy.*

*We come in to get a simple revision in price, for an obvious glitch to be fixed –and they are raising the price -and considering dropping the whole effort.*

Williams decides.

He speaks to Bill Quinn.

"Well, Bill, I guess the way I come out of this one is that we have given FAA our hand and said, 'Here's a deal.' We have shaken hands on the deal and said, 'Here's our offer.' To back out at this point in time seems wrong. I think we'll leave the bid in."

Williams calls Learson.

"Vin," he says, "what do you think about this whole thing?"

Williams listens. He acts surprised.

'You haven't been consulted?" Williams says in wonderment.

"Well, then how did these people get to me without having gone through you?"

*I am impressed at how polite Williams is. His tone and pace are gentle.*

"I wish in the future, Vin, you would not let this happen. I'm going to go ahead with what these Federal people are recommending – that we bid the small main memories instead of the large capacity memories, the LCSs. I am also going to have the system re-priced on the basis of 37 systems. Before I go ahead, however, I would like you to get personally involved and let me know whether you see any problems."

We leave the meeting. The problem is that we jumped over Learson and got to the president without briefing Learson. Pfeiffer is concerned, in deep thought.

"We're going up to see Learson," he decides. "Watts, I think you ought to be there also."

It is 5:30. We push through the rush-hour traffic and get on the Saw Mill River Parkway, heading for the Yorktown Research Center in Yorktown, New York.

We have not called Learson; he may have left the office. Pfeiffer and I get there before Humphrey.

Learson's secretary looks up and smiles.

"There you are. Mr. Learson's been expecting you. You can go right in."

"He's been expecting us?" asks a surprised Pfeiffer.

"Oh yes. He's been waiting for you," Kathy Merck says.

"Did he call my office?"

"Not that I know," she answers. "Shall I tell Mr. Learson that you are here?"

"No, no. Not yet," says Pfeiffer.

Pfeiffer walks into a nearby cubicle, lost in thought.

"Let's not go in right away," he says to me.

I recognize gamesmanship. Learson is apparently confident that Pfeiffer would react immediately to correct the breach of going to Williams without even informing Learson,

# A Brawl in IBM - 1964

Humphrey had set up the meeting. It was Humphrey's meeting. Yet Pfeiffer, being the Vice President in Charge of Federal Marketing, can not simply state that Humphrey had set up the meeting with Williams. Pfeiffer should at least have <u>notified</u> Learson.

Pfeiffer walks up and down, in thought, growing more relaxed as the minutes passed. Five minutes go by.

Learson comes into our little cubicle.

"There you are, Ralph," he says. "Good to see you," with a big smile. "How long have you been here?"

"Just arrived," said Ralph, "just arrived. We were passing by and decided to stop in"

"Yes, yes, I thought you would," says Learson. "Do you want to come in?"

"No," says Pfeiffer. "It's late and I don't want to keep you."

Learson is surprised.

"But you came to see me?"

"No, no. Just stopping by," says Pfeiffer.

"Well, come in and talk for a bit."

I smile.

By this time Humphrey is coming up the aisle and we all go into Learson's office.

It is approximately 7 P M.

"Explain the situation to me," says Learson.

Humphrey uses the flip charts he'd used with Williams. The first chart was a paragraph written in full English that stated the following: "IBM has bid to FAA a system containing five main memories and three LCS's. The LCS memory is priced as a standard memory. The main memory is priced as a special memory. As a result, it would be cheaper to have a system composed of all main memories and this would be our best bid."

Humphrey begins to read the chart.

Learson reacts.

"I can read. I can read. Show me something besides text."

For some reason, Learson always hates flip charts that have only English sentences.

Humphrey is a bit flustered. He flips to the next chart, which is again all text, and he flips to the third chart, which contains some numbers and he starts to explain the numbers.

Learson cuts him off.

"As I understand what you're doing," says Learson, "it is the following."

He proceeds to summarize exactly what it is that we are trying to do.

"That's right," says Ralph.

"This is a damn fool scheme." says Learson.

"*WHAT?*" Pfeiffer is angry.

"What do you mean, 'fool scheme'? This is the only thing that makes any sense under the circumstances. It's clear that if we want to win this bid, we're going to have to do something that common sense insists that we do."

"Why common sense?" counters Learson. "We decided to bid these systems at $105 million. No one has ever decided to bid them at 90 million. The answer is NO - we will not bid such a system."

"Why?" asks Ralph. "Why are we doing such a thing?"

"Because I want to," says Learson. "I've decided to bid this system at $105 million, and that's what I'll bid it at."

I speak up.

"Vin, we're going to look completely stupid in the eyes of the customer."

"Why? Why should the customer even know what's going on?"

I swallow before I speak again. I clearly do not want to tell Learson that I had, in a meeting with FAA, practically guaranteed that IBM would change its bid and replace the LCS memories.

"Because," I say, "the cover letter of our price proposal submitted on January 23rd states precisely that a system can be configured without LCS memories. The statement goes on to say - further, Vin, - that IBM would be most willing to supply systems without LCS memories."

Learson explodes again.

"How dare you put that in a letter. How dare you?" His voice rising.

# A Brawl in IBM - 1964

Pfeiffer attacks.

"What do you mean, how dare we? What do you pay us for – to be damn fools or to win this business. We're not in this game to be tricky. We're playing to win. If you did not want us to go below $105 million, you should have made that clear. We have been given no such direction. We have been told to win the business. I don't understand this whole damn thing, Vin, and I don't understand why it is taking us so damned long to make such a simple decision."

Humphrey has been sitting quietly, ill at ease, not speaking.

Learson picks up his coat from his coat rack and begins putting it on.

"I'm not going to discuss it any longer tonight," he states. "I'll think about it overnight and talk to you in the morning."

Learson and Pfeiffer are then alone for a few minutes.

Learson leaves and Watts and I are with Pfeiffer

We sit in a nearby office. Silence reigns.

"I'll have to change jobs." announces Humphrey.

I almost fall out of my chair.

Pfeiffer is inscrutable.

"Why?" asks Pfeiffer, calmly.

"I've never been treated like that," Watts says quietly. "Vin has lost confidence in me."

"Not at all," says Pfeiffer. "Vin is just emphatic. There was no condemnation."

I agree.

Humphrey just shakes his head.

"I'll change jobs." he repeats.

"I don't think Vin has lost confidence in anyone."

"I don't know," says Humphrey. "I just don't know."

We leave Armonk. 9 PM.

Pfeiffer and I go to "dinner" –a hot dog at an all-night joint in White Plains.

"Ralph, I love Learson. But I sure don't understand the role he played today."

Ralph chews down a bite.

"He's worried about Burroughs."

✻ ✻ ✻

Three days later Humphrey and I are down at 590 Madison Avenue in Manhattan talking to the group vice president in charge of the Product Division, John Gibson. George Kennard's boss.

We are clearing up the last sections of the letter that must to be submitted to FAA, changing the LCS memories to main memory. We have gotten that agreement – BUT- we are going to raise the price because of the 37 versus 47 system bids.

Gibson approves the letter without much discussion. While we were there, Gibson gets a phone call from Learson.

Gibson is chatting on the phone with Learson. He then hands Humphrey the phone to talk to Learson.

"Hello"…pauses – "Yes …yes… OK"

Humphrey is brightening.

''I will be there at 8:30. yes…yes… fine…I'll call your secretary for directions."

He puts down the phone and tells us that he has to hurry because he is having dinner at Learson's home at 8:30 that evening.

I see Pfeiffer the next day.

"The Humphrey-resigning crisis is over," I tell Ralph. "He's gone to dinner at Learson's."

"I know, Joe".

"Ah, ha! I thought you were in the middle of this."

Ralph just smiles.

Pfeiffer had told me earlier in the effort that the Chairman of the Board, Tom Watson, Jr. had interviewed and hired Humphrey. Personally. Watts was related to some very powerful people.

Learson would not want someone connected to the chairman resigning. I had surmised that Pfeiffer had let Learson know that Humphrey was not comfortable with the encounter, - to say the least - and now Learson was smoothing things up.

# A Brawl in IBM - 1964

Pfeiffer is driving towards LaGuardia. He is philosophical, thinking.

"Joe, did we have an unfair advantage in this bid?"

I smile.

I can tell by now that Pfeiffer has at least two modes of operation –(1) "I am the Executive" and (2) "I'm Ralph."

He is just Ralph now.

"No. Why?"

When he was 'just Ralph,' I do not have to be on guard. I relax too – but not too much. The Executive at times comes leaping into the picture at an instant's notice.

"Well, we knew everything –everything. The size. The delivery. The multiprocessor. Every damn thing."

"So did a lot of other companies, Ralph. We had no proprietary or sensitive data. We don't know their budget. Gray told you in August that what he was telling you was what he told every company that came to talk to him. You pointed that out to Evans in the letter after the lunch in August."

"Yeah."

We drive across the Whitestone Bridge in silence.

"But, Joe," Ralph is clearly mulling something over, "what about all the little companies. Or companies that have not been tracking the FAA. They couldn't possibly bid. That's not fair."

"Sure it's fair. This is not a child's game we are playing. You've got to be <u>big enough</u> to play. You've got to understand real-time systems. Many companies don't. You've got to understand government contracting rules and procedures. Many companies don't. DP doesn't understand those things, Ralph. You either enter the game fully or you are never really in it. And it <u>costs</u> to play. We've spent a lot of money betting that we will win. We may lose it all."

We head for La Guardia and the shuttle.

"Ralph, the government has competitions - not in a sense of fairness or obligation to companies, but to get the best deal for the taxpayer! And there are reams of rules that those guys at FAA live by. The process of inviting bids is precise and laborious. Remember how the RFP was always 'next week'"?

"Yeah."

"Well, they were going through all the wickets – touching all the bases. The competition must withstand protests from the losers, lawsuits, and irate congressional queries. So <u>every</u> base is touched. These people at FAA earn their pay."

"Are they good?"

"Damn good. They get it done –and I admire them. And, Ralph, if there are no bidders, or only one bidder, well, then there is no competition.

And then they may be forced to redo the whole thing- and at least one year is lost and maybe more. But they got competition. Look at what we did. Our pencil was sharp."

"Yeah. Well, stay away from FAA for awhile."

"*What?*"

"Stay away from FAA for awhile. Don't see them."

*The Executive is back; a slight change in tone signals the transfer.*

"Okay. Can I ask why?"

"Learson says we are in collusion with FAA."

I laugh.

"I'm serious."

"I know you are –but it's funny."

"Well - stay away."

"Okay."

There was nothing to get from talking to FAA at this point anyway. We are in wait mode.

✯ ✯ ✯

"What's the matter, Joe?" asks Collins.

I shake my head.

"Heads you lose; tails you lose."

"What?"

"Learson thinks we're in collusion with FAA. We have been told to stay away from the FAA."

"What? WHAT?"

# A Brawl in IBM - 1964

"You heard me."
"That's idiotic."
"I know – you know. They don't."
Collins is wide-eyed –and a bit hurt.
"COLLUSION?"
"In a way it's a compliment. We must look good as salesmen."
"It's crazy."
"Stay away."

I thought I should tell Pfeiffer about the <u>bad days</u> at FAA –1961 and 1962. When IBM had almost nothing going, –we were the outsiders. How we had slowly wedged our way in. We got a 7090, IBM's largest computer at the time, ordered by one faction in FAA over the dead bodies of another faction. And one Navy Captain- on loan to FAA- grabbed me by my tie one day - and growled -"We'll get you, you son-of-bitch. IBM will never get another order here."

I should tell them how over years Whitney and Finley and Lawson and Houltman had edged FAA slowly, slowly around –till now we were trusted. White had put together a top team. And it had paid off –but it had taken years. YEARS.

"How can they think that?" repeats Collins.
"Look how close we were to FAA. You yourself said we'd done the perfect job."
"Yeah, but..."
"You do everything right - you look suspicious."
"What do we do?"
"Nothing. Stay away from FAA. Hear nothing for a while. There is nothing going on at the moment."
"Okay."
But we get the prices of the memories fixed in the proposal.
Again, the memo I write "to file" tells the story - to document what was happening.
Pfeiffer signs the letter to FAA. I hand-deliver the Pfeiffer letter to the procurement office of the FAA. I write a memo to file.

The bid now made sense. The price went down a bit, to about $95 million.

The rest of February –eleven days –were tranquil.

Nothing doing on FAA.

We all feel we've lost – because of price.

On March 3, I get a call from Jay Rabb, FAA.

"We'd like to visit your plant to assess if you are 'off-the-shelf' or not."

*HURRAY ! ! !*
*FAA would visit only if the IBM price were within the competitive range.*
*The price is "OK". Compeitive.*
*We're not out of it!*

We set March 5 for the visit. WE -Collins, Oldani, Kowalke and I – immediately get the Shuttle to New York and drive to Poughkeepsie.

Collins and I- and Manson from DS - spend the entire day of March 4 rehearsing the presentation DS would make. We go through every presenter, every piece of the presentation. We leave nothing to chance.

At 3 PM the next day Collins and I drive to LaGuardia, pick up the FAA people, in two rented cars, drive back to Poughkeepsie and have dinner with the FAA visitors at the Treasure Chest restaurant on Route 9, from 7 till 9. Then we leave the FAA visitors and go back and rehearse again - till midnight. We do not discuss the bid.

We meet for breakfast at 7 and arrive at 8 for the presentations. Pfeiffer is there, and Whitney. They'd come in late the night before and had not been in the practice sessions. We are told that Evans will not be there.

We are in a classroom setting, with tiered seats. The FAA evaluation committee sits in the front seats.

The agenda:
Presentations        9 till 10:30
Break                10:30 to 11

# A Brawl in IBM - 1964

    Presentations               11 to 12
    Lunch                          12 to 1
    Tour of the production facilities   1 to 3

FAA would tour the Solid Logic Technology production line– SLT -the new circuit packages.

Pfeiffer and Whitney sit in the middle in the rear. Collins and I sit in the back on opposite sides of the room.

*We've practiced it all! It should go well!*

After ten minutes, I know something is wrong!
Very wrong!
It doesn't sound right.
Key adjectives are missing.
*"Maybe it's me."*
I look over at Collins. Collins is looking at me –with angry eyes.

*The bastards have changed the presentation! We are caught napping -helpless. They did not tell us.*

We must let the presentations run on –to interrupt will not only be embarrassing, but damaging.

Pfeiffer gets up from the back of the room and goes outside to make a phone call. I follow him.

"Ralph, we're in deep trouble. They're making the 9020 sound like a complete new development. They..."

"It sounds fine to me, Joe."

"No, no, no. They are changing the whole emphasis. They're changing the whole agreed-to theme - the 9020 is to be a part of the 360. They..."

"You're imagining things, Joe. Calm down."

"Ralph, we practiced all day yesterday – they are killing us with the changes to the presentation."

I pause.

How do I <u>illustrate</u> that the pitch is wrong?

There is no way. It is subtle; it is in the adjectives; in the 'slant'. It isn't in any one sentence!

Collins comes out.

"They've changed! It's no good."

Manson comes out.

"George, why have you changed the pitch?" I ask – with some heat.

Manson looks surprised.

"We haven't changed. It's the same pitch we practiced."

Pfeiffer begins to leave.

"Relax, Joe –Jack. It's Okay."

Collins and I look at each other helplessly.

Collins and I talk alone.

"They've changed, Joe."

"How can we show that?"

"I don't know. It's not something you can pinpoint..."

"Let's go back in and listen some more. Maybe it is us."

We go back in and listen. And we are in agony!

It is wrong! It is coming out WRONG.

We now can see glances being exchanged by the FAA people.

IBM is sliding off a cliff!

We are in freefall.

But wait - Whitney seems relaxed. And Whitney is never relaxed!

Maybe it is our imagination.

I decide not to risk it.

I tap the Guest Services coordinator on the shoulder, and beckon him outside the room. Guest Services schedules the tours through the factory.

There were so many tours that a special group, Guest Services, sets up the whole thing – speakers, tours, path, time –everything.

"Pete," I say to Pete Klinger, "I want the tour right after the 10:30 break. Okay?"

"Oh, Joe. That's almost impossible. I..."

"Pete." I grasp his arms.

"Please. Pete. It's critical, Pete. I'm going to announce at the break that the tour is on at 10:30. I don't care if it is ragged! Sloppy. Just do it."

"Okay," reluctantly, but in agreement.

Manson is about to go back into the meeting room.

"George, I've changed the schedule. The tour goes on at 10:30."

"You can't do that. We've got a schedule."

"It's done."

I walk back in.

Collins rolls his eyes at the ceiling –it is BAD. Whitney now looks concerned.

The presenter is covering the SLT production. It is 10:15.

Pfeiffer reenters.

"I guess it's time for a break," says the speaker. "Any questions?"

I speak.

"We have a slight change of schedule. Rather than have you sit all morning, we're going to have you take a tour right after the coffee break. Then lunch. Then a wrap-up. That way we'll be able to answer to the group any questions that arise from the tour –and you don't have to sit for the whole morning."

It sounded logical. It bought us an hour to straighten things out.

Collins is nodding!

They mill about the coffee urn. I go like a bee from one group to the other, to sample reaction.

I pick up politeness. That's all.

Damn. I need evidence!

I ask Pfeiffer to meet with Manson and me during the tour.

The group moves off for the tour.

Pfeiffer, Manson, Collins and I meet in a nearby empty office.

"It's changed, George." I accuse.

"No, Joe. It has not," Manson states calmly.

"George, it's changed," states Collins.

Manson looks long-suffering, looks at Pfeiffer as if to say 'look at what I have to put up with!'

Pfeiffer is puzzled.

"What has changed, Joe? What? What statement? What presentation?"

"The thrust, the tone, the emphasis. It sounds like the 9020 is a brand new machine. It's supposed to be 50% or more 360! It's supposed to be SLT, the same instructions, the same architecture..."

"It sounds like that to me," says Pfeiffer.

"Right," says Manson.

I am perplexed – lost - befuddled.

*What the hell was happening? Maybe it is me,- but I trust Collins. We are seldom both wrong.*

We go around the same conversation once again.

Suddenly, the door bursts open. A breathless Whitney enters.

"You guys are going down the tubes! Seitz (an FAA technical man) just told me his vote at present is to declare the 9020 not a current machine, not 'off-the-shelf.'"

"That's too bad," says Manson evenly, relaxed. "But if that's the way it is, well...that's the way it is. It's their call."

Pfeiffer's whole attitude now changes. He now knows we were in trouble - the customer has told us so. Now he bores in to find out why.

"George, you all practiced all day yesterday. Did you change the pitch."

"No."

We all look at each other.

"It's changed!" I declare.

Manson glares at me; I glare back.

Again the door bursts open and in comes Bob Evans.

He's not been expected.

"Looks like a funeral," he observes. "What's wrong."

"We're sliding off a cliff," I say. I repeat Seitz' judgment.

Evans nods knowingly.

"I thought so. Had to happen. When we got the message to our people late last night, I knew this would be the result."

"What message?" asks Pfeiffer.

## A Brawl in IBM - 1964

Evans is surprised. "Didn't George tell you? We got word last night from Al Williams' office [IBM president] to 'paint the 9020 special'. So we are! We changed the thrust of the presentation."

I glare at Manson. "Why the hell didn't you tell us?"

Manson says nothing.

"Let's get things straightened out first, Joe," says Pfeiffer.

Within minutes, we agree that IBM is about to lose the Air Traffic Control contract.

And that DS's hands are tied –they cannot go back to their original script without relief from Williams' directions. But we have some time – the FAA is on the tour.

Pfeiffer and Evans will call Williams.

Those two go into Evans' office to call Williams. Luckily, they find him in his office!

A half-hour goes by...very slowly.

The FAA is on the tour of the production facilities.

Pfeiffer emerges .

"It's back on track. Evans will present at 1:00."

Pfeiffer explains that Williams was concerned about the price for the 9020! So he'd given the word late last night to not have it look too similar to the 360. When Pfeiffer explained to him on the phone call that they were about to be judged 'unresponsive,' Williams had paused for a long time, and then said, "Tell the truth. It's the right thing to do. Present the facts!"

We rejoin the FAA group. The tour had been fine –impressive. But the FAA eyes are either guarded or full of warnings.

Pfeiffer addresses the group to announce yet another change.

"We did not expect to have Bob Evans with us, but he is here, and he'll tie together the facts you've heard this morning."

Evans gets up, and as usual, he has magic!

Once again, I am mesmerized! The magician is casting a spell, relating facts, building hypotheses, showing relationships, cause-and-effects, subtleties, technicalities. He shows how the 9020 was the same as the 360, how it was different.

It is a masterpiece. He spoke for an hour and a half.

At 2:30 we take a break.

It is in the eyes of the government people –we have recovered!
Evans has done it!
Again.

※ ※ ※

At 3, Collins and I drive the FAA people back to LaGuardia.

Before we go, I walk with Pfeiffer. We walk past Manson, who is standing alone.

Pfeiffer stops.

"George, I understand you were just following orders. No harm done."

I am outraged!

*'Why the hell is Ralph so nice? This idiot almost cost us the whole thing! And he LIED to us All morning!!'*

Manson stares through Pfeiffer - into some other world.

"I didn't change the pitch," he says in a monotone.

Pfeiffer and I exchange glances and walk on.

We are firmly "on the shelf".

We are in the competition.

## CONGRESSIONAL PRESSURE

We are picking up comments from the FAA people that there is a lot of congressional pressure for other companies to be awarded the contract.

'Do something.' the FAA people are telling us.

I undertake to convince Pfeiffer that IBM should call one of the U. S. Senators or Congressmen from New York. "Tell the FAA that they should not be pressured by Congress – to go by the merits of the proposals only."

"IBM does not sell that way, Joe."

"We're not asking for support of our stuff – only that no pressure be put on FAA. These are life and death systems. At least equalize the pressure by having the New York guy say, 'Hey I want this to

# A Brawl in IBM - 1964

be clean –up and up –and if there is any congressional pressure, let me know.' Lives are at stake on this stuff, Ralph. "

"No."

I go at him again and again.

"We're being hurt."

"How do you know?"

"Our friends tell us."

"Who?"

I name two or three people.

"What do they want us to do?"

"Have our New York reps weigh in for 'no political decisions'."

Finally Pfeiffer agrees to discuss it with Learson. I am delighted. We take the shuttle to LaGuardia.

And a taxi to 590 Madison Avenue, at 57th Street, to see Learson. We go to 16th floor, the executive suites, and through a set of lush offices. All top executives had an office here as well as in Armonk. Midtown NYC had been Headquarters for many years.

We wait outside Learson's office for a half-hour. The secretary calls, "Mr. Pfeiffer."

"Stay here a minute, Joe; I'll call for you in in a few minutes."

Ten minutes go by.

I hear yelling!

I recognize Pfeiffer's voice yelling.

*'Must be a beauty.'* I think.

I no longer get upset that I am not in the meetings.

And I am totally confident that Pfeiffer will do the job. Pfeiffer is totally prepared for these meetings. He hadn't dropped one yet –if you didn't count the 'orange- soda' meeting.

The yelling continues.

The secretary looks at me - and we both smile.

It is fun, not work. She is bright as hell, and obviously enthralled by Learson's style, as am I.

Finally, after a half-hour, Pfeiffer exits. He is a bit flushed.

"Let's go," to me; "Thank you, Kathy," to the secretary.

"Well?"

"He said we're insane! That IBM doesn't work that way, not only no, but hell, no. He said Watson is in Israel on a trip, and he's going to send him a telegram to stay there till this is over - to keep him out of this mess.'"

I laugh.

It was worth a try. And we tried!

"You were really going at it in there, Ralph."

"What do you mean?" Pfeiffer says, surprised.

"The yelling. I could hear you yelling."

"You could?"

"Yeah."

"Me? Or Vin?"

"I could hear both of you."

An embarrassed grin spreads over Pfeiffer's face.

"I didn't realize I was yelling," he muses.

"You were".

✧ ✧ ✧

Unbeknownst to me, Pfeiffer and Humphrey are considering other sales strategies. IBM and American Airlines have jointly pioneered the airline reservation system called SABRE. SABRE is to handle 65,000 agents on line simultaneously. A revolution in airline reservations. Instant reservations.

IBM is doing the programming for the system - at IBM's own expense. Once American Airlines gets going, all the other airlines should begin to buy systems. So the money expended was well spent. It is a mammoth undertaking, and to this day a huge business venture is based on the software.

But - at this point in time, using the 7090 computer, IBM's largest in-production system, they still do not have the reservation system working.

A. K. Watson, brother of the IBM chairman and chairman of the IBM World Trade Company, apparently has suggested to Humphrey that they get the chairman of American Airlines to call the FAA

Administrator, Najeeb Halaby. And tell him of the massive effort underway to help the airlines, and in so doing show competence in the management of creating large systems.

I find a letter from Humphrey in the files years later. Dated March 10, 1964. The idea is no go. The major FAA concern with IBM is its ability to meet schedules. The original schedule for total system cut-over was May, 1962. This has not yet been accomplished. *22 months late.* The system did not perform as planned, and IBM provided additional storage capacity. American Airlines situation is becoming a success, but not a card to play.

*SABRE is a milestone success of a large software-dominated system. Such efforts being two years schedule is commonplace – to this day.*

☆ ☆ ☆

In March, IBM announces a new, big disk file. For people with systems that need such disks, it is a big step. For insurance companies, social security or IRS, it is almost as important as the 360 computer line itself.

The FAA Sales team look at the specification, and yawns –it is not for us.

I am giving Pfeiffer an update on the FAA- "No news."

"What do they think of our new disk?"

"There are no disks in this system, Ralph."

"The new disks show technological competence across the board. How did they react?"

I see danger ahead. The Executive is talking.

"I haven't told them about the new disk."

"WHAT?"

"I haven't told them."

I am relaxed. *(I am up to my neck in alligators and this is just not important.)*

"Look, young man. It is your job to tell your customers about <u>every</u> announcement IBM makes. You go do your job."

Unconverted, I leave and go through the motions. The FAA yawns when we describe the new disk.

But this little episode isn't over yet.

A full day meeting of all of the Washington Federal sales force is held. About 2 to 3 such meetings of 400 or so sales and technical people were held each year.

I attend. My mind is on the FAA, but I have to keep up with what was going on. I do have other accounts –National Bureau of Standards, the Weather Bureau, the weather branch of NASA.

Suddenly, in front of 400 people, the speaker – Kilner's boss -Weiland - attacks!

Attacks - ME!

*What the hell?!?*

"... and we know that you <u>competent</u> sales people have let your customers know immediately about the new disk –not like some people who –because they have some special situations –have *ignored* their duty."

A small titter goes through the 400. They know it is FAA. Collins is next to me muttering.

*"What the hell is this for? Don't we have enough on our plates?"*
*I don't need a public chastising.*
*FAA is not interested in the goddamn new disk.*

I am sure Weiland has been put up to this by Pfeiffer. The meeting continues. It enters a little rah-rah phase. Weiland is asking for pledges from the floor for sales commitments.

One after another, managers stand.

"I'm so and so and I have the Social Security and my team pledges sale of 40 disks."

"I have ..." and so on.

*Are these plants? Rehearsed?*

I jump up. "Carl, I'm Joe Fox - I have the FAA and I commit... "

I am drowned out by a roar of applause from the sales representatives.

They also judge the reprimand as nonsense.

We never discuss disks again.

April 1, 1964

March ends. We have stayed "on the shelf". We are in the competition.

On April 1, the entire sales force of the IBM Company goes to class for two days to learn the new 360 system. It is to be announced to the world on Monday, April 7, 1964. The proposal team attends the mammoth sessions too. We spend the morning of April 1 with the other 400 Washington, D.C. marketing people at the Twin Bridges Marriott Hotel, across the Potomac in Virginia.

I have difficulty in understanding the presentations. It is not that the instructors are bad, but just that the systems now all have new names, numbers and letter designations.

Before the afternoon session, I call the office, "*to see if FAA had called.*"

"Yes. There is a note here for you to call Mr. Tibbet at FAA."

Tibbet is the procurement man on the bid. ! ?

" April Fool! You're kidding," I say.

"No! No, I'm not!"

I call Joe Tibbet, the FAA negotiator.

"We want to start negotiations with you and with other bidders. No final decision has been made –and the negotiations will help us make that decision. When can you come down?"

"This afternoon."

I do not care if I sound anxious.

"No. I'm tied up. Tomorrow."

"Okay."

"At 10. "

"Okay."

"See you then."

I barely suppress a war hoop. I go back to the meeting and talk to the team and to Kilner.

"Tibbet just called and they are going to start negotiations with a couple of companies, and we are one. We meet tomorrow morning."

We all grin at each other.

All the months, all the fighting, is coming to fruition.

*Our price is in the ballpark. We are "off-the-shelf"! Or On the shelf. Whatever.*

I rush back across the 14th Street Bridge to see Ralph at the 1111 Connecticut Avenue facility.

I had no trouble getting into Pfeiffer's office.

"That's wonderful." grins Ralph.

Then his smile fades.

"Now what? What do we want to do?"

"Get a negotiating team, Ralph. DP is not prepared to do this kind of negotiating."

*99% of all our contracts -even with the government - are standard –agreed to once a year in a marathon negotiation with GSA (–the Government Services Administration) – and that is only for standard -priced, and publicly announced equipment.*

"This contract is not for standard equipment - and the only people who are experienced in negotiating in this arena are the Federal Systems people."

"We can do it," says Pfeiffer.

"We can't," I answer.

"We got us this far."

"We can't negotiate this contract."

"Why?"

"There are a thousand details to a contract of this size. We'd take your whole legal staff and swamp them."

"I'll get you people from Harrison -DS, Group."

"There's the rub. They're not in the same game. It'd be like putting soccer players into a U. S. football game."

"Those guys are good, Joe."

"Yes they are. I said it wrong –they just haven't been in the Contracts-Custom equipment game. They understand the standard GSA contract for the standard announced stuff!"

Pause.

## A Brawl in IBM - 1964

"That is a different game, Ralph. You can be great in one and not even understand the rules of the other."

Ralph is not convinced.

"You can do it." He repeats.

"Ralph," I lean over his desk, "I would if I could. I can't."

"This is your game, Joe. Run it."

"I'll drop it; I'll screw it up. I need the FSD professionals."

"You're good."

"I'm not superman. We have to get one of the FSD negotiators assigned. Now! The crisis is here."

"No! Not yet. You and Jack Ford go down there tomorrow and see what the issues are. Then I'll talk to you about a team from FSD. Let's be sure it's needed before we ask."

Ford is the IBM Federal Region Lawyer. He and I go down to FAA the next morning.

"You took a lot of exceptions considering this is a competitive procurement," comments one of the FAA contract people.

"Well, it is our standard line."

Ford makes it clear-that IBM will in no way give to FAA cost data on the computers to be procured. The FAA says that would not be a problem.

The issue of third-party liability comes up. Ford mentions that IBM would very much like to have a clause in the contract which states that IBM would be indemnified against damages for any accident.

The FAA lawyers and negotiators nod. They understand. They sympathize. But they state that the FAA has no legal authority to indemnify any contractor against liability. An Act of Congress would be required before they could do so. And Congress is enmeshed in the Civil Rights Bill. They state they have requests for this indemnity often, but no one has insisted upon such indemnification.

Ford points out that Atomic Energy Commission and some of the military agencies do indemnify their contractors. FAA understands, but they do not feel that this is necessary for FAA conduct of business, and they repeat, "We do not have the legal authority to indemnify". Ford drops the issue. Ford later tells me not to worry about it.

At 1 PM we go to a second meeting with FAA procurement, with Joe Tippet and his boss, Ray Mulari, and an FAA lawyer.

Pfeiffer, Whitney and Collins join us for this one. There are technical FAA people there. It is a friendly meeting. Tippet wants to know if the IBM statements in the proposal were firm.

Ford states we will have to go through them one by one.

There are a few technical questions – easy stuff.

They want to understand IBM's organization. Who is to negotiate?

I shoot Pfeiffer a glance.

He begs the question.

Oooops ! ! The front-end equipment is in question -the units that connect to the radars, and the telemetry and other devices. The part of the computer that accepts and gives information to the outside world is a critical part and usually very complex. In most new large systems, the details of the data will not be known until well into the project. It will be radar data, yes, but will there be 18 binary digits (bits) of information per radar scan; or 20 bits? Will the range information be first in the stream of data? Be before the altitude or after?

To avoid buying the wrong equipment, the government usually contracts for these "unknown" boxes on a CPFF basis (cost plus fixed fee).

Thus, the bidder estimates that the box to handle the radar data inputs will cost about $75,000, and with an 8% profit. The government writes the contract that way, with the agreement that the company will allow the government to audit all costs to assure that all costs are justified. If it turns out that they (the government and the contractor) have underestimated the job, and it costs $150,000 (twice the estimate) the government pays the $150,000 plus the originally estimated profit amount –8%. The contractor is now only making a 4% profit. This is CPFF.

CPFF is the only fair way to procure these items. Small companies frequently go out of business accepting such development contracts on a fixed price basis.

But IBM does not give the government visibility into the costs of its commercial line. It does give the costs for equipment built in the Federal Systems Division.

## A Brawl in IBM - 1964

BUT WAIT - IBM had bid the unknown boxes on a fixed price basis.

TILT!

We had seen this hole in offering and had spent some time worrying and thinking about it, but to no resolution. It was put on hold –and never resolved inside the company.

Now, on Thursday afternoon, at 1:00, it blows up.

"How much is your cost estimate for the PAM boxes?" asks the FAA. Peripheral Adapter Modules.

"Well, we can't go CPFF on those!" I reply.

There is a silence - a stunned silence.

Whitney speaks up.

"We have a way of fix-pricing small segments of the PAM, and giving you a set of options so that you can pick and choose, combine and delete, and build up a PAM from the pieces."

The FAA technical people whisper to each other for a few minutes. One speaks.

"This is crazy. We can't do business this way. Maybe we could if in your proposal you had described this building-block approach, but it is not even mentioned."

The speaker holds up his palms in a gesture of bewilderment.

Whitney again.

"We can describe the building-block approach, but we'll have to get the engineers down from Poughkeepsie. How about first thing tomorrow?"

He sounds like he knows what he is doing. I don't.

But Whitney is good. Difficult- but good.

The FAA evaluation team looks at each other - and says OK.

What could they say? If IBM could explain it tomorrow morning, great.

We talk in the hall, outside the meeting room.

"I've called Cousins and Keeley," says Whit. "They are coming down with two or three others. We'll meet them at 1111 Connecticut Avenue at 6:00."

At 5:45, in come the engineers. They understand the problem, have been discussing it on the way down. All they need to do, they said, was to explain a basic building-block plan to the FAA, where the building blocks are all priced and described clearly.

The problem was the combinations, the number of combinations.

"You guys leave us alone," says Whitney. "I'll give you progress reports."

I remember the long weekend at Islip.

The technical group is using the executive offices on the third and top floor of 1111 Connecticut Avenue. Collins and I camp out in a nearby office.

About 7 P M Pfeiffer comes in, returning to his office from someplace.

I explain to him what is going on.

Ralph wishes us well, and asks if he could help.

No, nothing to be done.

The engineers are deep in discussion and debate. Whitney leads it.

It gets to be 8 P. M.

I call home – I'll be late; very late!

Collins gets some sandwiches for the team.

Ralph goes to his hotel –the Mayflower, next door, and comes back around 8:30 in a tuxedo. He is going –as IBM's representative –to some formal dinner. He says he'll stop in after the dinner. His home is still in the Westchester area. His house is abuilding in Montgomery County Maryland, but it is not ready yet,

Hours go by.

I go in and listen a few times to the technical discussion and I understand very little of it.

"Are you making progress, Whit?"

"We're getting there, we're getting there!"

About 1 AM, Pfeiffer comes back, still in a tuxedo.

"You guys are still here?"

"We'll be here a while, Ralph," I say. "Maybe all night."

Pfeiffer sits in his office for an hour. He is a picture sitting there in his tuxedo in the middle of the night! He comes out at 2 AM.

"I'm going. I'll be back at 7 – I hope you guys get some sleep."

Over and over. 4 AM.

# A Brawl in IBM - 1964

"This could be a show-stopper," says Collins.

"Yeah," I say.

"We're in a Catch-22. We can't give cost data – and we can't fix-price the thing because it doesn't know what it has to talk to!"

"Yeah."

"It could be over."

5 AM.

At 5 AM, Whitney stops into the office Collins and I are in.

"We've got it," he says, and briefly described the modular, building-block approach. I understand a bit of it.

At about 6 AM, Collins mentions that the new approach has not been priced, nor sanctioned, by Manson.

My spirits sink! I'd forgotten that part. I'd been concentrating on how to sell the thing to the FAA –I'd forgotten we had to sell it to IBM!

Pfeiffer comes in at 8. At 8:30 we call Manson.

He agrees!

And he agrees he'd do it within the cost limits of the old approach! No need to re-price.

Now to get FAA to like it.

We wash up and shave with the one razor one of the Poughkeepsie people has brought. We look slightly seedy and rumpled, but there is no choice –we must go right to FAA.

"Whit," I say. "You carry the meeting. You run it –it's yours."

"Of course it is." he says.

Pfeiffer comes with us.

We present to the FAA evaluation team. Whitney controls the meeting. It goes beautifully. They'd come up with a marvelously simple set of building blocks that fit what the FAA has to get into the computers. Whitney's years of working with the FAA and his deep knowledge of the Islip system are paying off!

The FAA people are nodding approval by 10:30.

No one tells the FAA we have been up all night - that might shake confidence a bit. And the FAA people do not seem to notice our rumpled looks. I sit along the wall next to Pfeiffer. We are out of the main line of communications. Since the only issue was the I/O system, I do not have to interact but once an hour or so. I keep dozing off when things get deep. Pfeiffer nudges me awake.

At one point, Pfeiffer points to my ankle, crossed over my other leg.

"What?" I ask.

"Your socks."

I am confused. I raise my eyebrows and make a confused face.

"They're too short." They are ankle length. My leg skin showed between the sock and the pant edge. I look at Pfeiffer's ankle. No skin showed there; Ralph had on calf-length socks.

It occurs to me that Ralph is trying to help me.

Image was so important in IBM. So important!

"Right," I say, "I got it."

That weekend I'll buy calf-length socks!

At lunch, Pfeiffer tells me to come with him to White Plains on the 3 PM Shuttle –"to see Learson –to get the FSD negotiation team on board."

My heart sinks.

I feel like a wet rag. I love meetings with Learson, but not today!

"Ralph, you go –I'll be in your office and if you need me –just call."

"You're going. I need you."

"Ralph, I've been up all night! And it is Friday, for God's sake."

"Joe, you have been at me forever about getting a negotiation team. It's a crucial meeting. You are coming with me."

The FAA meeting ends well; it is 2:40. We have survived the fixed price PAM issue.

*Whitney is the hero, and in retrospect I wonder why I never even thought of having him join the effort earlier. It never entered my mind.*

*He is a mixed blessing in his work. It is always a battle with his outsized ego, but as this effort by him shows, it is worth the effort to cope with that ego.*

*Collins was my conscience most of the time, (like it or not) and he never suggested adding Whitney. We were focused on the multiprocessor technology challenge and Oldani was focused on the processor speed and*

# A Brawl in IBM - 1964

*capacity. We had no one looking at the front-end channels and devices. Whitney saved us.*

Pfeiffer and I grab a cab to make the 3 PM Shuttle at National Airport. That will get us to White Plains at about 5:15.

*"Another Friday night and I'm heading the wrong way. My poor family."*

"National Airport. We're getting the 3 o'clock Shuttle." Ralph tells the driver - who must be 80 years old. He drives at a snail's pace. We creep along. I think I might escape yet.

"I'M A BIG TIPPER," yells Ralph to the driver, apparently assuming he is also hard of hearing.

"I'VE GOT TO MAKE THAT FLIGHT."

This seems to penetrate; we move a bit faster –but still slower than 90% of all traffic.

We are going to have to run for the Shuttle!

"Ralph, I'll pay the cab. You run. I'll run after I pay the cab. If I miss the plane, I'll be in your office here."

"If you miss the plane, get on the 4 o'clock."

There is no way out, except to refuse –and that never enters my mind.

I pay the cab, catch up with Pfeiffer.

We would get to White Plains at about 5:15. Ralph's car is at LaGuardia.

The old four-engine, propeller-driven, three-tailed Super Constellation drones through the northeast sky. Pfeiffer works on his mail; I sleep a bit. I am very tired –I've been going since 7 AM Thursday, and the tension has been heavy.

We start down.

Suddenly, we are in <u>turbulence.</u>

The plane pitches and bucks and groans. Down, up, down.

Suddenly, its engines go to full power – it shudders and writhes!

I am petrified!

Pfeiffer is deep into his paper work! The plane slowly gains altitude.

"Ah, folks," the pilot comes on the speaker, - nonchalant, of course. "We've got crosswinds at about 50-60 knots. We'll go around and have you down in ten minutes."

My palms are sweating.

Pfeiffer works on his mail.

They come around –and the same damn thing!

Down, down, then full power. It struggles to gain altitude.

This is a very old, big, unwieldy, four-engine, propeller airplane.

The cabin is deadly quiet. You can feel the fear.

"Ah, folks." He is back again. Nonchalant –of course - they practice that.

"We're going on over to JFK. They are reporting less wind, and we'll have a much longer runway. We'll put on full throttle and put her down!"

The tension eases a bit.

We make a gamey, full throttle landing at Kennedy. As the plane touches down, the sigh of relief from a hundred-plus people whooshes through the cabin.

Some people clap; Pfeiffer looks up from his mail, raises his fist and intones, "Yeah, yeah!"- like a cheerleader!

*'He's human after all.'*

We call White Plains, tell Learson's secretary we'll be a little late, catch a cab to LaGuardia and pick up Pfeiffer's car.

As we walk into the IBM DP HQ building at 112 East Post Road, everyone else is streaming out. It is 5:45 <u>Friday</u> night. The weekend.

*'Oh damn,' I still have to go back to Washington in the damned wind and the tin can Super Constellation.'*

I toy with staying overnight, but I've not seen much of my family. I will stomach the wind.

We arrive outside Learson's office - a borrowed one- he is visiting the building - and say hello to the secretary.

## A Brawl in IBM - 1964

"Oh, Mr. Pfeiffer," she says, "Mr. Cary would like to see you before you see Mr. Learson. He said to go on down to his office." Frank Cary is Pfeiffer's boss. Pfeiffer beckons me to follow. We walk to the opposite end of the building.

I am curious about this request from Cary. Pfeiffer works for Cary, but Cary has not been involved at all on the FAA effort. I had gotten a letter from Cary when we had successfully got the proposal submitted, but I have never met him.

(Cary will become chairman of IBM in January 1974, succeeding Learson.)

We go right into Frank Cary's office. I feel a little disheveled. I've been in the same clothes since 7 AM Thursday morning.

Perhaps because of the weariness, I find myself standing too close physically to Ralph and Frank. Ralph introduces me to Cary. We shake hands.

"What are you meeting with Vin on, Ralph?"

"We want to have FSD negotiate the contract for FAA. We think the people at Group are fine, but this is a very complex <u>Federal</u> buy and FSD is far more capable in this area."

*I love it – he is using the right words.*

"Well, I'll join you in the meeting." says Cary.
Ralph beams.
"Fine."
"But we may get into personalities, so Joe should wait here."
I suppress a smile.
I think, *'Ha. You don't know how bad Ralph wants me in this meeting.'*
"Fine," replies Ralph, and he and Cary walk out of the office.

*What happened to 'I need you? It's <u>your</u> meeting'?*
I just stand there.
It is 6 PM. Friday night. *And then I realize - I do not have a car to get to LaGuardia. Are the planes even flying?*
I pace for five or ten minutes.
Then I go to the reception area for the office Learson is using.

The secretary has left. I am too tired to read. I sit and glower.

Jack Ford, the Washington IBM lawyer who had been with me at the FAA meeting on April first, walks up. He's been in White Plains on other business. I like Ford.

"Holy mackerel, Joe, you look like you just lost your best friend! Cheer up - it can't be that bad."

I tell him the story.

"...And I've been up all night, Jack. And I've got to go back to D.C. yet tonight."

"That's awful, Joe. Listen, I've got to go back tonight too. I'll wait for you and we'll go together. I have a car. Maybe we'll even get some food. Come get me at legal when you are ready."

I have a ride to the airport and a companion for the trip. I feel better.

I sit outside the Learson office. 6:30.

At 6:40, Vin, Ralph and Frank come out.

All smiles; all relaxed.

*"No trouble here!"* I conclude.

Learson beams at me. He holds out his hand.

"Congratulations, Joe. You did it. You won the FAA order."

"Thank you, Vin," and I smile, as he pumps my hand. "But we don't have it yet. We could still screw it up."

"You won't; you won't." Vin smiles. "Why didn't you join us in our meeting?"

Learson gestures to the office behind him.

"You're not afraid of me, are you?"

Still smiling, happy.

My mind is formulating nine different answers, all of which clearly cast Cary as a villain, when I feel a vise-like arm encircle my shoulder. Ralph has me in a just-short-of-ferocious clamp. I am being tugged toward the elevator.

"This man's afraid of nothing, Vin; nothing." says Ralph.

He pushes me into the elevator, whispers in my ear.

"Everything you wanted - we got. I'll see you Monday; Frank and I have more business. Good night."

The elevator doors close.

# A Brawl in IBM - 1964

Pfeiffer has saved me. I had been about to 'stick my finger in Cary's eye' –which would have served no purpose whatsoever. And which would have been a mistake I might not be able to overcome.

I meet Ford; we eat a light dinner and we have a surprisingly smooth flight to D.C.

I get home at midnight.

White calls me.

"What's happening?"

I relate the events of the last week.

"Hank, be ready for a request to take over the negotiation."

"We're ready. I've talked to Spaulding." (The president of the Federal Systems Division). "We'll spring Laguzza, and maybe me."

Laguzza is a great contracts man – this is good news.

"You, Hank? Why do we need you?"

"Shut up. You need me. You just don't know it. Who's going to run this thing after we win it?"

"Not me. I want out."

"I'm going to run it. From FSD. As a project."

"That's good."

"Yeah, so I'll get aboard now."

"Good."

# APRIL 7 IBM ANNOUNCES THE 360

IBM announces the 360! Meetings are held in all major cities. A new generation of computers has arrived. Press Conferences are held in New York, where Watson, Bob Evans, and Fred Brooks describe to throngs of news people and business invitees the family concept and the new computers. For Evans, it is a monumental achievement.

For the FAA team, the announcement is very important. It adds credibility to the 9020. The same instruction set, components, devices! All are now the IBM standard. And the announced prices are a total of 2 million dollars *less* than those in the 9020 bid –a price reduction we rush to the FAA! These are prices for standard tape drives and memories and the like, bid for every one of the En Route Centers.

Pfeiffer tells me that after the announcement, he and I are going to Westchester again –<u>by train</u>!!

We are going to meet with all the other major parties of all the divisions and Group Staff and Corporate Staff and be sure that everyone agrees to the new FSD role as the negotiation team. As we roll through New Jersey, I tell Pfeiffer I want White to run the negotiation.

"A man named Jim Laguzza is the chief of the negotiators at the FSD, Rockville, Maryland, location. He'll be the one to negotiate, but White should run it."

"I understand why you want Laguzza, but why White? He'll push you out. You're abdicating?"

"There is so much to do, Ralph. If Laguzza and I disagree on an issue, I'm in trouble. He's there at my request, and I can't disown him. But he has no allegiance to me. White can control Laguzza, and I can not."

"But White'll be in charge."

"I can control him."

I was abdicating! I was replacing one czar with a second; White is moving into Humphrey's spot.

## A Brawl in IBM - 1964

Why didn't I grab it for myself?

I didn't want it! I correctly foresaw that whoever headed the negotiation <u>should</u> be the FAA program manager for the next several years –and I was tired.

And White would be better than I during the wrap-up of the negotiations –and better as the program manager. White had lived through dozens such efforts; he was an FSD veteran. I was from DP, the commercial marketing division, with the standard product line. I had touched on and witnessed negotiations of special systems –but I'd never lived through one!

It was not all downhill –not yet! There are still 'show-stoppers' on the road ahead. I just didn't know how many!

## FEDERAL DIVISION- AND CORPORATE - TAKE CONTROL

I meet Pfeiffer the next morning at Armonk IBM Headquarters, April 8. I had made some flip charts to present to the group.

It is a high-level group indeed!

Learson and Gibson, the two Group VPs. And Spaulding, the President of FSD. And Kennard, President of DS, to whom Evans reports; and Manny Piore, Spaulding's boss. And Dick Bullen, financial VP of IBM. I meet him for the first time.

I bring them up to date on where things stand.

"Time is of the essence. FAA wants to work concurrently on technical issues and terms and conditions.

They must sign a contract by June 30, the end of the fiscal year- or they lose their funding. FAA says they are negotiating with other companies, but they are not."

Eyebrows go up. Surprise. A few "hms."

Learson is not going to let that pass unchallenged.

"How do you know? Did they tell you?"

"No. We can tell. They are spending all their time with us. They have no people to be conducting a simultaneous negotiation, and we can tell from the way they talk."

They accept that. I have credibility.

"FAA hopes to have a contract in two to three weeks. The sooner they sign –the earlier they get a machine.

"The 360 announcement reduced our price $2,000,000. We'll go to double-density tape drives, and that'll save us another $300K off our price."

I cover some technical details, and then put up a chart –which states that the present organization shouldn't negotiate the contract. I describe the proposed liaison to FAA.

IBM PROJECT OFFICE
Promised in Proposal -17 people – charged to Division overhead.
Full Time, Authoritative, FAA Contact. Many small decisions some major ones.
Several Contracts
Several IBM Divisions
Deal with Other NAS Contractors, Subcontracts, Legal Issues
Constant Changes to Contract
Reliability Model and Definitions for Acceptance Tests
"No Marketing Support for This System"
Present Organization Cannot Do This

Pfeiffer states that DP wants FSD to do the negotiations – specifically White and Laguzza.

Spaulding puts on a show of reluctance.

"These aren't spare guys you are asking for – White and Laguzza are stars. It is going to hurt bad to give them up to this."

But it is accepted - Laguzza and White are to the negotiating team full time.

I wonder why they needed the meeting at all. They all agreed to everything; it seem as though it had all been agreed to in advance.

Ah ha. Not so fast. There are two new conditions. Corporate Finance and Corporate Legal each wanted to put one of their corporate level specialists onto the negotiating team.

This is quite a departure.

"Is that a problem, Joe?" asks Ralph, privately, at a break.

# A Brawl in IBM - 1964

"I don't think so. It should be a time saver. Besides we won't have many issues."

I had never been more wrong.

✯ ✯ ✯

Now there is a major difference in the effort. The professionals have arrived!

White and Laguzza had been through huge negotiations –and they had a willing, supportive professional staff in FSD in the Washington area to do the necessary back-up work.

For the duration, the new team was:

White -FAA Project Manager
Joe Fox -Marketing manager
Laguzza -Negotiator
Collins -Marketing
Joe McCann -Legal –from Corporate Legal, recently from FSD
Peter Wall -Finance –Corporate Finance, a FSD veteran
Whitney, Kowalke, Oldani -Technical, Washington
Davis, Burnstine, Keeley, -Technical, Poughkeepsie

The technical representation is to cycle from Claude Davis to Keeley to Burnstine to Whitney to whomever. As needed.

Both corporate representatives have been in FSD during their careers –there is no learning time for them. McCann had, only a month earlier, moved from FSD, Kingston, to corporate in Westchester.

## A NEW TEAM

Then on Friday, April 11 White, Collins, Laguzza and I are on the Shuttle back to New York, to meet with McCann and Weil and Group Finance, and go over the items on the table.

It goes VERY slowly! A foretaste?

"Is Humphrey still involved?" Collins had asked.

"No. He's disappeared from this one. But he did a great job for us. Managed a lot of stuff in Corporate that I would not have been able to do."

We are street fighters among wizards – Humphrey leaves the FAA effort at this point – and he too is awarded a United States Medal of Technology. This is for his achievements over many years, and the bulk of the announcement states it is for his work at the SEI at Carnegie Mellon University.

White has been out of the FAA furor since September. He'd not been in the weekly Learson meetings, the firehouse, the design, and the FAA technical meetings. He'd been in just once, to testify to the research committee, on the day President Kennedy was killed. I am delighted he is back. Things were piling up, dozens of details.

Individually, they are good. As a team, they are superb. We leave the details to the experts. There is little wasted effort. A myriad of items that had to be reduced to clauses and statements of fact on paper get onto paper.

"I was right," I think as I watch the size of Laguzza's "control book" grow beyond one inch thick. The control book contained every clause and everyone's position on that clause –FAA's, FSD's, Legal's, DS's, Finance's.

When I was first 'allowed' to sit in on a negotiation, in 1959 at the Air Force base in Rome New York, I'd been told, pointedly, not to speak. I was DP- sales; FSD –federal - was the negotiator.

I was shocked at the nasty, blunt talk between the customer and IBM. After the meeting, I'd expressed dismay.

"You can't talk that way to a customer," I wailed.

The older negotiator, whom I respected, explained.

"This is not sales, Joe. It's negotiation. There is a point at which both sides will be satisfied, but it is found through a process of give and take, of bluffing, intimidation, and bravado. It's an art form."

I had now sat through enough such sessions to realize that indeed that was the way it was done. I didn't like it, but it worked.

I had once sat in on negotiations for seven hours, as the two sides debated endlessly one clause.

6 PM. 7 PM. Over and over the same ground –on a tax clause!

# A Brawl in IBM - 1964

At 8, one side suddenly switched to the price. Bing, bing, bing. In rapid sequence, the price changed. Accepted. That was it. It was over.

They never went back to the tax clause.

Outside I asked what happened to the tax clause they'd spent all those hours on.

"Oh, hell, that was a decoy. We were filibustering, getting them tired. Then we switched to the real issue."

Both sides play these games.

✲ ✲ ✲

Laguzza was the head of the negotiation section of a large part of the Federal Systems Division. He is smart as hell, and nimble minded. He is thorough and professional and accomplished. The first team is finally on the field.

Manson never came to any meetings. Indeed, he seemed to disappear. I talked to him only once or twice. I was happy to "see his back".

## NEGOTIATING WITH FAA – AND IBM

Laguzza fires off dozens of memos.

Every day during the week of April 14 we meet with the FAA.

On Monday, April 21 we take the Shuttle to LaGuardia and meet with Group Finance again.

Finance, we find, is <u>AGAINST</u> EVERYTHING!

"They are not being reasonable on anything," Laguzza states flatly.

We shuttle back to Washington and meet Tuesday through Friday with FAA again. All day, every day.

There are now "sides" being formed –"our side" and "their side".

IBM Westchester is <u>against</u> this bid. They are fighting everything!

Third Party Liability comes up again. The lawyers explain to us that juries are awarding huge settlements in cases against manufacturers of products. For example, in a General Motors case, Buick had to pay a huge sum for "defective brakes" even though the car had been in use for several years. In the accident, there were two parties. Buick Division became the third party in the suit, and thus the name Third Party Liability. In case of a mid-air collision, then, airline companies and the Government would be the first and second parties, and then IBM could become the third.

"Suppose we do build a defective machine?" asks one of the working team.

"Then we pay. That is defective workmanship. But the court cases tell us that even if there is no defective workmanship, the jury is awarding penalties simply because the company is rich –richer than the airline, say. They get the 'deep pockets' to pay".

"But FAA says they <u>can't</u> indemnify. They do not have the legal authority to do so.

The solution of getting liability insurance is explored.

Corporate Legal checks with the IBM insurance people. IBM has $40,000,000 product liability coverage, which would cover this system the day it went into operation.

This seemed to solve the problem. But no, now the Data Systems Division wanted to (I) increase the coverage, and (2) *charge the new premium to the FAA.*

This is nit picking –it means we would have to change the price yet again.

And they weren't talking about that big a premium. IBM already had a lot of insurance. The premium wouldn't be but another 25 to 50 thousand dollars –and on a bid of $95 million, that is peanuts.

We argue that –and get nowhere.

It is as though the staff wants to <u>punish </u>FAA –as though FAA has been responsible for the jury and judgments in this case.

April is trailing to an end –and there is not much visible progress in negotiation!

✯ ✯ ✯

# A Brawl in IBM - 1964

April ends –troubled but happy.

We are in negotiation, in contention; our price is in the competitive range!

The 360 has been announced.

We fixed the pricing problem on the front-end input/output units.

We brought in the professional negotiators!

But –a big BUT- the IBM legal and financial people are causing trouble.

※ ※ ※

This is easy duty for me. I am coasting; the others are doing the work. White and Laguzza are spearheading the negotiations, making the key decisions and coordinating with the corporation. The technical team is more than competent to do its own thing.

I am almost an observer.

There seems no danger; it seems to be inexorable. Oh, finance and legal are being difficult, but they would get out of the way soon. The crest of this wave of energy built between the two large organizations would sweep it all along. The die was cast; the switch was thrown.

All we had to do was not let a major screw-up occur. Without a major screw-up, these two bureaucracies would find a way to contract.

"All the battles have been won!"

I feel good. There had been so many brawls; so many close calls.

But ... I am naïve.

# THIRD PARTY LIABILITY

DS Legal is NOT about to simply accept the FAA assertion that they did not have authority to indemnify.

The DS lawyer writes to McCann, the corporate lawyer who is now on the negotiating team. The DS lawyer is more senior and has more clout than McCann.

McCann answers that insurance would take care of it.

He copies Laguzza, who then writes to the DS lawyer.

TO: Mr. G. M. Newmann (DS Legal)

Attached ... is a copy of McCann's memorandum dated April 27, 1964, which covers the subject of third party liability.

I feel that the result of Mr. McCann's conversation with Mr. P. J. Hopkins (insurance) eliminates the problem of third party liability.

If you do not agree I would appreciate your so advising me.

McCann's letter said IBM would get insurance! Laguzza's said, "...eliminates...third party liability."

But legal is not going to let it end.
Group legal answers Laguzza.

REFERENCE: Your Memorandum dated May 4, 1964
I do not agree.
G. M. Newmann

He offers no clause. No reason for his position. WHAT?
I had met Newmann in January, during the effort to send in the final price bid. We'd gotten along well.

# A Brawl in IBM - 1964

I speak with him now, by phone, trying to break the jam.
"George, FAA can't indemnify."
"Then FAA has a problem."
I stay friendly –it takes effort.
"<u>We've</u> got a problem, George. <u>We've</u> been trying to get this contract for a long time."
"Then get FAA to give us an indemnification."
"I <u>can't</u> George –you've got me in an absurd loop."
"FAA has a problem."

*Ford's (Washington DP Legal) prediction - on April 1st when he and I first met with the FAA,- was wrong.*

*In meetings, we point out over and over that IBM has no such protection on the 1401-1410 at Islip, nor did the competitors. No one in Westchester pays any attention.*

*The issue is 'new', they say; the law has been changing; the courts are 'punishing' big corporations.*

The third party liability issue is now a monster.
"We are going to lose on this issue, Ralph."
Pfeiffer has heard something like this from me on a dozen different issues.
"What do you want me to do?"
"Go to Learson."
He mimics me in a singsong: " 'Go to Learson, go to Learson.' Don't you know any other solution, Joe. 'Go to Learson.' We've got to bring him solutions."
"If I had solutions, Ralph, I wouldn't need Learson. I'd be Learson."
Pfeiffer glares at me.

✫ ✫ ✫

On May 14, Laguzza writes in his status summary:
"15. <u>Third Party Liability</u>

DSD Legal will provide us with a copy of the proposed clause covering this problem and which must be incorporated in any resulting contract."

"I'm worried, Hank."

"Why, Joe?" ".

"I just heard McCann –(the corporate lawyer assigned to our team) talking to Trimble on the phone. He called him 'Mr. Trimble.'"

"So?"

"Hank, it tells me he doesn't know Trimble. We're going to have to whisper to Trimble now and then, off line, private. We're going to have to say, 'Hank, look...!' - and Trimble has got to listen. Otherwise he'll try to stand in front of this speeding train, thinking that it'll stop –like 99% of them have done. And he'll get smashed –and WE may get smashed too."

"What? WHAT?"

"Hank, the guy calls him 'Mr. Trimble.' No one calls anyone 'Mister' in IBM."

"Joe's good. He's a good troop. "

"I agree. And we can't change him for a different lawyer. Not now. But, Hank, watch out."

"Relax. You're seeing ghosts."

"I hope so."

✳ ✳ ✳

There are two old contractual items outstanding between FAA and IBM: The outright purchase of an IBM 7090 computer installed at Atlantic City, in FAA's facility there, and 2. The outright purchase of the 1410/1401 at FAA in Islip, Long Island.

I had been trying to clear up these items with Joe Tibbet-FAA Procurement - for several weeks.

I had gone out on a limb and committed in writing that the purchase date would be March 1 for the 7090 and April 22 for the 1410/1401. No rental fees after these dates. It was now mid-May.

# A Brawl in IBM - 1964

I was on shaky ground –the rent billing had been stopped on the earlier dates –and the longer Mr. Tibbet delayed giving me something in writing, the more stretched my neck became.

On May 14th, Tibbet calls.

I say, "I hope you're calling me about the 1401/1410."

Tibbet says, "No. I'm calling in regard to NAS. "

"Oh, hell," I say.

Tibbet is taken aback.

I quickly add, "What's up?"

"We want to sign a <u>'letter contract'</u> and we want to do it today or tomorrow, at the latest," he says.

I am speechless. This is too good to believe.

"What?"

"We want you to sign a letter contract."

"Serious?"

"Very."

"Call you back."

I run into the office where Laguzza and White are talking. We are all in the Connecticut avenue DS office so as to be close to the FAA buildings.

"They want us to sign a letter contract!"

They look at each other.

"It's too good to be true," says Laguzza.

We decide to head for the Shuttle – we'd have to get Corporate Finance and Corporate Legal to agree.

I explain to Collins the significance of a 'letter contract.'

"It is a great deal for the contractor, for us. On many negotiable items we now can hang tougher, because a letter contract is a short letter to us from the government authorizing us to spend money. It's a bit rare. It is often called a 'license to steal'. They get committed to us. We're spending money, underway. They are obligated to pay us what we spend. It gets harder and harder for them to back away from us with every day that passes. We become entrenched as we negotiate."

Laguzza has called the FAA contracts people, but he cannot pin down why they are willing to give IBM a letter contract. FAA indicates that since the delivery of the first machine was 19 months after receipt of contract, that maybe they'd get the machine earlier by signing a letter contract a few months before a definitized contract.

"I don't believe that's why, though," muses Laguzza.

The taxi goes down Connecticut Avenue to 17th Street to the Tidal Basin, over to 14th Street, and over to National Airport. It is a gorgeous day, bright and cool. The forsythia has begun to pop. We get the shuttle.

Obstructionism awaits us in Westchester, N. Y.

Finance does not like the idea of a letter contract - and the delivery is not going to improve with an earlier contract. The delivery is fixed.

"Tell them the delivery is quoted based on a June contract."

Laguzza and White look at me.

Their eyes said: 'Want to fight that?'

"Let's live with that - for a moment", I say.

I sense there are more problems.

"There are several items that must be in a letter contract," says the head of Group Finance.

"First, IBM will give no cost visibility into the product. No cost reviews. This is commercial product plants, commercial people, commercial components —we do not want to show our costs to FAA."

Laguzza immediately agrees.

"We agree. We will be able to take the letter contract and not give costs."

"It must be in the letter," Finance insists.

"Why?" Laguzza is puzzled.

"Why not?"

Oh –oh.

"Look," Laguzza explains, "we give away nothing – NOTHING –when we sign the letter contract. We can put in the DEFINITIVE contract (which would come later) a clause that protects us."

"How long after the letter contract?"

"Three months –six, maybe."

"No. No work, period, without that clause."

Two sides look at each other.

# A Brawl in IBM - 1964

Stalemate.

"What other clauses?" Laguzza asks. The meeting has turned somber.

"All computers must be under one contract."

I remember this as a Williams' dictate in January. No reporter could look at a profit report and slam IBM for unconscionable profit on the last machine, and ignore a huge loss on the first machine. IBM was gambling that <u>all</u> the computers at all sites would be bought and installed. If not, IBM could lose a lot –millions.

Again, there is agreement that that condition will apply, but not now, not in the letter contract.

"Let it wait" – Laguzza stresses over and over that IBM will be in the driver's seat.

"I'll guarantee you those clauses in the final contract," he says.

Finance insists -" In the letter contract! In the first one we sign."

We leave very down. We check into a motel and in the morning take the shuttle back to Washington.

We try to convince the FAA to put these conditions into the letter contract.

Laguzza struggles valiantly, to no avail.

FAA tells us "You are introducing clauses that we'll have to run through the system. You are not accepting a letter contract." Almost Laguzza's exact words of the previous evening.

We rush to the airport –yet again, jump on the shuttle -and up to Harrison. We meet from 6 till 10 with Group Finance and the lawyers. Stalemate.

We get the last shuttle back to the DC and drive home to the suburbs - and to FAA in the morning to start the cycle again. We are living on hot dogs at the airports.

Collins, Kowalke, Oldani Whitney are solving technical issues.

The "letter contract" offer had come in on a Tuesday. We'd rushed up to Harrison, back to Washington, back to Harrison. Back to Washington again.

On Friday night, we arrive home about 10. Exhausted. With no progress!

On Saturday, May 16, the negotiating team meets with Don Spaulding, President of the Federal Systems Division, from 10 AM to 5 PM.

We go over the terms that "must be put into the letter contract." Maybe Spaulding can break through.

On Sunday, May 18, we work all day in Washington with the engineers from Poughkeepsie. It is the day the Salk polio vaccine is being give out, free, by the Government. We all troop down to the high school ad-hoc vaccination center, around the corner from the IBM building and we all get inoculated. We work until 10 PM.

On Monday, May 19, the negotiating team meets with FAA. Now the FAA lawyers are objecting to a letter contract.

Mulari, FAA's chief of contracts, is incredible that IBM has proposed "changes" provisions. He shakes his head that IBM will not leap at a letter contract!

When we were alone, Laguzza muses.

"You know, we're really negotiating with IBM, not the FAA."

"What do you mean?" I ask.

"We have no problem with FAA. We could finish this thing in a week! A week! ...if IBM Finance and Legal would get reasonable."

Now we are bringing everything to Corporate Finance! And Corporate Finance will not accept any questions from the negotiating team until Group Finance has reviewed it and taken a position. Group finance services DP and the product divisions.

We go over and over the same conversation. Over and over with two levels of IBM staff. No progress at all is being made.

Spaulding acts!

We are to see Al Williams, president of IBM, the next day.

At last, progress! ? Perhaps.

# IBM'S CORPORATE OPERATING BOARD -The "COB"

We get the Shuttle, Tuesday, May 20.

We arrive at Armonk to see Williams and are told to go to Yorktown Heights to meet with the Corporate Operating Board. The new IBM Headquarters building at Armonk is still under partial construction and IBM Corporate personnel are scattered all over Westchester county. The Yorktown Heights facility is the location of the IBM Research Organization. Recently formed, this "COB" is a convocation of <u>all</u> IBM Corporate Vice Presidents.

There is little time to get to Yorktown.

We rush out of the new Armonk headquarters. We have three cars – Pfeiffer and I are in one; White and Spaulding are in a second; Quinn, the Corporate financial man, is in a third.

Pfeiffer speeds through the narrow roads of Westchester.

I am totally lost, happy that Pfeiffer is driving. At one stop sign, I see the car Spaulding and White are in - crossing in front of us, <u>right to left</u>.

At the same instant, at the same intersection, I see the car Quinn is in crossing in front of us, <u>left to right.</u>

We continue straight.

Three cars rushing to the same place are going in three different directions.

"Ralph, Ralph…"

"I see them."

We all make it to the meeting on time.

Pfeiffer tells me, "Say nothing unless I signal you".

I am awed by the clout in the room!

T. V. Learson, A. K. Watson, Manny Piore, Gil Jones- head of IBM World Trade, Hank Trimble (the chief lawyer).

## A Brawl in IBM - 1964

Then *mere* divisional presidents and vice presidents like Spaulding and Pfeiffer. And me.

A. K. Watson, known as 'Dick', is Vice Chairman of IBM and the brother of the Chairman. Later he will be Ambassador to France for the United States under Nixon. Learson will be the next Chairman of IBM. Gil Jones –whom I had never met – is Chairman of the IBM World Trade Company.

Tall, thin, gray, distinguished, Dick Watson is in charge of the meeting.

"Thank you all for coming –on such short notice. I know most of you had to leave meetings. I did, too –but this is important. We're here to discuss whether or not we should insist on certain clauses in the FAA contract."

He explains Finance's position. He explains that the IBM controller is out of town, or he'd be there with them, and Bill Quinn would represent Finance. Quinn had recently been promoted from Group Finance to Corporate Finance.

Then Watson gets to the issues.

"Let's remember in all our discussions that we want this contract. It is important to us. We'll do the job right. The team in Washington has done a great job getting us here," --a nod and smile to Spaulding and Pfeiffer --"so we want to find a way to contract for this business."

I glow! With that kind of kick off, this is going to be duck soup! The stalemate is about to be broken!

This is the top of IBM. There are only two higher than these guys. Eight years out of Brooklyn, and I am sitting with the highest level of the seventh largest company in America, the blue chip IBM.

Dick Watson outlines the gist of the third party issue and then turns to the lawyers.

The lawyers explain the recent rash of court cases that have them concerned about the third party, and how the government in some cases would indemnify the contractor if the hazards were grave.

I speak up.

"FAA has told us that we are the only contractor asking for this indemnification. All the other bidders are willing to take the contract without indemnification."

I am throwing the fear of competition at the group, showing the unreasonableness of IBM.

Watson glowers at me - and yells "LET THEM THEN! Let them give the contract to the other people. They can't coerce us into this!"

Stillness. Dead silence.

My mind is going 200 miles an hour!!

*Where is the man who a minute ago was saying we had to find a way to do this?*

Watson is glaring at me, defying me to respond.

I look at Pfeiffer. Pfeiffer was staring at me with cool, not angry, eyes, which say clearly: "I warned you not to speak; get yourself out of this."

Spaulding's face has the same message. Panic is setting in on me when one of the other members changes the subject back to the legal issue. Watson finally looks away from me.

*"How can this company be the seventh largest in the U.S.?" I think. "This is absurd. Every other competitor would stand on their heads to be where we are on this."*

The lawyers continue to paint nightmares, aided by the financial people. They repeat all their arguments. I keep my mouth shut.

A midair collision scenario is hypothesized - over New York City –at rush hour –traced to an error in the computer. And, another –suppose an IBM computer fouled up air travel for hours. The airlines could sue for wasted fuel.

All the executives are inscrutable – only interest is on their faces. Learson abruptly throws out a word. Almost a shout.

**"OM –I –UM."**

"What, Vin?"

"What?"

None of us seem to have caught it.

"OPIUM!" he says, 'Opium'! The lawyers are smoking opium. We solved this problem five years ago –with insurance. It is the same problem we addressed when we were concerned about a computer failure causing a mis-design in a nuclear plant. This is the same problem."

"I agree."

"Right."

"Yeah."

"Vin is right – it is the same".

All seem to remember- no one fights it.

They discuss IBM's insurance position. The lawyers know the facts. IBM was insured for about $40 million per incident.

Learson asks how much the biggest airline was insured for.

$50 million.

"Raise ours to 100 and get on with it," says Learson. "Sign the contract."

The discussion continues - briefly.

The Finance man gives a short rationale as to why they should insist on the indemnification. Low profit, special pricing, and high risk of bad press –all these in addition to a profit risk.

Watson calls for a vote.

UNANIMOUS to accept the contract without indemnification!

I cheer - inwardly; outwardly, I am inscrutable. I hope.

*"Say nothing, Joe."*

A.K. now graciously thanks them all again for interrupting their schedules. I am sitting next to Gil Jones. Gil was president of DP years ago; now he is chairman of IBM World Trade.

I have never met him.

A. K. Watson now begins to sooth the feathers of the vanquished.

"And I want to thank Mr. Quinn for a fine job today, representing Finance."

But - Mr. Quinn is not through yet!

"Thank you Mr. Watson, but I did not do a good job here today. If I had, you all would not have voted the way you did."

Impassive outside, I rage inside.

*"This damn guy gets away with..."*

A crash at my elbow made me jump.

Gil Jones is inscrutable no longer; he has smashed his palm on the table.

"I <u>resent</u> that," he declares with vehemence. "I resent that."

"Now, Gil," Watson is soothing. "Now, Gil."

Jones is not to be quieted.

"He questions my intelligence. I understand these issues. And if he doesn't present it correctly, then he doesn't deserve to waste my time trying to explain it. He doesn't belong in this meeting."

Spaulding and Pfeiffer are as inscrutable as I hope I am.

Quinn scribbles a note on a slip of paper as Gil is talking.

"If Mr. Quinn has additional facts, I'm willing to hear them. But he has <u>no right</u> at this point to question <u>my</u> vote."

Gil is forceful, emphatic.

Quinn pushes the slip of paper over to me –I am between him and Gil - and I push it to Gil, - who reaches out – takes it - and immediately crumples it into a small ball and leaves it on the middle of the table.

That ends the meeting.

> *The COB did not last long as a mechanism within IBM. It was just too unwieldy to try to get that many vice presidents into one room. They were all too busy. To coordinate their schedules was too difficult.*

Upon adjournment of the meeting, Dick Watson, Manny Piore, and Don Spaulding go into Mr. Williams' office to discuss the results of the meeting.

White and I wait outside for about two hours. Spaulding would hurry out and grab one or the other of us, ask a question, and then go back in.

# A Brawl in IBM - 1964

It is becomes clear that the issue has not been totally resolved by the Corporate Operating Board!

Mr. Williams has reserved the right to make the final decision.

We are still in danger!

About 5 o'clock that afternoon, the decision comes out - we would continue to press for "clarifying language" on the third party liability issue.

We start back to LaGuardia and the shuttle, in order to meet with FAA the following day.

Pfeiffer drives to the airport.

"Gil is beautiful," I offer.

"He is that! By the way, you walked into a fire storm."

"Yeah." I am sheepish. "I thought with Watson's opening it was safe."

"Not in this league, young man, not in this league."

Back In Washington, we meet at 7:30 AM and prepare for a negotiating session with FAA at 10:00.

## THE IBM PRESIDENT'S REVIEW

At 1 PM, Pfeiffer calls me at FAA.

"Yeah, Ralph?"

"Come to White Plains! Now!"

"Why?"

"We have all been called to a meeting tomorrow with Al Williams –he wants to review the third party liability issue. And the Islip system printer is dropping strips again. We've got to tell Williams tomorrow about the Islip printer."

"No Ralph."

"Yes Joe."

"I'll meet you at 9 tonight at White Plains HQ."

I rejoin the group.

"Hank, tomorrow..."

I get no further.

"I know. Spaulding just called me. I am in the meeting too."

"What's up?" I ask.

"It can't be good. Every time we go up there it's Russian roulette. One of these times we are going to die."

We call everyone they could think of. We get no hint of "what is up".

I catch the 7 P M Shuttle. I get a hot dog at the terminal, and meet Pfeiffer at 9 p.m.

We review the facts on the IBM flight strip printers in the FAA en route control center in Islip, Long Island, New York.

Pfeiffer is very concerned. He <u>has</u> to tell Williams –and I say "that just might get the vote of the COB overturned"!

"The printers are acting up again," Whitney had told Pfeiffer on the phone.

Should we tell Williams?

"No," I say. "Let FAA handle it. Don't label it a crisis. FAA has not called you."

Pfeiffer is very worried.

"We have to tell Williams."

"No." I keep reassuring Ralph that the FAA will handle the thing. I pull out a letter from FAA from September, where they complained that they had to put extra people onto the system to compensate for the errors.

I show Pfeiffer the letters, pointing out that "FAA has had to put additional people on the correlation of information –i.e., the checking and certification that the information gotten from the printers was correct. "

This is <u>proof</u> that FAA realized that electronic and mechanical printers could fail! And they put people on to check it. I argue strenuously that this, in effect, absolves IBM should a tragedy occur.

My argument is –

1. Nothing is 100 percent fail-safe. Everything fails, no matter how reliable it is, no matter how many times over you put it in duplex, triplex, or quadruple; equipment fails! Any group responsible for using equipment in a real time system must take this into account.
2. FAA has taken this into account and had so stated in their letter.

# A Brawl in IBM - 1964

3. Although everyone would be appalled by a disaster, one can do only his best.

IBM can do only its best and FAA then, in turn, must take the tools given to them by the manufacturers and do their best.

"The letter said that they had to put extra people and procedures into place. They were stating <u>not</u> that the system was unsafe, but that the errors were costing them <u>extra people</u> to be sure it was safe."

"So?"

"So that means there is no great problem. **We** are making it a big problem. We shouldn't."

Pfeiffer just looks at me.

"Look. Has anyone called you, Ralph."

"No. "

"Tom Watson?"

"No. "

"No one's called anyone but <u>Whitney</u>. The FAA administrator hasn't called anyone. They aren't upset."

Pfeiffer finally agrees. There is no need to raise the Islip printer issue with Williams.

✳ ✳ ✳

I leave Pfeiffer at 2 AM in the morning. I meet Pfeiffer at 7 AM for breakfast.

We drive to Armonk, IBM corporate headquarters, for the Williams meeting, the president of IBM.

This is a mysterious meeting.

"What's the agenda, Ralph?"

"Don't know."

We drive.

"I don't like it, Ralph. What is to be done? Why are we meeting?"

"Relax. If the President of IBM wants to call a meeting on FAA, he can."

I don't relax. I worry.

"Meetingmanship" overrides "right" when right is not well represented and fought for. "Right" might not even get into the meeting! The proponents of right had to be ready to present well -and fight well! What is the agenda of this meeting?

We assemble in a large conference room. We were all invited by name, specifically –Spaulding, Trimble, Fox, Kilner, Pfeiffer, Laguzza, White, Whitney, George Newmann–DS's lawyer, Carl Weiland, (Carl is Kilner's boss and reports for Pfeiffer-and has been not in the loop and has been very patient. And C. B. 'Jack' Rogers–assistant to Williams, and Gene Richards, the controller of FSD. We chitchat.

Al Williams enters a half-hour late.

He goes around the table and introduces himself to those he does not know. He shakes hands with every attendee. His demeanor is friendly, interested in each person. Each attendee mentions where he is from; if not, Williams asks. He sits at the head of the long table.

"I apologize for being late. I do not like to keep people waiting –and certainly not as large and talented an assembly as this."

He is gracious. He explains why he is late, telling us about the meeting he'd just been in. He then gets down to business, saying he is "immensely distressed that the IBM company has to be run personally by its president", in what he considered a relatively routine negotiation.

He cannot understand why we are hung up on this third party liability problem.

"Obviously, gentlemen, we are interested in getting this business because I, personally, have spent much, much time on this proposal. And you have spent much more. I don't understand why we are delaying and why we are not on the ball on this issue."

He pauses.

"Let's list on the chart all the key dates on third party liability," he says.

"Hank," he addresses Trimble, "you list the dates on the chart for us. You be the recorder. Who's got the dates?"

Trimble stands and approaches the chart holder.

Spaulding speaks.

"The first mention of third party is in the January 23 proposal."

Trimble writes on the paper chart:

*January 23 Proposal*

"What does it say?" asks Williams.
"Nothing. Just states that a clause covering third party is to be included in the contract."
"What's after that?"
"April first. Jack Ford, our lawyer in Washington, and Joe Fox meet with the FAA negotiators and they want to know what IBM desires."
Trimble writes.

*January 23 Proposal*
*April 1 FAA Meeting*

"Ralph," said Williams, "what went on at that meeting?"
"Jack Ford explained to the FAA what we wanted. And..."
"Is Mr. Ford here?"
"No, sir," said Pfeiffer. "He's in California and..."
"When I ask that people who had contact with the FAA be here, I mean just that."
The rebuke was gentle - but clear.
"Yes sir," says Pfeiffer.
"And then what?" Williams addresses Spaulding.
"FAA explained they did not have the authority to indemnify us. That an Act of Congress would be needed."
"Write 'Act of Congress', Hank."
He writes:

*January 23 Proposal*
*April 1 FAA Meeting*
*Act of Congress*

"And then?"
Spaulding continues to read off the events and dates.

It is becoming clear why they were there, and why Trimble has been selected to do the writing.

It is a public wrist-slapping.

Williams is going to make it clear to all that the lawyers have not done well on this one.

About two hours into the meeting, Mr. Williams asks, "Mr. Trimble, it was obvious that FAA would have to pass a bill through Congress in order to indemnify us."

Trimble: "Yes."

"It is also obvious that the Civil Rights filibuster going on in Congress is still going on."

"Yes."

"It is also obvious that we must have a contract by June 30th, and Mr. Trimble, how did you possibly expect that FAA would pass any law in time for us to get this contract?"

Silence.

Trimble states that what he was trying to "put the pressure on the government through this contract" in order to highlight the developing nature of the law with regard to third party liability.

Williams said, "In other words, Mr. Trimble, you were 'playing school'?"

Silence.

"Yes, sir, we were 'playing school.'"

Williams looks at the group at the long table.

"I'm ashamed. I am truly ashamed that the IBM Company could operate in such a fashion."

Williams was either a consummate actor or he was truly ashamed.

*I believe he really is ashamed.*

But Williams isn't quite done yet.

"Still, there is merit in the concerns that the lawyers have been raising. And although we will not insist on indemnification, I do want the negotiation team to get into the contract language that will signal to a judge or jury, sometime in the future –if it is ever needed – language that will say, "See -we knew this was a worry' - and will help us in that case."

"Call it 'bell-tinkling' language."

"Can you do that?" he asks the group. Several of the people nod or say yes.

"Fine. Thank you all for interrupting your schedule..."

Suddenly, Newmann –the lawyer for the DS product division - speaks.

"Mr. Williams, I would like you to ask Mr. Fox what his understanding was with regard to the position that IBM had to take on third party liability."

A short silence falls; Al Williams knits his brow.

My mind races.

*A trap! Damn you, Newmann,- but you're smart.*

*If I say, 'yes, I understood from the beginning, 'that third party had to be in there, then it is my failure; DP's failure! It <u>is our job to raise issues early and</u> resolve them.*

*I am the guilty party here. DP failed to do it's job.*

*If I tell the whole truth, that the Federal Regional lawyer, Ford, told me not to worry, that IBM would be reasonable, then I get Ford into deep trouble with the legal fraternity. Ford will be honest and back me up. He'll confess.*

*But he's in deep trouble. I can't go there.*

*If I say 'yes,' I knew it was my job to fix this, do I reopen the whole issue? Or just take a fall for a day or two? I can survive a fall!*

*But maybe it will be a rallying point for the lawyers to turn the whole momentum.*

*But maybe Williams will close the meeting; maybe –just maybe, he will not ask me to answer.*

This was the other side of the coin for marketing –one side was clout. We controlled IBM's face to the customer. The bigger the customer the more clout. But the other side was responsibility –it was marketing's job to raise all issues, to force solutions, to blow the whistle.

This is what Newmann is trying to force into the open - that I knew about the third party issue, and it was my responsibility -not legal's -to move it or remove it. And I had not.

I see instantly what Newmann is doing –it is a masterful meeting move!

Williams looks at me and asks, "What about that?"

Rather than answer the question, I evade it!

I state not my understanding, but my belief. They are different.

"Mr. Williams, I believed, as was just said, that IBM was 'playing school' and that we would not allow this contract to go down the drain in order to set legal precedent."

Williams nods, thanks us all for coming, and leaves.

Ford tells me later that Newmann was disconsolate.

"He says he thought you 'were an honest man,' Joe. He thinks you lied."

"I didn't lie. I didn't answer the question, but I didn't lie."

Newmann never spoke to me again.

This saddened me! I liked Newmann.

But I had seen no reason to confess, to stand and say, 'yes, it was me –my fault –my responsibility.' The lawyers were being arrogant (Newmann's letter with one line in it.) and sloppy, and I'd not blown the whistle for many reasons. I'd not been exactly loafing, with free time on my hands. And I did not believe that the lawyers would allow themselves to be cornered like this!

The lawyers had brought US all here to this juncture

*"THE FAA has a problem."*

Pfeiffer drives us to the airport.

"I'm learning, Ralph."

"How?"

"Did you see me in that meeting today?"

"You didn't say anything."

"Right."

We catch the 7 PM Shuttle back to Washington. Friday we are to spend negotiating with FAA.

We have gone back and forth to New York six times in eight days. We have worked Saturday and Sunday –this is our twelfth straight day of work.

## A Brawl in IBM - 1964

✫ ✫ ✫

We meet with the FAA at 10 the next day. We can tell instantly - something is up. Facial expressions and demeanor trumpet the fact - a change has occurred.

Mulari tells us, "No letter contract. We'll push all the way though."

We are not surprised; we have been completely unresponsive!

We have missed a golden opportunity to sign it! But my sadness is overcome by optimism. We should be able to push it all the way home! The COB has voted –unanimously! The president has slapped the lawyers' wrists! Finance has been routed.

It should be finished easily, even though we missed the letter contract gift.

Once again, I have completely misjudged the situation.

✫ ✫ ✫

I get back to my office and open a letter - on Bob Evans' personal stationery.

Bob 0. Evans<br>Box 390, Poughkeepsie, N. Y.

May 14, 1964

Dear Joe,

> I understand we have been notified that IBM is the choice for the major FAA task ahead. You and I have had our differences and I certainly do not agree with many things you do, as I am certain you do not agree with my own actions, but there is no question but that the success of IBM in this key task is a function of your imagination, aggressive leadership and endurance. My hat is really off to you in respect.
>
> Regardless of our differences in systems organization philosophy, you can be assured that the resources of

DS-Development will be applied as required to the FAA task.
I hope we can succeed.
Congratulations !
Sincerely,
Bob Evans

*Evans is a class act.*
*I reply.*

May 26 To: Mr. Bob 0. Evans
Dear Bob:
Thank you for your note. We hope to have the order within a week. I'm sure that you are aware that we still have several minor problems with FAA.
Our differences you mention in your note are past, and I am sure that I will enjoy working with you on any occasion in the future.
Joe Fox

Although it may not seem so, there is much detail left out of this story. The efforts the 50 person IBM group toiling in the FAA Development site in Atlantic City, the FAA side of the question, the personal lives of the main characters, and many, many subsidiary issues that were fought over with passion, clause by clause are not in here.

Price guarantees, price protection, most favored customer clause, reliability guarantees, resistance to radiation guarantee, inspection, shipping, packing, insurance, passage of title, etc. etc.

On the technical side it never stopped. Reliability equations, how to measure, definitions, probabilities, reconfiguration, recovery procedures, tape speeds and sizes and specs and printer speeds and specs and fonts –and on and on.

And the negotiating team went through each of these - professionally and quickly. There is no drama in them. They were the necessary work to be done to put in place a new national system of air traffic control. To prevent mid-air collisions. They are the ordinary stuff of big contracts.

# A Brawl in IBM - 1964

The FAA did a superb job in getting all of these settled despite the erratic behavior of the IBM Corporation as it thrashed about.

While the main persona of this story rush back and forth to the airports, to New York LaGuardia and to IBM Armonk, the others make steady progress through the mountain of details needed for a $95,000,000 contract.

✯ ✯ ✯

I am in IBM Harrison, late in May.

Almost all people are rational. So why did finance fight this order so ferociously?

"Marty," I ask Foley, Group Finance manager, "why do you all want to kill this project? It's 100,000,000 dollars!"

"There's no profit in it, Joe."

"Well, there is if we install all 37 systems.

JOE!!" smiles Foley. "That is what you marketing people said about the 1401-1410 system you installed at Islip. How many more of them will we get orders for?"

He is right and totally logical! The Islip bid had priced certain units based on sales of five to ten systems. Now it is clear, with the acceleration of NAS, that there will be no more orders for the 1401-1410!

"But the profit of the 1401 and the 1410 – the standard boxes –" I emphasize, 'That will outweigh any loss on the special units."

"Ah, Joe, you are evading the question. How many more sales?"

"I don't know."

"None," says Foley!

"And now you people want us to do it again."

"Watson wants to win."

I am retreating.

"Fine. We just want him to know what it is costing him to win."

"And," Foley continues, "it is costing more than just money."

I can't argue with that.

"And, then, if there is a disaster, we're exposed again."

I cannot refute any of those points. But I still argue.

"The likelihood of IBM being sued is so small ..."

"Fine," Foley interrupts. "That's for the executives to decide. Our task is to be sure they see the downside risks."

I change the subject.

Later I would understand that our roles are structured to create conflict. Marketing and finance were never to agree! This "fruitful friction" pushed real issues to the top, and made for better, clearer decisions.

I worked at the art of attacking positions and not people. My constant speech to the people who were fighting the contract went like this:

*"Look. You and I are paid to see this issue differently. And your conclusion and mine are different. That's okay! You argue your position; I'll argue mine. If you win, so be it. If I win, okay. But when it's over –either way –we'll still respect each other. We'll go have a beer. It's not personal."*

## GET MORE INSURANCE

White gets a copy of a letter from finance dated May 18$^{th}$, 1964

Memorandum to: Mr. Hoskins Subject: Insurance for FAA
This will confirm our telephone conversation of Friday, May 18th, in which we discussed the FAA project and insurance coverage in connection with this project. Etc etc … The coverage is in place.

## IBM REORGANIZES

On May 27, the following notice appears on the bulletin board:

EXECUTIVE PROMOTIONS ANNOUNCED
Thomas J. Watson, Jr., today announced the election of T. V. Learson and A. K. Watson as IBM senior vice presidents– a newly created position.

Frank Cary succeeds Mr. Hume as president of the Data Processing Division.

Earlier this month a Corporate Operations Board, consisting of the six group executives, was organized to provide company-

A Brawl in IBM - 1964

wide review in the areas of technology, product development and marketing. The senior vice presidents will also be members of the operations board and will alternate its chairmanship every six months.

Reporting to T. V. Learson will be:
W. C. Hume, IBM V P and group executive for the Data Processing Division.
M. B. Smith, IBM V P and group executive for Electric Typewriter, Industrial Products and Supplies Divisions, and for the Service Bureau Corporation.
L. M. Spencer, president of Science Research Associates, Inc.
Reporting to A. K. Watson, who also continues as board chairman of the IBM World Trade Corporation will be:
J. W. Gibson, IBM vice president and group-executive for the Components, Data Systems and General Products Divisions.
G. E. Jones, IBM vice president and group executive and president of the IBM World Trade Corporation.
E. R. Piore, IBM vice president and group executive for the Advanced Systems Development, Federal Systems and Research Divisions, and the Systems Research and Development \Department.
The Corporate staff, under Mr. Bullen, will report to the chairman and the president.

See Organization Chart page 303

The reorganization does not affect the FAA effort.

# THIRD PARTY LIABILITY –IN OR OUT ?

The effort to get "Bell Tinkling" language in begins immediately after the Williams "playing school" meeting.

At first it is slow, but then we get some words! There seems to be no problems, but to the Washington team, this is a wild card, a strange entry into a standard game, a new deal that we do not control. It makes us nervous! But things are moving.

On May 25, Laguzza writes to FAA a summary of where we stood. The opening sentence:

"As a result of our recent negotiations, the following reflects our agreements...

...

Item L: <u>Third Party Liability</u>
"If and to the extent that the Congress in the future authorizes the FAA to include such a clause in this contract the Government will include a provision to indemnify the Contractor against the liability for injuries and/ or damages to third parties arising out of the Government's use of the equipment furnished under this contract."

The bell-tinkling clause has been agreed to! There finally is a third party clause and it has been agreed to!

But - someone in New York is pushing the lawyers. They now sheepishly tell the Washington team that we must get <u>better</u> "bell-tinkling" language.

We go to the next negotiating session. We hold our breath.

Joe McCann introduces a new clause, not under third party, that says that FAA is "doing design."

FAA is instantly on guard.

## A Brawl in IBM - 1964

The FAA lawyer states that "that sounds like the third party liability issue through a backdoor".

The FAA lawyer proposes a clause:

"The parties agree that IBM is not responsible hereunder for delivery of any software (except as required by contract) and/or for the operation of the ATC system (which incorporates equipment provided by the contract)."

FAA has proposed <u>great</u> "bell-tinkling language". IBM accepts it. It clearly states IBM was not responsible! It is changed slightly and included in Laguzza's summary.

We all breathe a very large sigh of relief!

May ends!

And there are but thirty days to go. We must sign by June 30 or the FAA will lose its funding for the effort. That would be a public relations disaster for FAA. Congress would bludgeon them. Most critical, a major delay in getting an updated En Route Air traffic Control System would be a major disservice to the public.

And we all fly.

Frequently.

✻ ✻ ✻

The Washington sales team is tough to take these days. We occupy offices and desks at 1120 Connecticut Avenue, the Bender Building. We are in with our peers, but our minds had been captured by the effort as effectively as if Martians had stolen them.

We were totally absorbed by the FAA contract. That is all we think about, talk about. We are an island in the midst of all the other sales people. We barely say hello. We do not talk with old friends. The project is too complicated to explain –so we don't try.

We are like foreigners who don't speak the language.

The outsiders see what was happening. Pfeiffer is spending more and more time on the effort. The secretaries and other executives are funnels for the information that Fox is 'with Learson,' 'with Williams,' 'with Trimble'.

A visit to the Learson level is perhaps a once-a-year event for those who report directly to Pfeiffer. I am two levels below that, seeing Learson weekly!

Carl Weiland is the sales executive between Kilner and Pfeiffer. He is totally left out of fray - for the simple reason that there are too many people in it already. Kilner has phased out. Weiland and Kilner handle this exclusion with maturity and poise. They could have resented my constant high-level exposure.

They never show a sign of it. They make life easier for me in every way they can. There is almost nothing I ask for that I do not get.

Negotiations continue. And all the corporate level staff organizations are fighting every clause.

Spaulding-President of FSD and in charge of the negotiating team - now reports to Manny Piore.

# MORE OBJECTIONS

I get a call from DS finance at 6 PM on Thursday, June 5.

"You can't accept the Changes clause. If you want, you can appeal to Williams."

Laguzza explodes when I tell him.

"The goddamn Changes clause is in every contract for every typewriter IBM sells to the government. This is too much."

He glares at me.

"What is the Changes clause, Jim?"

"It says simply that the government is the sovereign and if necessary can order you to institute changes in your product. They'll pay for the changes, but you must institute them immediately. It's for emergencies, will almost never be invoked, and is in every damn IBM contract with the government."

We go to the FAA meeting the next day. Laguzza acts as though FAA will accept the deletion of the clause as a natural event.

The FAA contracts people are amazed! After a whispered conference, Ray Mulari looks at Laguzza.

"Has IBM _ever_ signed a contract with the U.S. Government?"

We are embarrassed.

White calls a recess.

"Let's go north and fight it."

We get the Shuttle –as always– and arrive at Harrison at 3 PM. We argue with the finance group till 1 AM –to no avail.

The next morning we fly back to D.C. – on the Shuttle.

We meet again with the FAA, avoid the Changes clause issue, and arrive back at 1120 Connecticut about 5 PM.

"We can't go back to Williams," says White.

We sit and look at each other. We phone the old boy network of assistants.

# A Brawl in IBM - 1964

"It's Russian roulette – and we may not survive."
I try to call Spaulding.
He is traveling.
Pfeiffer? Traveling.
Finally I announce: "I'm going to call Piore."
Manny Piore is the group Vice President, boss of Spaulding.
It is 6 PM.
Piore has left the office.
I have his home number.
All executives' home numbers are in a directory I had been given at the start of the proposal.
I call the number and explain the problem to Piore.
Piore asks several questions, and listens quietly to the answers.
There is a pause.
"Joe, you call finance. Tell them you've talked to me. Tell them, you –the negotiating team -are going to <u>accept</u> the Changes clause and if corporate finance wishes, <u>they</u> can go see Williams."
My eyes pop. I've never thought of that!
"Yes sir."
I hang up.
With carefully disguised glee (I wonder how well I acted), I call John Schwamb, group finance..
"John, you know the FAA has really come unglued over the Changes thing. We've raised the issue to Piore. I called him at home, told him your position."
"Yeah."
"Piore says we are to accept the clause. If finance can't live with that, you guys go to Williams."
Silence.
More silence.
"I'll call you back."
"John, we will hold off a day, but then we're going to tell FAA we accept."
"I understand."
"One day."
"I've got it."

I trust Schwamb. He would never deny getting the message.

We never heard again from New York about the Changes Clause.

We accept it two days later.

*The financial people always said no. They were trained to say no. A finance man who said yes didn't last long. The IBM business was so good and growing so fast, IBM's position so strong, that growth and profit were inherent in the way things were. "No" to new ideas kept things the way they were. "No" was safe.*

*If finance said no, and the new idea was killed, good. If they said no and were over-ruled, and the new idea failed, well, they had predicted it, fought it! It had been passed over their objection. If the new idea worked, well, it was because finance had forced the implementers to commit to it in blood, because finance had scrubbed it. That was if anyone ever bothered in the euphoria of success to look back at the beginning and see that finance had opposed this new marvel.*

*The financial people said no to every new idea.*

✫ ✫ ✫

A beautiful June morning. June 5. We are all in the 1120 Connecticut Avenue building, preparing to go to the FAA for the negotiating session.

I notice McCann the lawyer talking to White.

Something's up. I walk over.

White makes a face.

"Joe, the people in New York want stronger words than those agreed to for third party liability."

"Again!", I mutter.

We meet with the FAA and propose new words to "tinkle" the bell a bit louder. The team holds its breath!

The first sentence states that, "The FAA recognizes that computers fail."

"Why is that sentence in there?" FAA asks.

# A Brawl in IBM - 1964

"That is the result of 'rump session' agreements," answers McCann.

He was referring to the fact that the IBM lawyers and FAA lawyers are discussing the language in separate meetings. I am not aware of this. I assume that White is.

"But why put it in there? It's obvious."

"Because a court or jury might look at it and be influenced by it," answers McCann.

"That doesn't belong in a contract," says one of the <u>technical</u> FAA people.

But, on June 5, FAA accepts the wording. Amazing.

But IBM is insatiable. We want more words, more protection.

On June 9th, McCann proposes to the FAA yet more language about liability.

Silence.

Then the FAA lawyer adds, "Except that is not to be interpreted as indemnifying the contractor."

This is a positive sign. Anytime they are willing to 'word-smith,' things at least might move forward.

Then the IBM lawyers propose a new <u>maintenance</u> clause.

"This is third party again," says the exasperated FAA lawyer.

"No, no. It's consequential damages," says IBM.

"We've never done this before," says the FAA man.

Then we get back to the new third party clause. No agreement.

FAA wants to drop the third party clause out. Totally. Period.

They agree to leave it as an open item.

White steps out to call Trimble at 2:00 PM.

Trimble - IBM's top legal executive, - is now in Washington, D.C., interacting with the negotiating team on third party clauses.

At the break, I chat with the FAA contracts manager about third party.

"We don't *control* traffic, Joe," explains Mulari. "We advise. The statues so state. We must prosecute if we feel a pilot took incorrect and dangerous action, but he is in control –the pilot."

I nod.

"And - a contract is not the place to state the role of the FAA. A contract is an agreement between two parties. Our mission is spelled out elsewhere –in legislation, in presidential letters and in executive orders.

A contract should not intrude on those."

How logical –how succinct.

Trimble had come to Washington with an attaché case. He'd told the team after a day that he had to go buy a toothbrush. Then he'd bought some shirts. Then more items. A one-day visit is turning into a career!

We do not like this. Trimble is a 'loose cannon' on <u>our</u> ship. We have no control over this wild card. He reports to the president. He could dump the whole thing and we'd never even know it.

I learn what is happening from White and McCann, who talk to Trimble.

Nothing is happening!

As far as I could tell, it was all talk, talk, talk. They seem to be lost in the woods of legalities, which seem to me to have nothing to do with the real world. They ARE *playing school*! They keep getting better and better words for an eventuality that has an infinitesimal chance of happening! And we are insured!

Trimble is having hour-long phone calls with Williams.

The Washington lawyer, Jack Ford, is not in the fray. I comment to him that having Trimble spend hours at a time on the phone with Al Williams is totally baffling. How can anything ever get done?

"You've got to understand what's happening to you, Joe," explains Ford. "Williams is a brilliant man. He thinks in the large. Trends, futures, currents. He looks far forward and has a great impact on IBM because of that. He's very stable. He is a balance to Watson's brilliant and sometimes spontaneous temperament. If Williams were to leave, the legal community in IBM would despair. They count on him to stabilize the corporation."

He continues.

"Williams loves this kind of problem. It fascinates him. He studies it, absorbs it, internalizes it. He understands every facet of it. He is milking Trimble of knowledge when he spends hours on the phone with him. Knowledge of far more than just this situation. He is getting the whole view of this area of unfolding law."

# A Brawl in IBM - 1964

This seems to explain what is happening. From my meetings with Williams, I judged him brilliant and stable.

"But what about Trimble? If he doesn't fix this thing he's going to get caught between the legal rock and 'the chairman who wants to win'."

"You're right. Trimble is in a tough spot. He's raised the issue. His lawyers have set up the roadblock. He can't now say it is trivial. So he's got to find a -a <u>middle</u> - that says 'this is very important to IBM, this legal principle but we can accept it on this one BECAUSE. And he can't find a because."

I stare at him. "Oh, shit!"

White beckons me out of the meeting with FAA.

"Trimble wants <u>the limits</u> of our responsibility spelled out."

"Shit."

"And he wants clause 4M to stay in - McCann's new words."

We go back in, take a break, and brief Laguzza and McCann.

We reconvene with FAA.

Laguzza proposes that we return to the 4M clause that was in the May 26 agreement.

FAA says no.

Then they said –"We'll go back to that if IBM accepts the maintenance clause."

That seems promising –they are negotiating.

But FAA starts to close ranks.

"No third party clause at all."

On that note, we adjourn for the day.

# IBM PRESIDENT FLIES TO WASHINGTON

June 10. The negotiating team is milling around the seventh floor of 1120 Connecticut Avenue. Everyone working on this clause, that clause, list of equipment for the Atlantic City Test Site, list of spares, list of, list of. ...whatever.

The secretary calls Laguzza to the phone.

"What? WHAT?"

His tone carries the group to silence.

"I understand. I understand."

His face is grim.

He hangs up and announces:

"That was Mulari. The FAA has suspended negotiations with IBM. They will reopen them - only if IBM agrees to drop third party liability clauses and language."

There is a long silence, then everyone speaks at once.

"Shit."

"It's a ploy."

"Oh, oh, oh."

"It's no ploy,' says Laguzza. He is grim.

White, Laguzza and Collins and I have a meeting. White is to call Spaulding and White will also find out where Trimble is. I am to call Pfeiffer and also call Williams' assistant, C. B. Jack Rogers, to fish for any information.

Collins is to go touch base with FAA technical people.

We split up for a half hour; then we meet again.

Trimble is en route to our office and is due any moment. Spaulding is in New York and has been sucked into FAA deliberations going on up there.

He had taken White's call; he would inform Williams of the FAA ultimatum.

## A Brawl in IBM - 1964

We have quickly decided to use that word. *Ultimatum.*

The clock is close to midnight on this contract. Even with full speed ahead we have our hands full getting a contract written. There is no time to massage this issue.

We sit and fret for the afternoon.

On Thursday June 11, Trimble is with us. He spends an hour on the phone with Williams.

We wait. We wait.

We chat with each other, are polite to each other.

The 7th floor looks like the fathers' maternity waiting room in a hospital.

We all watch Hank Trimble. We <u>watch</u> him. For clues. For body language.

And we see nothing. He spends <u>hours</u> on the phone!

He tells White about the calls.

"That was Williams."

Everyone knew that!! –it was a one-hour and 40-minute phone call. Who else could it be?

"He wanted to understand the details of the Buick case and to review the FAA arguments."

"Again?" asks White - incredulously.

Trimble looks at White –"Be careful." his eyes say.

The day drags on.

At 11:30 Collins comes in with news from his meeting with the FAA technical team. "They are serious - and they are mad as hell! They think we <u>planned</u> this. That we would get them against the wall and demand indemnity"

White talks to Spaulding on the phone. Spaulding is with Williams and A. K. Watson and Manny Piore in Westchester, NY. A summit meeting, of sorts.

White had talked to Spaulding the day before. Spaulding had gone to Westchester to see Piore on some other matter and had gotten caught in the FAA issue –or he'd attached himself to it. He spent the night in Westchester, even though he'd not planned to. Now, at 3 PM, he is still there.

"I asked him," White tells us, "when he was going to return here. –and he said –'When sanity returns up here.'"

*Realism seems to be a victim of power. The higher people get, the more they lose touch with the earth –with what really happens. "Power corrupts, and absolute power tends to corrupt absolutely," wrote Lord Acton, the British 18th Century historian. And Eric Hoffer, the longshoreman philosopher, wrote in <u>The True Believer</u> that "nothing stimulates credulity more than absolute power or absolute helplessness."*

We wait. Collins is almost running, not pacing, back and forth.

"There's no time, Joe, there's no time. Their money goes away July 1."

The FAA money is Fiscal Year 1963 money. If the contract is not signed by June 30, it is a disaster.

"I know, Jack. I know."

"Does Al Williams know? Does Watson? This company doesn't deserve to win! Joe, if it weren't that it would leave FAA high and dry, I'd almost like to see us lose. We *deserve* to lose."

"Jack, maybe IBM deserves to lose, but you and I deserve to win."

"Well, <u>we've</u> won it, Joe. We know that. That's enough for me."

"Not for me, Jack. I want everyone to know it. We –you and I –deserve that. If we lose, within a year it will be known as my loss - and yours. People don't know the details."

Collins switches back to the June 30 deadline.

"What are you going to do to meet June 30: We're running out of time."

"I don't know, Jack."

Pfeiffer calls me.

"Come over and talk to me."

"I hate to leave Trimble here. I'd like to be right here if something breaks."

"I'll come over there." Ralph replies.

We use Kilner's office.

Sam Kilner, Pfeiffer and I talk.

## A Brawl in IBM - 1964

"Get Learson into this, Ralph. We are going down the tubes."

"He wont' get in it. I've told you. This is Williams' baby. Anyone getting into it against Al is going to get sandwiched between Watson and Williams. Few survive that."

"We're doomed," I moan.

Ralph smiles. He exudes energy and confidence.

"You've been in tougher spots on this one, Joe. We'll survive."

"How can you be optimistic?"

"It works."

We chat about other things.

Trimble finally comes out of the other office. He'd been on the phone an hour.

"What's the verdict, Hank," I ask.

"Jury's still out."

"If we turn this down, at this late date, someone high up is going to have to explain it to FAA. I can't."

"That is why the IBM airplane is being warmed up." Trimble tells me.

White gets a phone call.

"That was Spaulding. He said they are getting on the IBM airplane at 1 o'clock. Williams, A. K. Watson, Piore –coming here.

He says -that Williams says - that FAA is not standing up to their end of the bargain. They control air traffic. They should be willing to state that in writing, - and they won't. 'What's right is right.' They should be willing to sign that."

I tell White.

"We can't fight on the issue of whether or not FAA is willing to *admit* it 'controls' air traffic. It is a bottomless pit. We'll get all caught up in laws and the English language and not get to what is really happening. We've got to fight fire with fire – fight 'what's right is right' with more 'right'."

White asks "Yeah?"

"Our position is we <u>misled</u> FAA. We've lured them into an untenable position, and now we're blackmailing them."

"What?"

"Blackmail. They can't sign with another vendor in 18 days. They sign with us or lose their money. And be publicly humiliated and torn apart by Congress."

"That is true," agrees Laguzza.

"Our thrust is that IBM is being sneaky – unethical. We said 'yes' three times; now we've lured them to this untenable position."

"I like it." Laguzza states.

White nods. "Let's call Spaulding."

I get on the call. " Don how much time before you must leave for the plane?"

"A minute."

"Just listen, then. We'll never get Williams off the 'what's right is right' theme! How do you argue against that? We've got to fight fire with fire –we've got our own 'what's right is right.'"

"What is that?"

"We had a handshake with FAA on the bell-tinkling clause. Then we changed. We did that three times."

"We did?"

"Yes. We misled them. We kept changing the deal. We <u>reneged</u> on a deal. That ain't right on our part. And there is no time for them to switch contractors."

"Yeah?"

"Play on that on the way down in the plane. We can't fight 'Right' head on, Don. We'll get killed."

Spaulding rushes "Got to go," and hangs up.

The message comes down through channels that Laguzza and Trimble are to meet the airplane at National airport. Laguzza knows the contract details cold. Trimble is IBM's legal chief.

On the IBM plane are Williams, IBM president, A K Watson, vice chairman, Spaulding and Piore.

Laguzza holes up in an office and reviews the happenings of the last several days. White and Collins help him. They rehearse questions and answers...what did FAA say on June 6...they stated "...," etc –etc etc.

Pfeiffer sits in Kilner's office with Kilner and me.

Pfeiffer looks serious. I am hammering at him now.

"I'll tell you this, Ralph, if we don't get back to that original language, IBM is out. And if we are out, you'll have to replace every man on the FAA team –me, Collins, Whitney, ..."

"Later, Joe, later. Let's cross that bridge when we have to."

We review what we know of the meetings that had been taking place in New York.

I sum up.

"As Spaulding says, Williams' argument is that 'what's right is right.' If they are responsible for air traffic control then they should own up to it and sign the contract."

"You can't argue with that," says Kilner, sinking into his chair.

"Well, yes, we can", I say. "You could argue that a contract is the wrong place to set out governmental job descriptions. But, -we won't win with that argument."

We sit in silence.

I stand up and start scribbling on the easel chart.

"Look, let's not argue with Williams's "What's right is right."

Let's fight fire with fire. He's saying that FAA isn't standing up like a man and signing the contract.

Let's drive home the point that IBM doesn't look good either. We've backed out of the May 28 and June 2 wording."

I scribble:

### IBM RENEGES ON 3$^{RD}$ PARTY LANGUAGE
May 28 agrees
June 2 retracts
June 2 agrees
June 6 retracts
June 6 agrees
June 9 retracts

"The point is that all FAA wants us to do is go back to the May 28 wording."

Pfeiffer and Kilner are listening intently.

Trimble has come in and sat down, but he isn't paying much attention to us.

"The point," I say, "is that IBM will look like it is acting in bad faith. I'm not saying, Ralph,..." Ralph has started to shake his head.

"I'm not saying that we are. But that is what it is looking like to the FAA. It's June 18. They think we are doing this deliberately to force indemnification.

Pause.

"FAA will never be able to get a contract signed with another firm by June 30. They'll lose the money for this year. The IBM company will have set back the air traffic control of the country by six months at least...the time we've been negotiating plus the next year funding problem. A new RFP."

"I like that reasoning," offers Ralph. "Who else have you told this to?"

"Spaulding –on the phone."

"Hank," Ralph addresses Trimble, "listen to Joe's thinking on this."

I go through it all again, but Trimble isn't paying much attention. I add to the chart,

"FAA set back six months -1 year".

"We've blackmailed FAA," I say. "They must sign with us."

"DON'T...use that word," Pfeiffer intones.

"Okay."

We go back across the street to 1111 Connecticut Avenue. The big guns are due in one hour –about 4 p. m. Elegant hors d'oeuvres appear.

The third (top) floor is neated up.

Pfeiffer takes me aside.

"You are not in the meeting."

"Okay."

For some reason, I accept not being in the meeting.

I hand Pfeiffer the hastily drawn flip chart, showing IBM "reneging".

"Here. Use this. It'll work."

"Okay."

I want to say more.

# A Brawl in IBM - 1964

"Ralph, if we lose, if we decide to withdraw, I want a shot at meeting with either Williams or Watson, okay?"

"Okay."

"Promise?"

"Promise."

I believe him.

Why was I so relaxed when I was not being allowed in the meeting? Was I exhausted?

No, I don't think so.

Normally I'd scheme and fight to get into these meetings. And if I didn't get in, I'd fret and chafe.

Perhaps it was that if the decision was to back out, I would get a personal audience with Williams, and maybe even Watson. This in effect is a safety net. If Pfeiffer, White and Spaulding couldn't do it, I had a shot. They owed me that. I thought.

And I am confident in our team. White is superb. Pfeiffer too. And Spaulding. And Laguzza. Those four are four very, very competent IBM executives.

I can think of only one other person I'd rather have in there -Learson. And I couldn't get him.

I go and wait in an office three down from the conference room. I tell Pfeiffer where I'll be, if I am needed.

It is 2 PM.

The four executives arrive and go into the conference room.

At 2:02 Pfeiffer enters the office I am in.

"They want you in."

"Okay," I say, still oddly calm.

It seemed perfectly natural to me to go to this meeting with the president of the "best managed company in the world", the multi billion dollar, computer industry-dominant IBM, and the other senior vice presidents.

The president of IBM has flown to Washington to meet with us.

White, Laguzza, Pfeiffer and Spaulding are there. So is Trimble. From corporate headquarters are Manny Piore, Spaulding's boss, and Piore's boss, A. K. Dick Watson, now senior vice president in charge of the product division, Vin Learson's counterpart.

I enter the room, nod to everyone, who all 'hello'.

Pfeiffer is furthest from the door, at the head of the table. Across from me are White, then Spaulding, then Dick Watson, then Piore. The president, Al Williams, is on my side of the table and next to Pfeiffer. Then Laguzza and then an empty seat, and then Trimble.

I take the empty seat between Laguzza and Trimble.

I see that Pfeiffer has the folded up "We Misled Them" charts.

Williams, President of IBM, starts.

"I've come here to tell you all face to face that we are going to turn down the FAA contract. I know you all have worked feverishly to win this contract, and I thought you deserved to hear my decision face to face."

I have my practiced, inscrutable look on my face -I think to do this now in all these meetings. All the others I could see without swiveling my head are inscrutable as well.

My mind is racing.

*Has it come to this? Is this company insane?*

And yet, I admire Al Williams' style.

Williams pauses and looks from one participant to another.

"Now, on the way down in the plane, Don Spaulding was saying we have misled the FAA..."

*'Hooray, Spaulding, you are good.'* I think. But stay inscrutable.

I nod my head, signifying agreement with Spaulding. Trimble next to me sees this and shakes his head, no.

"Now I don't quite understand this argument", continues Williams.

Dick Watson, sitting across from Trimble and me, interrupts and says, "He says yes; he says no. Let's listen to the one who says yes." Meaning me.

I sit very relaxed. This isn't my fight. Pfeiffer will take it from here. He has the charts.

Suddenly, Laguzza is handing me the folded-up charts.

I stand and put the charts on the easel. I am on my feet for the next two hours, the most junior of all in the room in age and title.

# A Brawl in IBM - 1964

I am not about argue the <u>role</u> of the contract versus the role of enabling legislation.

I am not about to state that the "FAA doesn't control air traffic; only advises."

Those arguments are losers.

Too esoteric; too defensive.

Too open to everyone's opinion.

The only argument that might win is "we misled them".

I start.

"If we do not sign, then FAA is in deep difficulty. They've been negotiating only with us. They can't possibly negotiate a new contract with anyone else by June 30. That means they would lose their money, the funding for the year. A major delay. Requiring a new RFP - and great embarrassment."

They all listen, very patiently.

"If so, we might say 'it's their problem. We were straight with them and that's life'.

But –we misled them!

Three times WE proposed language on third party, three times we had a handshake, and three times we reneged."

I had chosen the word deliberately. *Reneged*

Trimble says, "Oh, no."

The others listen.

I continue.

"On May 28 we agreed to this set of words."

I show the chart with the statement.

"They agreed. But on June 2 we tried to up the ante, and we gave them a new clause."

I show it.

"They agreed! We changed again. On June 8 the same thing. We want more -and they agreed again."

Williams asks technical questions. What did this phrase mean? That one?

I keep trying to get through to the end. It is the pattern I am trying to show, not the detail.

Finally, I ask Williams, very politely; "Al, please let me get to the next chart and then we'll go back over for details. It's the pattern that's the key."

"Okay," says Williams, quiet and gentle as always.

"So on June 6 we had agreement for a third time –we had a 'handshake,'" I say, deliberately using the same words that Williams had used back in February when Finance was trying to withdraw the bid –a 'handshake.'

But Trimble is not going to let that one go by. He says evenly:

"It is a negotiation. You propose; they react. There is no agreement till the contract is signed. No 'handshake' till signing."

"We proposed," I answer. Ignoring the point he makes.

"They accepted. We can't raise the stakes on our proposal without reasons. Even so, they went along three times. But we went to the well once too often."

"It is a negotiation. They're used to this," Trimble says calmly.

"Not to this," I say. "This is not a normal negotiation by any stretch."

I get to the end.

"We signed up –then we reneged –three times. We had <u>three</u> handshakes, and three times we reversed ourselves."

I am done.

Williams asks White: "Were you represented by counsel when you accepted these clauses?"

White sees a chasm opening and tries to evade, to protect McCann.

"Well, it was very complex and..."

Spaulding stops him.

"You can answer that 'yes or no'."

"Yes," says a reluctant White.

"Who was the lawyer?" asks Williams.

"Joe McCann."

"Why is he not here'?"

"He is moving his home from Poughkeepsie to Connecticut today," answers White.

"And he is a corporate lawyer, not a division lawyer'?"

"Yes sir," answers Trimble.

# A Brawl in IBM - 1964

"And did you know your man was accepting these clauses'?" Williams asks Trimble.

"No sir. I would not have agreed."

I am a mess of conflicting emotions.

The meeting is going well for our side, but it is chewing up the lawyers!

I like the lawyers. Every one of them. Even Trimble.

But it is too late.

There is a short silence.

"WHOP."

Williams has slapped the table with his palm.

"IT STINKS," he says with emphasis. "The action of our legal department stinks."

No one moves.

It seems that no one even draws a breath.

Williams, usually so gentle, has caught us all by surprise. And he IS the president of IBM.

Trimble speaks- calmly.

"Shall I defend myself now or later?"

"Later." Says Williams. "Let's get the negotiations started again."

"*We've won yet again*", I think, but I am still practicing inscrutability –or trying to.

Williams speaks.

"We have led FAA 'down the garden path'. And we must get it back on track."

A pause. I am cheering inwardly. "… the garden path !! "

But inscrutably?

Then, Williams adds, "I'm willing to bend, but not to kneel."

"*What the hell does that mean? Are we still in the soup?*"

Williams addresses Hank Trimble.

"We'll back off to an earlier bell-ringing clause. Hank, I'd like you personally to do this."

"Yes, sir."

"I am willing to bend, but I am not willing to kneel." He repeats.

He gives us, again, some more words and phrases that we are to get into the contract. He says that we can go back to the June 6 wording.

We call the FAA chief negotiator and he says that he thought this should be acceptable to him.

The meeting breaks up. Williams, A. K. Watson and Manny Piore go into Pfeiffer's office, making phone calls.

It is 4:30. I am still standing. I have been standing since 2:10.

Laguzza, White and I huddle in a corner.

'Trimble's in deep yogurt," says Laguzza.

"Damn it," says White. "It sure doesn't look good for him."

At that moment Trimble comes over. He senses our distress.

"Fellahs, don't worry about Hank Trimble."

"Hank," says White, "we didn't want this."

"I know. You couldn't help it. I've been in deeper trouble."

We smile wanly.

Almost to himself, Trimble adds: "When Tom gets mad at you, it's okay. But when Williams get down on you, that's different."

I update Collins and Whitney and the others, and I go home - happy.

The next day, I sit with Pfeiffer, reviewing.

"Ralph, why did Trimble say he'd never heard of the three 'handshakes' before the meeting? I told you and Trimble about them yesterday afternoon before the meeting."

"He wasn't listening to you, Joe. His mind was elsewhere."

"By the way", Pfeiffer tries to be stern, "don't you ever tell the President of IBM to please hold his questions. I…"

"It worked."

"Don't you ever do it <u>AGAIN.</u>"

"Okay."

We both smile.

✯ ✯ ✯

A week later, I sit with Collins, almost relaxed, at 1120 Connecticut Avenue.

These last weeks of furor over third party liability, with a score of Changes clauses, the threat of backing out of the reliability

# A Brawl in IBM - 1964

guarantee, and dozens of questions on guarantees, etc. etc. has produced -absolutely -nothing.

I am glum, even though we are in the last days now.

"Jack, it is a staff out of control. These guys are paid to see ghosts. 'Watch out! Watch out! Watch out!' If you get hurt, they told you in advance. If it is nothing but their nightmares, and it goes fine, well, they kept you from getting burned by warning you to be extra careful."

"What's the point?" asks Collins.

"They got a cushy job. Say 'no' to everything and you'll never get in trouble."

"Are they built that way –or is it the job?"

"It's the system. It's the executive's fault. They encourage this nonsense. Look at the time they spend on the phone! Hours! Learson would never have let this nonsense go on."

Why does Williams let it go on?

"The lawyers tell me Williams loves this kind of problem. It fascinates him. I believe it from what we've seen. TWO-HOUR-long phone calls –over and over the same ground. It's like he's stuck on a sandbar."

"Who can move Williams?"

"Only Watson. And everyone is afraid to go over Williams' head. It's career suicide, they say."

## ONCE MORE TO IBM WESTCHESTER

We are meeting in Harrison N. Y. – an hour from LaGuardia - with Manson's replacement, Beeby. On technical issues.

White gets a call.

"Trouble," he says, in response to the questioning looks. "FAA just called the president of IBM."

"WHAT?"

"Yeah. Mulary's boss called Al Williams and stated that they could not accept the clause that they had agreed upon after the Williams meeting two weeks ago."

"Damn."

"The hell with it."

"It's hopeless."

"Shit."

"No, it's not that bad. Spaulding says that the company now has made up its mind. They want this contract. Williams is sending Dick Watson down to Washington to review the situation and to try to get new words. We are to meet with them tonight at 6:00 at the office next to the Mayflower hotel."

"Let's go! We have no time." We rush to get the shuttle –yet again.

Collins volunteers to stay. Beeby agreeing is not enough. Finance is saying no.

We drive back to LaGuardia, and get on the 3:00 Shuttle.

I am so tired, I don't even mind flying.

# THE POWERFULL FLY TO WASHINGTON YET AGAIN

At 6 PM, we start the meeting.

Hank Trimble has flown down with Dick Watson and Manny Piore.

And, a new player, *outside counsel* to IBM, George Turner, a partner in the prominent N. Y. law firm of Cravath, Swain and Moore.

That is a surprise.

"*They don't trust Trimble anymore*", I think.

Dick Watson starts, "What do we have to do to get this thing signed?"

We decide that we should send a letter to the FAA, stating that computers fail and withdraw that language from the contract. The letter could be used in any future court case. It isn't as good as having it in the contract, but we'd live with it.

Laguzza calls the head of FAA procurement. They agree to take the letter.

Everything seems to be settled. We take a 10-minute break.

I call Collins at 6:30. He is still in Harrison, N. Y.

"More trouble, Joe."

"I don't believe it! Beeby?"

"No. He's Okay. He backed off."

"Who?"

"Finance."

"They're going to fight us to the death, Jack. What now?"

"They non-concur on the reliability guarantee. We have to tell FAA we no longer guarantee the reliability."

"Do those bastards know..."

"I've explained it all to them, that the guaranty offer was explicitly stated in the January 23rd submission; that DS is <u>with us</u> on this one. DS states they can make it."

"What is Finance's logic? Why should we withdraw?"

"They have no logic. They just non-concur."

"Shit."

"How is it there, Joe?"

"No problem. They're in a 'fix-it' frame of mind. Barring a surprise, we should be okay. But they're about to call Williams. You know how volatile that can be."

"Yeah."

"You coming back?"

"Yeah. I've got no luggage. Might as well."

"Call me at home if you get in before 11."

"Okay."

"Thanks, Jack."

"For what?"

"For staying there and crisping up the issue."

"Okay. See you."

Laguzza and I are in the tiny men's room on the third floor of 1111 Connecticut Ave.

"Joe, I can't take much more of this – working all day -and then rushing to Harrison. I'm wearing out. And the FAA knows we're just errand boys. They know we can't commit."

A voice from the enclosed toilet area asked, "Why do you have to go to Harrison?"

It is Dick Watson.

Laguzza and I exchange glances. Neither of us knew he was in there.

"Well, we have to get each day's progress approved."

"Well, we'll see about that," says Watson, exiting into the tiny wash-up area. He is putting on his suit jacket, which is lined with beautiful, colorfully-flowered material.

"Hey," says Laguzza, pointing at the elegant lining, "Allll <u>right, </u>Dick."

"I'm not all gray," says Watson, grinning.

Back in the meeting, Dick Watson opens the conversation.

"Jim," he says to Laguzza, "tell them how you people are running back and forth to Harrison every day."

"Yes sir, Mr. Watson, we… "

"You called me 'Dick' in the men's room. No more 'Mr. Watson'".

"Okay, Dick".

Watson looks at the team.

"What else stands in the way of our getting this order? I like all you people, but I am getting tired of this particular effort."

"Dick, there **is** one more issue."

I explain that the financial people are now blocking the reliability guarantee, even though the Product Division had agreed to accept it and is still willing to accept it.

"Did George Kennard agree?" Dick Watson asks, referring to the president of the Product Division, Bob Evans's boss.

"Yes".

"Then we'll live with the thing. The staff can't overrule the line people. I'm chief of staff and I authorize you to go ahead."

Watson goes into Pfeiffer's private office and calls Williams - who is traveling. He then tells us that Williams agrees with everything, including the reliability guarantee.

While the phone calls are being made, I chat easily with George Turner, the outside counsel. I ask if he has read "*My Life in Court*" by Louis Nizer.

"I really was impressed by the role of the lawyer," I say. "I never knew that lawyers got that deep into the content of the issues."

"Yes," answers Turner, "I am familiar with it. I was on the grievance committee."

*Oh, I think, Nizer got into hot water with the legal fraternity for "advertising."*

I decide I am out of my depth and let the conversation drop.

Laguzza comes over.

"Thank you for your help today," he says to Turner.

"I did nothing," replies Turner.

"Oh, no, you really were helpful," insists Laguzza.

I try to think of what Turner had done.

*"Nothing! Turner is telling us that he isn't needed–that Trimble is perfectly able to handle this."*

Turner answers, this time with some intensity.

"Young man," to Laguzza, "I know when I am productive and when I'm not."

It is 8 PM. We say good night.

✯ ✯ ✯

Now we sweat about the calendar. The contract will be thirty pages or so in length. IBM needs time to take the <u>signed</u> contract and get it signed by an IBM official authorized to sign! This is common practice – but now there is little time to do this.

The last week of June is a paper blizzard –everyone is writing to everyone else.

Prices are still coming in on all sorts of items –PAM, sub-channels, standard units, spare parts. Clauses are still being hammered out.

# ONE WEEK LEFT

On Monday, June 23, less than 7 days from the end of the fiscal year, we are still getting details on the tools and test equipment that the FAA will need to buy in order to maintain the computers. FAA will at first have IBM maintain the computers, but it will train their own people.

Laguzza's summary is now 20 pages in length, and third party is back where it was!

L. Third Party Liability

If and to the extent that the Congress in the future authorizes the FAA to include such a clause in this contract, the Government will include a provision to indemnify the Contractor against the liability for injuries and/or damages to third parties arising out of the Government's use of the equipment furnished under this contract."

In almost a comic opera fashion, it comes down to an "exchange of letters."

FAA agrees to 'accept' a letter from IBM -and in turn will answer the IBM letter with one of their own.

Spaulding prepares the IBM letter to the FAA. His letter is "cleared" through the powers that be.

Spauding's Letter To The FAA June 22, 1964 states:

...

We assure you that the reliability and performance criteria of your specifications will be met...

...the design and operation of the air navigation facilities of which the computer systems are to be a part may have additional safeguards and crosschecks on malfunctions of equipment.

We believe, as we are sure you do, that such crosschecks and safeguards are necessary.

Yet plenty of loose ends need to be tied up. A myriad of details are being administered to by more and more workers. Several of Laguzza's subordinates are now in all meetings. More lawyers are at the meetings. Dozens of typists all over Washington and Rockville are pounding out clauses now.

One more confrontation arises.

White and I are waiting for the elevator in the Bender Building on Connecticut Avenue.

"Joe," says White, "FAA wants us to agree to a change in the cost guarantee clause."

He pauses. And adds "We will not do it."

"Why not?" I ask.

"Because they don't need it. They're pushing us too far. They think if they call Williams again, they'll get it."

"They will get it, Hank."

"They won't call Williams."

I look at White. "Okay." I say.

He is right; FAA backs off.

White is now the boss.

Everything seems to be in place. Nothing can go wrong –or can it?

We wait patiently for the FAA to call. We will pick up the contract from the FAA, drive it out to Rockville, Maryland, to be signed by Spaulding, then run it back to FAA at Independence and 9th.

ON JUNE 30, 1964, THE CONTRACT IS SIGNED.

✫ ✫ ✫

# POSTSCRIPT

**There has been no mid air collision in the space monitored by the en route air traffic control system of the U. S. since 1960.**

The first U. S. National Airspace System En Route Center with the 9020 went into operation March 1974.

Letter:   To: Frank Cary, Chairman of IBM. March 14, 1974
FROM: J. B. Jackson President of FSD
   cc Evans, Pfeiffer

Today at 1:00 EDT the IBM NAS Radar System went operational at Kansas City and Los Angeles FAA En Route Centers. This is the culmination of ten years of effort and will significantly improve the Air Traffic Control System.

I wanted you to know that this milestone has been achieved. Other Centers around the country will follow. FAA is not, repeat, not publicizing this because of current negotiations with the Air Traffic Controllers over salary and job conditions.

✫ ✫ ✫

The 9020 works. A 4 CPU system. It met all the reliability guarantees.

IBM wins the competition to write the software for the 9020. Hank White was in charge of the bid. 500 IBM employees work at the FAA site outside of Atlantic City N J for 10 years. Joe Fox is the V P overseeing this contract From 1970 to 1977. The system – the computers and the software are installed in the UK control system.

A Brawl in IBM - 1964

**9020 Passes ALL Tests**

Bob O. Evans is moved to be President of the Federal Systems Division in Maryland.

Pfeiffer goes on to higher-level executive positions.

Learson, Cary and Opel become the chairman of IBM, in that sequence.

IBM REVENUES FROM FAA CIRCA 1976 –Estimates by author

```
Revenues on the FAA contract to April 1976.
9020 Hardware ...............................................$209,800,000
Maintenance....................................................9,000,000
Estimate Spare Parts...........................................7,000,000
SUBTOTAL....................................................225,800,000
Application Software..................................est. 50,000,000*
TOTAL.......................................................275,800,000
```

*This is the revenue for 500 IBM people at Atlantic City creating the software.

360 CLONES REPLACE THE 9020'S

The 9020 performed for over 20 years. It was replaced by another 'family' descendant of the 360, a 370 *software compatible* system called the "Host". Another IBM contract. The roughly 600,000 lines of code – the 'operational' software - were reused on the replacement IBM computers.

**People Careers**

Ralph A. Pfeiffer- President of the Data Processing Division , and then Chairman of the Board, IBM World Trade Americas/Far East Corporation, and IBM Senior Vice President.

Bob Evans became President of Federal Systems Division in late 1964 in Gaithersburg, Maryland, outside Washington, D C. He loved the FSD job, but he missed the "big tent" work of the product strategy and development. Joe Fox became his Administrative Assistant in 1969.

## U. S. NATIONAL MEDAL OF TECHNOLOGY

In the White House on February 19, 1985, Bob O. Evans received the U. S. National Medal of Technology from President Ronald Reagan, for:

> His contributions to the development of the hardware, architecture and systems engineering associated with the IBM System 360, a computer system and technologies which revolutionized the data processing industry and which helped to make the U. S. dominant in computer technology for many years.

Dr. Fred Brooks and Eric Bloch, both of IBM, receive the same medal along with Bob and with the same text.

**Watts S. Humphrey. 2003 Fellow of the Software Engineering Institute (SEI) of Carnegie Mellon University**
For his vision of a discipline for software engineering, for his work toward meeting that vision, and for the resultant impact on the U.S. Government, industry, and academic communities.

✭ ✭ ✭

Both Bob O. Evans and Frank T. Cary had first names that were usually nicknames, but were their given names. It was Bob Evans not Robert, and Frank Cary not Francis.

Hank White became Vice President of IBM's Federal Systems Division in 1967. In 1970 he was promoted to V P of IBM's Service Bureau in New York. When IBM transferred/sold/ the Service Bureau to Control Data Corporation in 1972, Hank White became Vice President of the Control Data Corporation, in Minneapolis.

A Brawl in IBM - 1964

## Joe Fox - FAA gives me a reputation –"street fighter". A bum rap.

A week or so after the contract was signed, I sat and chatted with Pfeiffer in his office in 1111 Connecticut Ave. We were casual with each other.

Then he said, "Joe, you have to learn to finesse situations. You attacked *everything*. You need to get smoother."

"O. K." I answered.

I went across the street to my office and thought about this message.

I went back and got in to see Ralph - no waiting. I told him of the meeting with the Poughkeepsie people and the threat that Evans had made – "… we are going to put your neck in a wringer, Fox. We are going to get you. And Evans made the motion of wringing a towel."

I paused.

"Ralph, I do not know how to finesse that."

He looked at me for a few moments.

"Why have you never told me that before?"

"There was no reason to." I answered.

But that was not the end of my 'reputation'. In 1966, in D .P, Headquarters in White Plains N. Y. – I had been promoted - my annual appraisal was conducted by C. B. Jack Rogers , who was -during 1964,- the assistant to the President of IBM, Al Williams.

Jack asked me what I aspired to in IBM.

"I want to be a vice president."

"Do you know your image –how you look to others?"

I guessed right then and there that I did not.

"No".

"You are, 'Joe Fox - *Street Fighter.*'" My eyes widened.

"That's not all bad, Joe. We've got a lot of fights going on, and when we throw you in, you perform. You're valuable. But you won't get to be a VP with that image."

But in 1976, I still ran into it. I sent a copy of my first published book, - Executive Qualities, - to David T. Kearns, then a V. P. at Xerox Corporation. He became Chairman of Xerox in 1982. He had been V. P. of the IBM Eastern Region of D. P. of IBM in 1966 and my direct boss.

Kearns wrote me in 1976, "I was shocked to get a book written by Joe Fox, street fighter". The letter was gracious.

✯ ✯ ✯

In September 1964 I was promoted to be in HQ of the marketing division of IBM, Data Processing. In 1967 I returned to Washington in the role that Sam Kilner had when I was there during the FAA proposal. Director of SSO –Scientific and Special Operations. FAA, Weather Bureau, CIA, National Security Agency, NASA.

In 1969 I became the Administrative Assistant to the President of the Federal Systems Division of IBM - Bob O. Evans.

✯ ✯ ✯

White and Evans were promoted to New York - separately but within months of each other in late 1969. White at this time was Vice President of FSD working for Evans, and was managing the FSD Systems Center. I replaced White (again) as General Manager of the Federal Systems Center in February 1970.

For over seven years I was General Manager of the Center, a profit and loss center of 5000 employees.

Somewhere in the next year I was titled *Division Vice President.* I took on the responsibility for the contracts with the FAA, with 500 IBM employees on the FAA site near Atlantic City N.J. They were creating the software for the U. S. En Route ATC system. White had won the competition for that contract while I was up in New York. In 1966.

I left IBM in May 1977. I started a three person software company in Washington DC in 1978, took it public in January 1997 as Template Software, sold it in December of 1999, and retired after 43 years in the computer field.

A Brawl in IBM - 1964

Jack Collins went on to higher and higher management. For years he managed the FSD people who were doing the FAA programming. He left IBM in 1978 to be a manager in Maryland for the Service Bureau of Control Data Corporation. When I started a small software company in 1979, he joined me as vice president. He never tired of doing the right thing. Collins and I worked together for the remainder of his working life.

Collins. Feisty, proud, fierce, competent. Honest to a fault. Deeply concerned that right be done and it 'be done right.' Looking out for the customer and the people constantly! Gaining the complete confidence of the FAA people in an amazingly short time. Criticizing strategy, finding information, picking people, working day and night, accepting the number two marketing role because the project was big enough - so was he!

Without Collins, we'd never have made it.

Sam Kilner was promoted to the New York area to be Assistant to A. K. Watson.

## POWER IN A LARGE ORGANIZATION.

1. The Executive. He or she can do things, change things. Or say no.
2. The competent performer. The chief engineer sometimes tells the president "No." And it sticks.
3. The Bureaucracy. It gets to stop many things from ever getting to the executive at all. Many filter, as they see fit. There are many Vice Presidents who reply to everything with a 'No'. It is safer now that they are VPs. They are to be avoided and bypassed.
4. The Salesman. He/she uses the clout of the customer to oppose the power of 1, 2 and 3. With a big customer, an astute salesman has almost unlimited power.

There are two very different types of high-level managers –there are administrators, and there are entrepreneurs. Administrators are oil –they keep things going. Entrepreneurs are whirlwinds –they change the nature of the place. Too many administrators, you get stagnation. Too many entrepreneurs, you get chaos.

There are far more administrators than entrepreneurs. It is easier to be an administrator – and safer. Not easy but easier. Many can say no –and do. Few can say yes –and few do.

Sometimes the only way to get something done is by confrontation. IBM set up contention to foster via a series of checks and balances among departments.

## WHERE WERE THE WOMEN AND MINORITIES?

There were no women in the FAA proposal effort. Women and minorities would be promoted aggressively in IBM management in the 1970s. The program was serious and well executed.

## FAA COMPETENCE

There are many critics of "the government", but most of them have never worked closely with "the government". The FAA performed beautifully in all these trials and tribulations. They successfully got the contract signed, despite an aberrant IBM that fishtailed this way and that until the last moment. At least some of the FAA people believed that IBM deliberately lured them into a dead end and sprung the third party issue at the very last moment. The FAA installed the systems. They developed the new displays. They manage the entire system – the radars, the communications devices, the displays, the radios –the people.

## THE UK GETS AN IBM 9020 FOR AIR TRAFFIC CONTROL

In the mid 1970's, with 500 IBM people creating the software application for the En Route system for the IBM 9020s, we were one of the largest contractors for the FAA. By this time we had 9020s in most sites and the 500 IBM software development people were under the very competent Dick Hanrahan. He reported to Jack Collins who reported to me.

A Brawl in IBM - 1964

I lunched with the FAA Administrator monthly. He asked me if IBM would sell to FAA yet another 9020 - that he would ship to the United Kingdom and they would run the same software on it for air traffic en route control there. The FAA owned the control software; they paid for it. I did not answer quickly.

"Will the British pay for 6 IBM engineers to be on site, the same way we do it here in the U. S.?" I asked.

*Leaving a system 'unsheparded' in remote sites where people could change the code is not to be done in the systems that have catastrophic Consequences of Failure. Trained and trusted software professionals were at all the sites – and only one control program ran in all the multiple sites. Any other way of controlling the software would be flawed and irresponsible.*

The answer was yes. Britain got a 9020 system. This was despite a "Buy British" policy for computer procurements. Later I was again at lunch with the Administrator. He mentioned that the U. K. had paid the bill for the 9020. I nodded and continued to eat.

"They paid in 6 months, Joe"

I nodded again and said, yes, that that was quick.

"Joe, I had no authority to do what we did. I bought it from IBM, moved it to London and got paid for it - all within the (U. S.) fiscal year. I got it on and off my books."

I was very impressed.

Here was a fine executive at work. When people in the U. S. criticized the system, I suggested they go to London and visit the Brits.

# I MEET TOM WATSON - CHAIRMAN OF IBM -1971

I never met or interacted with the IBM Chairman during the furious efforts of 1963- 64. Then, regarding FAA, I met the chairman. It was not pretty.

For 1969 I had the enviable job of being Bob Evans's assistant – from September 1968 to September 1969. I loved every minute of it and I admired Evans. In 1970 I was made the general manager of the

Federal Systems Center – the software part of FSD – and in charge of the FAA contracts, among many others.

In 1971 the Vice Presidents of the Federal division –including me - hosted the IBM board of directors. It was a standard affair at which the executives of one of the divisions took a turn at briefing the board members. It was Federal Systems Divisions' turn.

My job then was Vice President and General manager of the Federal Systems "Center" – 4000 people doing software development, a Profit and Loss unit. Headquartered in Gaithersburg Maryland, I had been promoted to the job after a year as assistant to the President of FSD – none other than Bob O. Evans. I replaced – who else? – Hank White.

I was in charge of the 700 people under contract in Houston Texas supporting NASA, 500 people in New Jersey supporting Bell Labs on an anti-missile missile effort, 500 in Los Angeles supporting the Air Force Missile Command – and 500 at the New Jersey FAA site, doing the software – for the 9020 – to control air traffic. I had roughly 100 contracts at any time.

We had a superb manager running the contract, Dick Hanrahan, who had performed so outstandingly at Houston before taking the FAA effort on. I met once a month with the administrator of the FAA, and we were doing fine on the tasks. BUT – the display system was late. Raytheon Corporation was running late in 1972. The schedule to go live with the new system was changed 9 times as Raytheon slipped the delivery of the new displays 9 times. That is another story. Their display was a breakthrough, and though late it was a major improvement for the controllers and the air travelers.

In 1971 it was the turn of FSD to host a meeting of the Board of Directors of the corporation.

In the middle of my boss John Jackson's presentation to the Board, he stated that FAA might be criticized for lateness - and perhaps IBM would be mentioned too. *One sentence.* Perhaps none of the directors heard it. Tom Watson, the chairman of IBM, had not.

The next day an obscure paper in Chicago quoted Congressman Jack Brooks from Texas – an 800-pound gorilla in the U.S. Government

# A Brawl in IBM - 1964

use of computers - castigating the FAA for delays in the new system – and mentioning that IBM was also not on top of the problems.

IBM had a clipping service, and Tom Watson read the comment - and went ballistic.

I got a call at home that evening–'Be in Armonk, N Y, tomorrow morning. Present the status of our contracts with the FAA at the Management Committee meeting'. I take the shuttle. I arrive at Bob Hubner's office. My boss's boss. I have no memory of where my boss John Jackson disappeared to. I do not know how he missed this meeting. But I was the FAA contact.

Hubner explains the issue to me- the chairman is embarrassed that the Board was not told that the FAA and IBM might get some bad press. Dean McKay, Corporate V P in charge of advertising and publicity, is with us. I have worked with both over the years and we are comfortable together.

BUT - they are pacing the floor of the office like two caged tigers – back and forth, back and forth. NERVOUS! Apparently <u>no one</u> remembers the one line in the presentation to the board by my boss that said there may be some bad press "but all is well".

I go to the phone and begin to dial.

Who are you calling? they ask.

The FAA administrator, I reply

No no, they say - and I foolishly obey.

I start making charts on the contract with the FAA- the scope, the plan, the schedule. They like that –I am to present this to Watson – and others.

We enter the meeting room –and there at least 50 people in this sizeable room. This is a regularly scheduled meeting of the MRC – the Management Review Committee. Ranged in 15 or so rows are the key executives of IBM and their aides. Personnel, finance, sales, manufacturing, publicity, legal, maintenance - and Corporate V Ps for the product and the sales divisions.

And to my surprise, in the furthest back tables, key people from our FAA efforts in the past are there– Dick Hanrahan- now in the product division - after doing wonderful work as the director of the

FAA software contract in FSD. And Jack Keeley, and Pat Beeby, both of SDD.

We walk into the room – Hubner leading the way – then me – then McKay. Tom Watson –Chairman of IBM- in the second row, right side – waves his finger at Hubner –"Is this the FAA?" he barks, face red.

Yes, says Hubner.

"Don't you ever embarrass me again like this." says Watson.

Hubner shows why he is a corporate level V. P. He points over his shoulder at me.

"Joe Fox will tell you all about it, Tom." he says – and goes to the left and sits down – as does McKay.

I put the charts up.

| | |
|---|---|
| Contract value | approx $5 million per year |
| # of people | 500 in New Jersey |
| Contract ratings by the FAA – | Favorable |
| Key eople | Key ates d |

Watson yells at me, red faced -"Why are you here Mr. Fox?"

"I was asked to come up and brief this group on the status of the contract." I say…calmly.

"You should be in Washington with the FAA, Mr. Fox"

*Damn - if I could only say I had just talked to the FAA Administrator.*

"I intend to see them tomorrow, sir."

"Wait a month Mr. Fox. Wait a month – and all this will have blown over."

I go back to the chart and point to something.

But he keeps on. Angry. Red faced.

"If you had gone to sales school, you would know what to do."

I had gone to sales school – but I decide not to mention that.

By now I am watching the room – which resembles something out of a Fellini movie. Every person is frozen and unmoving any bodily part. Some are in weird postures – and had to be uncomfortable.

## A Brawl in IBM - 1964

One exec is staring at the left ceiling corner of the room – and has not moved in the few minutes of this tongue-lashing. Another is bent over a writing tablet - looking down at it – and frozen in place.

Another is staring strait forward- and stiff as a board.

*WHAT IS GOING ON HERE?*

I have looked at Learson several times – he is staring at me – upright, rigid. I had met with Learson weekly during the FAA proposal.

"If my father were alive, you would not get away with this." barks Watson, the IBM chairman.

My mind is cool. *Then I'm glad he is not alive - 'cause I am going to get away with this.*

Then I notice Learson is moving his eyeballs –<u>only</u> his eyeballs – rolling them straight up and down - he is telling me something. What?

*Turn The Charts!*

The chairman yells; Learson rolls his eyeballs; and I turn to the next chart.

I do not speak to anything on the chart – I just turn one and look back at Watson.

Who just keeps yelling at me.

I learn after the meeting that the frozen execs are in *avoidance* posture. When the chairman gets into one of these frenzies and he sees an arm move, or a head, or a pencil, he will turn on the "mover" and say- "Well, what do you think about this?" – and a perfectly innocent and perhaps totally ignorant of the issue in play – an innocent 'bystander'- is now the person on the carpet. Unless the *caught* mover has a brilliant insight or comment, it becomes *his* or *her* fault that this 'trauma' is upon the company.

IT BECOMES THE FAULT OF THE MOVER! ! The mover is guilty – and is asked - "What do you say to this?"

The mover may not have a clue about the issue. What does one say? If not something pertinent and helpful, the mover now is part of the disaster being 'examined'. A guilty party. No –THE guilty party.

Soooo -no one moves. But Learson.

Learson rolls his eyes – I turn the next chart.
Tom the chairman yells.
Learson rolls his eyes.
I turn a chart.
The chairman bellows - "We have never done right by this customer. I took Evans out of his job because of this account. If it had not been for that young man in Washington, we would not have this account."

Learson moves - sits tall. Swings toward Tom and says, "That young man is Mister Fox, Tom."

Tom is startled. Stares.

Learson is talking. To me and Hubner and McKay.

"Tom is absolutely right. Get down to Washington and determine what is the problem and come back to brief us again."

I have the charts off the holder before he gets out the last words, and we head for the door. The three of us.

Tom Watson calls after me.

"Mr. Fox." I stop and turn and face him.

In a friendly tone, he says, "I wont forget you again, Mr. Fox."

I smile and get out of the room.

I never did find out what 'again' meant.

## WE VISIT WITH THE FAA ADMINISTRATOR

I arrange for Hubner and McKay to join me in meeting with the FAA administrator, Jack Schafer - who listens to us asking him how we were doing etc, and then he sums up.

"You all are doing just fine. Let me tell you what I did when I heard about Jack Brooks' statement. I called Brooks.

'What are we doing wrong, Jack?' I asked."

"Brooks, answered me. 'Jack you all are doing just fine – just keep going. It is an election year and I needed a little publicity, that is all'."

We IBM people are speechless. We ask a few simple questions – "We ARE doing OK?" and the like and get out of there.

✳ ✳ ✳

A Brawl in IBM - 1964

## WATSON'S DEMEANOR

Watson's haughtiness is related in a 1993 book <u>BIG BLUES – The Unmaking of IBM</u>, by Paul Carroll, a Wall Street Journal reporter. He quotes an incident involving David Kearns -later to become chairman of Xerox. And, in the mid 60's, David was my immediate boss in IBM – and a fine, competent gentleman.

According to the author Kearns was presenting to the IBM Management Committee and a latecomer arrived and took a seat.

Watson greets the new comer graciously.

Then thunders: "David here is making a nice presentation – you'll enjoy it – not like Jack - who just made a presentation to us and who stood right there and told us lies."

The book has Kearns saying he wanted to hide behind the easel that held his charts.

✶ ✶ ✶

In <u>Big Blue</u> by Richard Thomas DeLamarter, 1986, on pages 60 and 61 cites a letter from A. K. Watson to his brother Tom Watson Jr. – the chairman of IBM –citing Bob Evans as the "most dangerous man in IBM" –as the man with world-wide responsibility for developing the 360 line of computers. The letter from A K reads 'I think B.O. Evans is one of the most dangerous men ever employed in the IBM Company".

✶ ✶ ✶

After the Watson meeting, Evans had called me on the phone within ten minutes.

"I heard it went badly."

"Badly?" I said. "It is a *DISGRACE* to see how this company is run. And – and the whole room – of fine minds – cowed into not only silence – but in holding onto some uncomfortable position so that they are not dragged into the penalty box for something they had nothing to do with. The man is a disaster."

Evans disagreed.

"Joe, when he was younger he would come to Poughkeepsie and spur us on to get into the computer business. He was great – an inspiration."

"Bob, I believe you. But now, he is awful."

When I told Bob about the …"out of his job because of FAA", he said his Federal Division job was a 'spanking' for having neglected time sharing and other technical aspects of the initial 360 models. He stated the FAA proposal events were not that crucial.

✯ ✯ ✯

In 1967 I was in IBM in the Westchester area, but the job was shrinking because the company had over planned new facilities based on a sales forecast they now knew was not to happen. So I was told to disperse my people, - and I was privileged to present a new business proposal to the MRC –the management review committee.

The idea was simple – take on development of new systems for a price for large customers. This indeed is a huge percent of IBM's revenue today and goes by the name "Services". But that was not to occur for several years. It was years ahead of the IBM willingness to get into this kind of business, now labeled "services".

I worked on this presentation for months under the management of Bob Howe – then the president of IBM's real estate division. Howe was a wonderful leader and mentor, an insider in the world of the top IBM executives. I suggested we invite the president of the Federal System Division – Evans - to attend the presentation, as that would save time if the MRC had any intent of going forward. The nucleus of the new business would require a sizeable group of FSD employees be moved from FSD to a new entity. It was likely to elicit an objection from FSD, and rather than have that arise after the presentation, I proposed that FSD weigh in at the presentation. It turned out that Evans, was to be at a meeting of a NASA launch team review the same day as the scheduled presentation. Neither meeting could be changed.

I suggested that we invite Evans's boss - ' a group V. P. in IBM headquarters in charge of <u>several</u> IBM divisions-Mr. Jones".

Howe said to me, "Oh, you are not aware of the problem with Mr. Jones."

He related that if Jones were in a meeting with the chairman, the meeting would explode, as the chairman would find a reason to 'beat up' on Jones, no matter what the issue was or what was being discussed. The meeting would fall apart and nothing would be resolved. As a result, one never wanted Jones in any meeting with the chairman. Yet Jones was a *group* V P. A few *Division presidents* reported to him.

I asked Howe "Why doesn't the chairman get rid of Jones?"

Howe looked at me as if I were a child.

"Do you think Tom is *cruel*?"

I was wise enough not to answer that.

✱ ✱ ✱

## WE BRIEF FRANK CARY IBM PRESIDENT

We needed to hire *secretaries* for the 500 IBM people doing the software outside of Atlantic City, N. J., in barracks-like buildings on the FAA National Facilities Experimental Center –NAFEC. My manager of the 500 people at the FAA site in N. J. came to see me. He had a 4-inch sheaf of papers under his arm. He had been working with FSD's personnel department for months – and all he had was this sheaf of papers regarding the effort to get the OK to hire –and no approval.

An IBM-wide hiring freeze was in place, but secretaries? – and outside of Atlantic City? The management of the Atlantic City organization had used temporary secretaries- and then been told that after 3 or so temporary gigs, the secretary could not be hired as a temporary employee again. I had not heard of the problem, and the file of paper impressed me. And I was informed that we were running late in our required reporting to the FAA because of the dearth of secretaries. We were getting lower ratings from the FAA. And our fee was based on ratings.

I went to my boss John Jackson and said I wanted to go to Armonk N. Y. – IBM HQ – and meet with the responsible exec and get a waiver. I was told the chairman of IBM – Learson – had just put the burden of enforcing the freeze on the President of IBM – Frank Cary.

I had worked for Frank for 2 years – with John Opel in between him and me. I was anxious to hire the people needed in N. J. - so we should go see Cary. And the airplane assigned to my boss was to take him to Armonk in 2 days.

Jackson and I called Cary's secretary and got a time to meet. Jackson and I and our FSD director of personnel –Jones- flew out of the Gaithersburg Md. small airport – in an IBM twin engine propeller King Air - and we got to Armonk at 11 am for my boss's meeting.

At 11:30 we met with the director of personnel for IBM, Walt Burdick. I showed him the charts that I was going to use with Cary – what did he think the reaction of the IBM president would be? Did the story make sense? Would we get approval? What did the restriction apply to? Had there been any recent appeals?

Burdick said he had no advice to give us – the restriction was new and the Cary assignment to manage it very recent. We went to lunch – each of us with a different local Armonk IBM people. I got back to the office we were using to find Jackson and Jones near panic. Jones had had a private lunch with Burdick and had been told we were going to get "killed" – that we were wasting Cary's time.

I got upset – "Why the hell could he not have shared that information with me and Jackson - we could have dug deeper – checked in with the assistant level in Cary's office?" Now it was too late.

Jackson wanted to cancel meeting. I objected- it was the only reason I had come up to N Y. I needed

the secretaries. We were missing our reporting dates with the FAA. And I would take the heat and carry the meeting.

## A Brawl in IBM - 1964

OK.

We walked into Cary's office at 3 p m. Jackson, Jones, Burdick, and I. Cary said hello to each of us. He asked what the meeting was for. I answered.

"I need to hire secretaries- full time – for the FAA contract at Atlantic City – we are missing our reporting dates and it is hurting our technical score on the incentivized contract.

And you are the man to see on this."

Cary paused and looked at us.

"I want to apologize to each of you that you had to come up here and see me on a issue like this."

He paused –"But this is way we are doing things now."

I put up the charts – perhaps 10 in all. We got to the second one – and Frank waved at us –

"Go hire the secretaries".

## OVERWORK ON THE FAA SOFTWARE?

In the mid 70's – getting ready to automate the ground system for NASA Houston for the new Space Lab Effort –we were having deep trouble meeting the schedule. We had never missed a software schedule in Houston. But the "lab" in space was sending down tons of data – and this was new to Houston.

Our people were heavily stressed – and some suffered breakdowns and family problems.

The corporate level personnel people discovered this and I was told that no one in my entire realm was to work more than 50 hours a week. It became clear quickly that the IBM people in Atlantic City on the Air Traffic Control contract were way over 50 hours a week.

I told them "no more than 50 hours a week".

O. K.

Within a month personnel came and told me the FAA people in Atlantic were still way over 50 ours a week.

We decided to lock the doors. The FAA site was outside Atlantic City in what used to be a U. S. Navy base. The offices were in two-story barracks-like buildings – a lot of them. We locked the doors.

A week later I was told our FAA programmers were climbing in the windows to work.

What should we do, I was asked.

Nothing. Do nothing – leave them alone.

And we did nothing - and we never had another directive from higher management.

✲ ✲ ✲

I left IBM in May of 1977. It had been a great 21 years. I was 42 years old.

# A Brawl in IBM - 1964

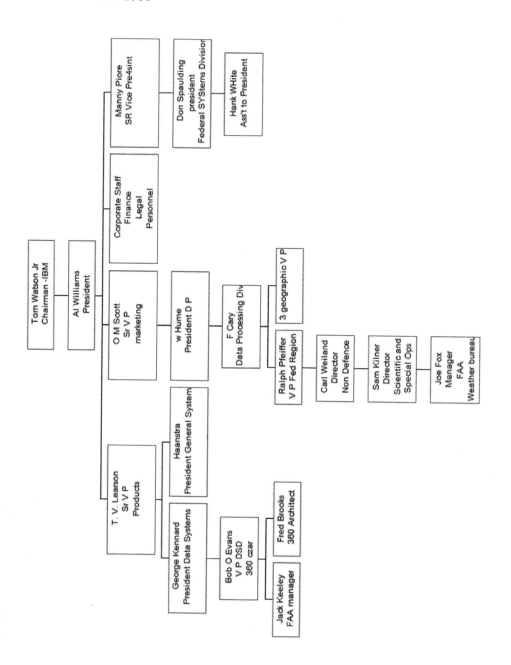

IBM ORGANIZATION CHART 1963

Joseph M. Fox

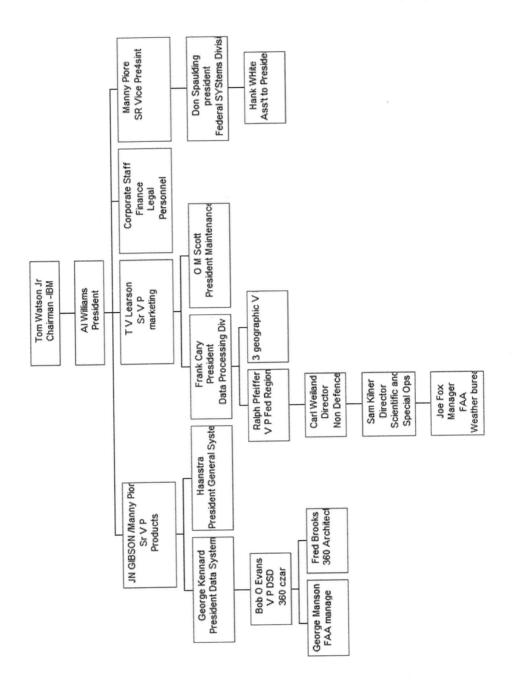

IBM ORGANIZATION CHART – 1964

Made in the USA
Charleston, SC
23 March 2012